On China's Road

Honghua Men
Editor

On China's Road

In Search of a New Modernity

palgrave
macmillan

Editor
Honghua Men
Institute for China & World Studies
Tongji University
Shanghai, China

The print edition is not for sale in Mainland of China. Customers from Mainland of China please order the print book from: Truth and Wisdom Press.

ISBN 978-981-13-7879-9 ISBN 978-981-13-7880-5 (eBook)
https://doi.org/10.1007/978-981-13-7880-5

This Palgrave Macmillan imprint is published by the registered company Springer Nature Singapore Pte Ltd.
The registered company address is: 152 Beach Road, #21-01/04 Gateway East, Singapore 189721, Singapore

Contents

List of Figures

List of Tables

PART I

Introduction

CHAPTER 1

Deepening Research on China's Road and Strengthening China's Discourse Power

Honghua Men

Since entering the twenty-first century, the global community has been discussing and paying closer attention to China. Thus, "China's Road" continues to be the focus of hot discussions, of which various perspectives emerge. From the "Beijing Consensus" proposed by Joshua Cooper Ramo to Martin Yacques' prediction of "China's domination of the world," the world both looks forward to China's Road and is concerned about China's future development direction. Regarding the evaluation and prospect of China's Road, there are various versions of the "China Threat" theory and "*the Collapse of China*." However, the "China Responsibility" theory is more commonly discussed and commentary about "China's Opportunity" and the "China Contribution" theory continue. This includes not only an objective analysis of China's Road but also many misunderstandings, exaggerations, and even intentional distortions. Many developing countries closely follow the experience of China's Road, while numerous Western scholars have used their inherent theories to explain the phenomenon. However, they are unable to provide an objective analysis and always present views mingled with ideologies and political bias.

Examining existing research findings on China, we can find relevant research but the atmosphere of political expression is generally strong. Such research always focuses on one point only and not others. Furthermore,

H. Men (✉)
Institute for China & World Studies, Tongji University, Shanghai, China

H. Men (ed.), *On China's Road*,
https://doi.org/10.1007/978-981-13-7880-5_1

many scholars are obsessed with and confident in China's bright future instead of problem analysis. In a general sense, the selection, initiation, and development of the country's road is the core problem deciding the fortune and destiny of the nation. China has initiated and is improving China's Road, whereby China has experienced hardships and twists and turns, as well as challenges and tests. Despite the above, China's future prospects continue to attract global attention. It can be said that, in the current climate, China's Road is one that should be intensively researched and paid significant attention by the rest of the world.

1 Exploration, Initiation, and Development of China's Road

Su Shi said, "If the world booms, the boom must come from certain consequences." Research on China's Road first began in the mid-nineteenth century when China began to emerge as a semi-colony society. In the last 170 years, China has experienced two democratic revolutions, a socialist revolution, construction, and reform. Many generations with ambitious ideals have advanced wave upon wave and untiringly searched as how to help modernize a poor and backward country. Through hardships and twists and turns, the main objective has been achieved. China's Road is a summary of the experiences whereby the Chinese people saved the nation from destruction, realized self-improvement, and strived for the rejuvenation of China's great nationhood. This included a democratic revolution with Chinese characteristics, and socialist transformation and reform with Chinese characteristics. China's Road is unique because the properties and the selection of the system, ideas, and development mode all comprise an unalterable socialist direction, government-led market economic system, human-oriented core ideas, and gradual reform.

The foundation of China's Road is socialism with Chinese characteristics. The first-generation central collective leadership with Mao Tse-Tung as the core provided valuable experiences, theory preparation, and a material basis for creating socialism with Chinese characteristics in the new period. The second-generation central collective leadership with Deng Xiaoping as the core successfully initiated socialism with Chinese characteristics, and the third-generation with Jiang Zemin successfully pushed socialism into the twenty-first century. In the first decade of twenty-first century, the central leading body of the Party with Hu Jintao as General

Secretary has successfully insisted on and developed socialism with Chinese characteristics. The report presented at the 18th National Congress of the Communist Party of China (CPC) showed the "three steps" of China's Road in the twenty-first century: to build a moderately well-off society by the time of the Party's 100-year anniversary; to build a rich, strong, democratic, civilized, and harmonious modernized socialist country by the time of New China's 100-year anniversary; and to realize the great rejuvenation of the Chinese nation during the twenty-first century. This great strategy is mobilized based on the further enrichment and improvement of China's Road.

Xi Jinping, *General Secretary* of the CPC Central Committee, discussed the implication of China's Road at the height of combining the "Dream" and the "Road." He pointed out that the realization of the great rejuvenation of the Chinese nation was China's greatest dream in modern times, while the socialist road with Chinese characteristics must be followed to realize China's Dream. The socialist road with Chinese characteristics is the dialectical unity of the logic of scientific socialist theory and the historical logic of Chinese social development. It takes root in China and reflects the will of the Chinese people. Furthermore, the socialist road is suitable to the development requirements of modern China and modern times, and is the necessary road to creating a moderately well-off society, realizing socialist modernization and achieving the great rejuvenation of the Chinese nation.

Since the 18th National Congress, the CPC with Xi Jinping as the core has been devoted to opening a new era of comprehensively deepening the reform and opening-up, implementing profound strategic reforms in various fields such as politics, the economy, society, culture, ecology, safety, diplomacy and national defense, and gradually forming a great strategy relating to the mid- and long-term development of China. In respect to system construction, China is energetically facilitating the construction of its state governance system while also focusing on combating corruption. It also seeks to establish a basis for long-term governance and the safety of the nation. Regarding China's economic and social strategies, a "New Normal" is proposed, and the reform of the economic system is advanced. Such reforms will positively safeguard and improve the livelihood of the people and ensure social health and stability. In terms of culture construction, China insists on the core values of socialism and emphasizes the importance of the rejuvenation of traditional culture. Namely, the future is created on the basis of origin, and innovation may be better realized if the nation is open to influences from its traditional culture. Regarding China's security strategy, an "Overall Concept of National Security" is proposed and a key focus lies on the improvement of China's national security system. Attention is also paid to China's diplomatic strategy, whereby the national strategic interests of China will be expanded, and the opening of a new diplomatic era with "common interests," "mutual benefit and win-win", and "Chinese responsibilities" are at the core of the reform. Thus, China's Road, with the above traits as the basis, with socialism with Chinese characteristics as the foundation, and with balanced development, peaceful development, cooperation, and mutual benefits as outstanding characteristics, will ensure that China walks firmly and calmly.

2 Basic Features and Strategic Values of China's Road

Since China's reform and opening-up, the economy has experience rapid development. Furthermore, its comprehensive power promotes stability, which has provided an inexhaustible impetus to global economic development and peace maintenance. China is considered the key power to reshape international order and its future strategy is attracting close attention from the international community. China also influences strategies of other major countries. Thus, China's national interests, responsibilities, and destiny retain global relevance in the new era. However, as various problems emerge during China's development, overseas reservations regarding the intention, speed, and scale of China's development have led to misunderstandings such as "China Threat" and "China Collapse", which to a certain extent influence China's image. Thus, there is an obvious scramble for the right to discuss China's Road.

Regarding relevant theories, China's Road is based on the inheritance and improvement of Chinese historical tradition and complies with the concepts of peaceful and win-win development since ancient times. China's Road represents the new development of Marxism and furthers the Chinization of Marxism. Furthermore, China's Road is the enrichment of Chinese diplomatic theories and international relationship theories, and endows them with both time and Chinese characteristics. This pathway is also a response to certain negative public voices in the international community and may provide supporting theories that act to cancel the negative influences.

In terms of China's practices, China's Road has provided a strategic path to China's future development as well as guidance for internal affairs and diplomacy. China's Road aims to promote national comprehensive power and further build the basis for the great rejuvenation of the Chinese nation. Furthermore, it promotes China's national influence power and provides assistance to the enrichment and innovation of global development modes. China's Road also seeks to promote the sound development of international transactions and investments and to help international political and economic orders to be both just and rational. China's Road further aims to establish a wonderful world with lasting peace and joint development and to highlight China's significant status as a "great responsible power."

China's Road, as the modern rejuvenation pathway of a long-standing and great power, is the most successful modernization development road of non-Western countries and can be considered the most dazzling example in the development history of the world's socialist societies. It is a road upon which China is connected to economic globalization rather than ignoring it to independently build a socialist nation with Chinese characteristics. It also enables China, with a population of 1.4 billion people, to achieve modernization based on socialism. Thus, it represents an unprecedented and brand-new road in the growing history of a newly developing great power. China's Road is also an unprecedented and brand-new road in both the world's socialist and Marxist history. To continually deepen the research on China's Road, we should obtain a much closer and deeper connection with the practices in the many aspects of China's reform and opening-up and its modernization construction. It is also essential to get a much closer understanding of the history, status quo, and prospects of the economic, political, and cultural development worldwide.

At present, Chinese economic development has entered a stage of the "New Normal," and comprehensive reform has entered a critical state. Similarly, China's state strategic layout has entered a material phase. In the face of the expectations from the global economy and international public opinions on Chinese development, China must continue to deepen and innovate China's Road in both theory and practice.

3 China's Road Needs Further Study

China's Road has grabbed the attention of the world. The fundamental reason for this is that China has designed an independent and automatic socialist development road with Chinese characteristics, while also taking into account the present realities of the state. This helps China to not only gain huge achievements and to lay a solid foundation for future development but also realize opening-up and tolerance in the face of future strategic designs. After a grueling period of exploration lasting more than 60 years, the Chinese people have realized that to achieve the great rejuvenation of the Chinese nation they must unswervingly insist on the leadership of the Communist Party. Similarly, they must demand reform in the direction of a socialist market economy and follow a development road that combines gradual reform and decisive advancement. It is also important that the Chinese people unswervingly adhere to a socialist economic system that is mainly composed of public systems and various ownership types. Furthermore, the people must adhere to the guiding status of Marxism, advance the localization of Marxism in China, and look to outside successes for reference.

The opening-up and forming of China's Road is closely tied to China's unique development course and historical culture. As pointed out by General Secretary Xi Jinping, China's Road emerged from the great practices of more than 30 years of reform and opening-up. It has emerged from continual exploration since the founding of the People's Republic of China more than 60 years ago. It has also stemmed from the profound summary of more than 170 years of development, as well as the inheritance of a 5000-year-old civilization. It has a deep-seated historical origin and a very realistic foundation. The report presented at the 18th National Congress of the CPC stated that China's Road is "under the leadership of the Communist Party, based on the basic conditions of the state and oriented to economic construction. It upholds the four fundamental principles and promotes reform and opening-up. Furthermore, it liberates and develops social productive forces, consolidates and improves the socialist system, and seeks to build a socialist market economy, socialist democracy, advanced socialist culture, harmonious socialist society, and a socialist ecological civilization. It also facilitates the comprehensive development of the people, gradually realizes the common prosperity of all people, and seeks to build a rich, powerful, democratic, civilized, and harmonious modern socialist state."

The brand-new layout of China's Road is being created. The *Book of Changes* comments that "Everything changes as time goes on and people should advance with the times." Since the 18th National Congress of the

CPC, the Party with Xi Jinping as the core has been promoting a strategic idea that closely combines domestic and international situations, positively advances the deepening of the system's reform, and promotes the construction of a state governance system. The Party is also focusing on the improvement of its governance capacity while carrying out the systematic design of a "five-sphere system reform," which includes politics, the economy, society, culture, and ecology. The Party has also committed to balanced national development, while proposing an overall concept of state development to build a moderately well-off society. This strategy also seeks to deepen the reform and the rule of law, and to strengthen Party discipline. Similarly, it will advance the modernization of the national governance system and governance capacity. The Party aims to begin a new journey in China's reform, opening-up, and modernization. Greater efforts to engage in international affairs are being made and the implementation of "international strategies" (e.g., Belt and Road Initiative) is helping China to integrate with the rest of the world and enjoy a significant international influence. Such actions reveal China as a constructive participator and leader in global economic governance and world order. Thus, the influence of China's great power is becoming more prominent. The exploration along China's Road has entered a new historical era. China's Road is China's rising road, the road to the great rejuvenation of the Chinese nation and the road to the realization of the Chinese Dream.

The initiation and development of China's Road has universal significance around the world. Most developing countries face the same problem: how best to implement modernization? All great powers have noticed that no matter which country produces certain innovations along the development road and becomes a world leader in that regard, another country may stand out and take the lead. On the one hand, China's Road has provided a road that differs from those Western roads available to developing countries and shows a beneficial enlightenment for exploration along the development road of human society. On the other hand, China's Road also shows the international community China's understanding of national development and offers its experiences to developing countries worldwide. China's Road has widened the way for developing countries to modernize, facilitated the diversified development of human civilization in an era of economic globalization, and influenced the road selected by other developing countries.

4 Promote China's Discourse Power on China's Road

As stated in the *Book of Changes*, "A wise man always comes at a moment's notice." In 2020, China will enter a crucial period: it will have established a comprehensive well-off society and laid a solid foundation for the great rejuvenation of the Chinese nation. This will be an important time for China, as its international influence will be growing and overall preparations will be made for the shift from a regional power to worldwide great power. According to the changes within the domestic and international environments facing China, it has been shown that opportunities coexist with challenges and that the opportunities are even greater than challenges. China's Road can only be improved by following the trends of the times, by ensuring that it is based on China's realistic conditions, and by focusing on the achieving the best results possible. It is also imperative that China implements bottom-line thinking and facilitates ideological innovation.

China's Road features strong Chinese characteristics, while relevant research and summaries should be further deepened. Research on China's Road generally provides a historical summary, and evaluates the status quo and future expectations. We should carefully summarize the combination of the cultural connotations of China's Road and Chinese historical traditions, and both the conceptual construction and scientific theory analysis of China's Road. Attention must also be paid to the realistic approaches taken by China's Road and Chinese strategic design to realize the innovation of research on China's Road in three dimensions, namely, history, theory, and strategy.

China ushers in a new era whereby it will make significant contributions to the international community and this is the proper time for China to promote its Discourse Right on China's Road. Research on China's Road is extremely active, with many commentators scrambling to put their opinions and views forward. The unceasing feeding of the China Threat theory and the gaining popularity of the Collapse of China theory prove that it is crucial for China to speak about China's Road. Thus, many academic circles are facing the important research task to properly tell "China story," and the task must be realized through the careful consideration of academic elites.

PART II

History and Reality of China's Road

CHAPTER 2

China's Road in the Light of Historical Continuity

Xu Yong

It is indisputable that China has developed from a weak to a strong country. Did this change erupt suddenly, or did it have deep historical roots? If the former, its vigorous ascent would be unsustainable, and would be followed by an abrupt decline. If the latter, this implies that China's long process of historical accretion enabled the country to seize the opportunity for a sustainable rise based on historical continuity. China's rise was accompanied by the gradual formation of the socialist road with Chinese characteristics following reform and opening up. This process was based not only on the social reforms that preceded reform and opening up but also on the long history of Chinese civilization. Only through a full understanding of the historical foundation of Chinese civilization and its tortuous course can we fully understand the great significance of the Chinese people's opening up a socialist road with Chinese characteristics and achieving China's rise under the leadership of the Communist Party of China (CPC). China's Road's most striking feature is historical continuity rather than rupture, and the main force behind this continuity is its intrinsic dynamism and vitality. The long history of China's agrarian civilization prepared the basic formal elements for the country's modernization. Once new elements were injected, the old civilization could be rapidly revitalized

X. Yong (✉)
Institute of China Rural Studies, Central China Normal University,
Wuhan, China

H. Men (ed.), *On China's Road*,
https://doi.org/10.1007/978-981-13-7880-5_2

and rejuvenated. Chinese "confidence in the road" was not a momentary intoxication but a "deep-rooted confidence with profound historical sources." Of course, the underlying continuity of China's Road contained elements of resuscitating the past that needed rational reform if they were to continue. The study of China's Road must analyze China within the coordinates of "world progress" and from the dimension of the longue durée in order to rediscover China through comparison, identify positive genes and genetic defects in the Chinese historical heritage and find the common values, unique functions and historical limitations in the underlying history of China's Road.

1 Time Never Stopped: The Driving Force and Institutional Genes of the Agrarian Empire

After the Opium Wars, Westerners "looked down" on China, entering the country with an overweening consciousness of superiority as well as a sense of exoticism. Back then, China and the Western powers were undergoing a period of "alternation of civilizations" and "rise and fall of national fortunes." Misfortunes never come singly. When China first experienced the challenge of an industrial civilization stronger than her agrarian one, the Qing Dynasty was in decline; it could be described as "a leaky roof buffeted by constant rain; a vessel, already late, sailing against the wind." Against this background, Westerners' knowledge and discovery of China was marked by the arrogance of their civilization's superiority and prosperity, giving them an attitude of Eurocentric condescension with regard to China. One could say that China's "developmental stagnation" was a common verdict of Westerners in the midst of the dramatic changes of modernization. A book on traditional China even has the title *The Immobile Empire*, signifying a cognitive bias arising from this historical gap.

Whatever opinions people had about China, there were some basic facts nobody could neglect. First, China had created the most brilliant agrarian civilization in the world. Second, it had the longest imperial history in the world. Third, the richness of Chinese theories of government had worldwide influence. All of these grew up in the course of China's history as the most enduring agrarian empire. An agrarian empire is not simply a "stagnant empire." The so-called stagnation is relative to modern industrial civilization. From the viewpoint of the staggering pace of today's modern industrial civilization, everything in the traditional world was "immobile" or even "barbaric." Therefore, based on the analytical paradigm of historical comparison, different countries should be analyzed over the same time and space. According to this paradigm, it is not appropriate to summarize China, one of the most ancient agrarian empires, as "stagnant": to do so precludes an explanation of the three basic facts above. The impetus behind the world's most brilliant agrarian civilization was mainly endogenous. This impetus was not an immediate "explosive force" but a sustainable institutional impetus that included independent farming households, endogenous government capacity and adaptive national governance. Its quintessence can be summarized as free people, strong government and effective governance, supported by the family system, the system of prefectures and counties and the imperial examination system. They not only created a brilliant agrarian civilization but also provided the basic institutional forms for China's entry into the modern world.

1.1 Independent Farming Households

Until the advent of the modern manufacturing industry, agriculture was the most advanced form of industry. The natural climate of the temperate zone and plain landforms provided a highly favorable setting for China's main industry, agriculture, which led the world from the outset. Its advanced productivity demanded equally advanced production relations, leading in the course of two thousand years to the family system, a unique economic and social organization, whose quintessence was the commitment that derived from autonomy. The gradual accretion of civilization was the result of continuous creation. Only autonomous manpower had the sustained awareness and commitment needed to create a civilization.

The family (jia) system was an economic and social organization in which the household (hu) was the basic unit. Unlike tribal, village community or manorial systems, it emphasized the role and function of blood relationships. Given China's natural endowments and distinctive production arrangements, the family was the organizational unit best suited to agricultural production, as history has shown. Even more important than this was the overlapping of "family" and "household." The household was an organizational unit unique to China. Its basis was in national administration, as the unit through which the government managed population and raised taxes. The family was an economic and social unit, the household a political one. The emergence of the household had revolutionary significance, in that it enabled the individual to emerge from the narrow regional community and become a member of a larger community, the state. This revolution, which occurred during the Spring and Autumn and Warring States periods, was inherited and institutionalized by the Qin Dynasty. One could say that the family/household system was the foundation of the Qi unification of China.

The value of this system lay in identifying the best organizational unit of agricultural production and at the same time enabling people to go beyond their narrow regional community to depend on one another. The peasant as producer had "formal registration" as an independent "free-man" with equal economic, social and political status. It was precisely the autonomous farming household that provided the basic impetus for China's creation of a brilliant agrarian civilization.

The first factor in this process was responsibility. For people to emerge from the regional community meant not only that they were independent but also that they had shouldered corresponding responsibilities. Families were composed of blood relationships: the most ancient, primal and basic form of relationship. In China, family units with surnames came into being very early, with village regional communities appearing much later. The freedom of the ancient Chinese was not the freedom of the individual natural person but freedom in which the family was the unit. All individuals were members of a family, and could only obtain their due recompense if they had fulfilled their family obligations. Internal family relations were not even but reciprocal, with a division of labor, as in "kind fathers, filial sons" or "Men plow, women spin." All family members shouldered their due responsibilities according to their status. The family system amplified and strengthened blood relations and bound family members to the fulfillment of their duties. The family had to not only feed its members but also transmit the family line. This made the family members toil by the sweat of their brow to obtain the maximum possible returns. In fact, the family system was a responsibility system, an inner identification transmitted by life itself, unlike the external pressure imposed on the slave.

The second factor was pressure. The independent farming household gained independence, but also faced competitive pressure for survival. In traditional China, agricultural progress and continuation of the family line led to a sharp rise in population. Having a large population but limited arable land was always a fundamental problem. The regular division of family land and assets under the household inheritance system resulted in a constant decline in the scale of operations. The price the peasant paid for independence from the state was taxes and corvée labor. All of these elements combined to strengthen the competitive pressures on peasant households seeking to survive. With no support or protection, they had to toil unceasingly and practice extreme frugality.

The third factor was hope. It was institutionally possible for independent peasant households to control their own actions. Because narrow regional relationships had been broken down, the ownership of land could flow freely in ancient China: "land does not have a fixed owner." Every peasant dreamed of making a fortune to bring glory to his ancestors. Although achieving this dream was impossible for most, it could bring them hope and spur their attempts to realize it. It was the combination of the above factors that made Chinese peasants so hard-working and enterprising. The ancient classic *Annotations on the Spring and Autumn Annals of Lü Buwei* describes the peasants as follows: "They cherish time, and only old age, sickness or death can keep them from their toil." Montesquieu recognized the Chinese people's diligence, and Weber spoke highly of the Chinese work ethic, regarding "the industry and capacity for work among the Chinese have always been considered unsurpassed." It was this diligence and capacity for hard work that brought forth China's brilliant agrarian civilization. At the same time, the family system integrated genetic inheritance, property inheritance and state continuity, providing an important basis for the millennial continuance of agrarian civilization in one nation. Since ancient times, however torturous the course of history, a country based on an agrarian civilization will last as long as there are people who live off the land.

1.2 Endogenous Government Capacity

Over the course of world civilization, governments and empires of various types have succeeded one another. Some of these empires have had a considerable size and strong government capacity. From the perspective of imperial history, however, none have lasted as long as China's. This is largely because the agrarian Chinese empire had a strong endogenous governing capacity and a high degree of institutionalization, which enabled it to provide continuing domestic public demand and capacity.

The first factor here was endogenous demand for public construction. The existence of the Chinese empire depended on agriculture, for which water conservancy is essential. The Yellow River and the Yangtze River, China's two large river systems, provide uniquely favorable agricultural conditions. However, their floods could be catastrophic, and the water conservancy works that would defeat them were beyond any single family or group. World history shows that it was precisely the need for flood control that inspired our ancestors to transcend the limitations of kinship and geography and form a larger national community. The legend of "Great Yu combating the flood" testifies to this need and to the enhanced governmental capacity derived from water conservancy.

The second factor was endogenous defense demands. An agrarian empire requires repeated cultivation of settled land. In China in particular, agricultural units were relatively small-scale family organizations. Conditions in the pastoral land of Northwest China were dry with low rainfall; this harsh environment meant that the nomads of the steppes often invaded the agricultural land of Southeast China. Since they acted as tribal units and were highly mobile, single agricultural clan or village would be unable to hold back the nomad onslaught. They thus needed to seek protection from a force that was stronger than the nomadic tribes, and this they found in the government. The Chinese empire developed during border wars with tribal peoples. The government had the function of protecting the population from invasion, as in the imperial Ministry of War.

The third factor was the demands of endogenous social management. The Chinese family was mainly an economic and social unit. Its political role was chiefly that of duty to the state rather than exercise of power as a political unit. Due to the uncertainty of the boundaries of such resources as land, mountain forests, rivers and dwellings, conflicts often occurred within families, enlarged families or clans, and villages composed of several families as well as among these bodies. Some of these conflicts were mediated by families and clans themselves, but a certain number required state mediation. This produced an endogenous social management capacity, as in the imperial Ministry of Rites and Ministry of Punishments.

As an agrarian empire, China's strong government capacity derived from endogenous requirements supported by the institutionalized system of prefectures and counties. This system and the family system could be said to be the two pillars of the imperial system.

The formation of the centralized state and the system of prefectures and counties went hand in hand. With the expansion of the empire, its rulers found that the direct management of land and population stretched their resources; this necessitated a stable system of local administration to exercise jurisdiction on behalf of the center. The system of prefectures and counties was set up under the Qin, who in a sense unified China via this system and thereafter used it to rule the country. The most striking thing about the system is that it enabled the central government to implement central power throughout the country through subordinate local government units and to ensure national unity via unified laws and systems. The government's ability to mobilize, absorb and organize depended for its implementation on the system of prefectures and counties. It is for this reason that China's county system, as a complete system of grassroots political power, lasted so long. Not a few counties have remained unchanged since their first establishment, a rare historical occurrence.

1.3 Adaptive National Governance

China's long history as an agrarian empire and a brilliant agrarian civilization was not automatic but the result of human operation or management. Unlike pastoralism and commerce, which are characteristically mobile, agriculture is stable. People can obtain their desired returns only by careful cultivation and good management on an affixed amount of land. In the course of cultivation, the peasants faced a variety of problems and needed to deal with them effectively, which brought into being the concept of management or governance. Governance held an important position in the formation and development of the Chinese state, as reflected in the legend of Great Yu combating the flood.

The emergence of the empire, a larger-scale national community, was accompanied by higher demands on governance. In general, empires have been ruled by family dynasties, as in Weber's "patrimonial bureaucratic administration." In the thinking of the agrarian empire, the family runs the country and the country is the family's patrimony. As such, it must be cultivated carefully to ensure its eternal continuation. This gives the governance of such an empire an adaptive character. The empire's rulers were well aware that the management of the country, like the management of the land, would encounter good times and bad. Imperial rule would have to change with the times and governance strategies would have to be continuously adjusted.

The first factor in this process was people-based governance.

The Chinese agrarian empire implemented a system of formal household registration that covered everyone under a national system and made them all subjects of the state. Rulers dealing with the business of governance had to recognize the importance of putting people at the center and having them accede in their inmost hearts to the ruler's authority. That is why ancient China emphasized the idea that in the relationship between the ruler and the people, the people outweighed the ruler: "The people come first, then the state, and last the ruler." This attitude was rooted in the idea that "the water that bears the boat is the same that swallows it up." The fact that the people were the yardstick of national governance gave them some encouragement to keep going.

The second factor was the flexibility of governance policies.

State rule was coercive, as is the nature of states. But there are two ways of governing a state. One is rigid rule enforced by violent repression and the other is rule by flexible and compassionate governance. Ancient China had examples of the latter kind of wise governance, as in Great Yu's diverting the flood waters rather than blocking them. With the formation of the empire, this ancient wisdom of governance continued to play a part. Despite their increased governance capacity, rulers adopted a flexible governance policy that put people at the center. They learned from previous experience and made adjustments according to different conditions and issues, which encouraged popular enterprise and raised morale, thus increasing wealth. Early Western Han rulers learned the lesson of the short-lived Qin Dynasty and following inter-dynastic chaos adopted a policy of "allowing the people to recuperate," whence derived "the enlightened administration of the Han emperors Wen and Jing." The same was true of the early Tang Dynasty, when a period of peace and prosperity was created in the "Zhen Guan era." Chinese rulers attached great importance to drawing lessons from previous governance experience. These lessons were embodied in concentrated form in the massive historical work *Comprehensive Mirror for Aid in Government* (*Zi Zhi Tong Jian*).

The third factor was that recruitment into elite government positions was through open competition.

In the agrarian empire, the state was family writ large and the family was the state in miniature. As the empire grew, just having a ruler in change was far from enough. It was necessary to hire "stewards" to run the state on behalf of the master, so a class of professional managers, that is, the imperial bureaucracy, came into being. This drew the best and brightest from all over the empire to manage the empire on behalf of the ruler. The imperial bureaucracy grew up via a fully competitive "political market." Its origins lay in the scholars (shi) of the Spring and Autumn and Warring States periods, whose positions derived entirely from their own knowledge and ability regardless of their place of birth or parentage. With the establishment of the empire, recruitment was institutionalized and elite government positions were filled through open competition. Thus was established the imperial examination system, under which regular examinations selected "stewards" to manage national affairs who were devoted to the people, loyal to the monarch and dedicated to the country. The imperial examination system thus became a pillar of the agrarian empire and "provided China with effective and stable government." Independent small-peasant households provided the impetus and wealth for social development, endogenous government capacity ensured its institutional protection and effective national governance provided it with a regulatory mechanism. As a result, a stable political community took root on Chinese soil and endured for millennia, a rare phenomenon in the history of the ancient world. John King Fairbank has said, "In spite of the immensity and variety of the Chinese scene, we need not be surprised that this subcontinent has remained a single political unit where Europe has not; for it is held together by a way of life even more deeply rooted than our own, and stretching even farther back uninterruptedly into the past." "But modern scholarship has made it plain that China was by no means a fossilized example of the world's early empires unchanging through the ages. Quite the contrary." "Continuity, in short. It had created inertia in the sense of momentum, persistence in established channels, not inertness." The impetus for change in China was endogenous, coming especially from wealth creation by the peasants. If it had not been so, there would have been no way of explaining why, before the advent of the West, China enjoyed the world's most enduring and brilliant agrarian civilization.

2 The Curvature of Time: Inertia and Genetic Defects in the Agrarian Empire

Human society develops in an upward spiral rather than a straight line, and this applies particularly to imperial China. In discovering China through comparisons, we cannot ignore the following facts. First, China once created the world's most brilliant agrarian civilization, but it also frequently destroyed that civilization. Second, China had the world's most enduring empire, but that empire was subject to dynastic alternation. Third, China had the world's most influential philosophy of government, yet its governance veered between stability and disorder. Thus, Chinese continuity had a strong element of recurrence. Chinese history often turned a corner; the country would seem to be poised before a new heaven and earth, only to be abruptly propelled back to the starting point. Fairbank divided change in China into two types: permanent (secular) change arising from "irreversible trends," and cyclical change, with its "simple pendulum-like fluctuations" and permanent "irreversible trends." What Westerners saw was the latter, and this shaped their prejudices. In pointing out our main theme, the "permanent changes" in China's development, we cannot ignore the secondary theme of cyclical change, which was likewise buried deep in the genes of the agrarian empire.

2.1 The Dependence of the "Freeman"

An independent population is the driving force behind the creation and accumulation of civilization. In terms of social relations, the ancient agrarian empire created many freemen, which enabled people to move beyond narrow dependency on other individuals. However, this was relative to directly subordinate and hierarchical relationships. At the same time as the empire endowed its inhabitants with a certain autonomy, it imposed on them relations of dependency that limited their initiative and creativity and led to inertia in the development of civilization.

The first factor in this process was the population's high level of dependence on the land.

Agriculture involves repeated production on fixed territory. This repetition, day after day and generation after generation, forged familiarity with and a feeling for the land. At the same time, in the old days, land was the only thing that could be counted on to provide a stable living and source of wealth. Fei Xiaotong called this dependence on the land "viscosity" or stickiness. Together with national population and taxation systems, the division of an inheritance among all sons further strengthened such dependence, institutionalizing viscosity. As land was divided equally among sons, each adult male in the household could hope for an equal portion of land, so the land was repeatedly divided and fragmented. This system precluded wealth accumulation and scale management, instead reproducing small-scale peasant cultivation generation after generation. However intensively and meticulously this land was cultivated, its produce and surplus were limited, so the small-scale peasant economy was generally a subsistence economy. At the same time, the state ensured the stability of tax revenues through the household registration system and other measures that kept the population on the land. The institutionalized viscosity of land made it hard for people to leave the land and seek a wider horizon for survival and development.

The second factor was the population's high level of dependence on the family.

Agriculture relies on the experience of previous generations, and this experience tends to be transmitted through the family's patriarch. Besides, life itself has to be transmitted through the family. This gave people a strong attachment to their families. The household system and national laws greatly magnified this dependence on the family, forming another source of institutionalized viscosity. Under the family system, a person was simply the member of a family, and this membership could only be gained by assuming the responsibilities appropriate to that person's status in the family. Within the family, everybody had a specific status and position that distinguished between senior and junior and male and female. Any violation of this order was regarded as a monstrous heresy. The joint liability system imposed on the family by the state created a situation in which "if one falls all fall; if one rises all rise," which again institutionalized the inherent order of the family. This confined people within the family order and made intergenerational breakthroughs difficult.

The third factor was the population's high level of dependence on the state.

In the agrarian empire, the emergence of the state responded to strong endogenous demand, so small peasants had a natural reverence for the state. In the agrarian empire, the ruler was the final owner of all land; he could not only distribute unowned land but could take over land directly by virtue of the state's monopoly powers. The two factors of land ownership and state control merged in the land system, further strengthening the awe people felt for the state. Even if someone dared to resist, he would only be changing the holder of power rather than institutionalized state power itself.

2.2 Bureaucratic Inertia

The agrarian empire governed the state through the system of prefectures and counties and the corresponding bureaucracy. A bureaucratic rather than a market system gave cohesion to countless small peasants, forming a strong state and strong state capacity. However, from the outset the bureaucracy was accompanied by an intrinsic inertia, which suppressed social development and even destroyed dynastic order, for the following reasons.

Firstly, bureaucrats were responsible to their superiors for centralized governance, which made them passive. As their main responsibility was to maintain order, collect taxes and provide men for military service, they failed to take the initiative in promoting local economic development.

Secondly, bureaucratic promotion channels were very narrow. Thanks to the open competition of the imperial examination system, the bureaucracy was a career open to talent from all over the empire, but within the system, open competition was absent. For one thing, a great many positions at the highest level of the court were not open to competition, being occupied by the emperor's intimates: imperial kinsfolk, eunuchs, and so on. For another, there was no performance evaluation mechanism for the official promotion, rendering promotion wholly dependent on "relationships" with protégés, friends and kinsfolk, people from the same native place, and other forms of personal client-patron relations.

Thirdly, the "household stewards" hired by the emperor feathered their own nests. Bureaucrats' official remuneration was low and they were indoctrinated with the Confucian idea that "the superior man esteems righteousness." But especially in ancient China, the bureaucrat belonged to a professional class. Anyone who wanted to become an official needed the support of the whole family; his success would shed luster on his ancestors and provide generations of patronage for his descendants. Being an official and making money, or being a high official and making lots of money, went together. Bureaucrats made use of their stewardship to get all sorts of informal benefits, but these generally ran counter to the interests of the public. This created a heavy burden for members of society, inhibiting their accumulation of wealth and even overturning dynasties.

2.3 *The Arbitrary Exercise of Power*

The fact that the agrarian empire was a patrimonial state led to a paradoxical relationship between theory and practice. Theoretically, "the world was for all" and governance "centered on people," but the patrimonial nature of the state meant that in reality a single family ruled the country and the emperor was supreme: that is, public power was placed in private hands. The theory that "the world was for all" and governance "centered on people" lacked institutional support and so could not check public power. This led to the arbitrary or capricious exercise of power, with the following features.

(1) *There was no clear boundary between public and private power*

The traditional exercise of state power had two attributes: it met public demand for large-scale water conservancy, disaster relief and military defense, and also met the demands of the rulers themselves, such as the consumption of the imperial household. But there was no clear boundary between the two.

(2) *Society had no power*

Traditionally, land ultimately belonged to the state. Ordinary people's possession of land and property was premised on recognizing and submitting to the rule of the state. Not only ordinary peasants but also the wealthier members of society could not defy the power of the state, which was thus exercised arbitrarily without any checks from society.

(3) *There were no constraints on the supreme power*

Traditionally, the exercise of power ultimately resided with the ruler alone, with no institutional checks. This put especially high demands on the man who wielded that power. Chinese politics particularly emphasized the "Way of governing": governance had its own principles and methods. But in institutional terms, those who could really master the "Way" did not have institutional commonality. It is undeniable that the protection the empire gave the population was premised on their payment of taxes and corvée duties, a burden which was among the world's heaviest due to two-fold expropriation by the state and the landlords. The peasants suffered not only economic exploitation but also supra-economic compulsion. However, their dream was always to lead an independent, unrestrained and self-sufficient life. When this ideal could not be realized, they did not totally submit to fate but fought to wrest concessions from the ruler, who would "reduce taxes and corvée labor" and "grant the people respite," or change land ownership by "dividing land equally," thus promoting a degree of social progress. However, this revolt was undertaken without advanced forces of production or ideas; it was a "revolt without a revolution." The dynastic cycle still determined the pace of Chinese progress. In particular, the random violence of resistance did great damage to civilization and affected the continuity of Chinese development.

3 An Unfinished Relay: An Innovative Chinese Road Taking the Baton from History

In spite of the repetition that characterized China's Road of development, overall it continued to forge ahead and did not stagnate. But in the nineteenth century, Chinese civilization encountered an unprecedented challenge: the industrial civilization of the West, which was already in the ascendant. The declining empire of the late Qing was not capable of coping with a strong industrial civilization. The inertia and ills that had accompanied the empire for thousands of years were all exposed by the challenge of the new industrial civilization.

Although the late Qing court was unable to cope with the challenge, China did not wait for the disposition of fate but generated a strong endogenous force for change.

Firstly, the integration of the empire had given people confidence in the continuity of the Chinese nation. Despite external challenges, this huge country's enduring unity and integrity and the cohesion derived from the integration of family and nation made it difficult for foreign forces from afar to rule China individually. As Marx described it, the Chinese "submitted after defeat with Eastern fatalism to the power of the enemy" after the First Opium War, but this was followed by a "universal outbreak of all Chinese against all foreigners" in a war pro aris et focis and "a popular war for the maintenance of Chinese nationality."

Secondly, faced with this challenge, the noble souls who led the way not only inspired the fight to maintain the continuity of the Chinese people and pursue the historical mission of making China rich and powerful, but also built a consensus on the revival of the Chinese nation, abbreviated as "the laggard gets the beating." Succeeding generations of intellectual elites whose "eyes were open to the world" dedicated themselves to accepting advanced ideas and with unprecedented energy mobilized the whole society to participate in a dramatic revolution; a revolution that would overthrow the imperial system and the old superstructure, and would attempt to eradicate the chronic evils of history. In terms of intensity and depth, the two revolutions—the overthrow of the imperial system and the establishment of the People's Republic—were unprecedented in world history and unleashed an energy that changed everything.

The powerful force of change generated from within was embodied in the birth of the Communist Party of China. Changes under the leadership of the CPC transformed the country, giving the old nation a jolt of new vigor and putting China on the new historical track to the socialist road with Chinese characteristics. During this process, positive historical elements played an important role. The founding of the People's Republic of China (PRC) in 1949 achieved unprecedented national independence and unity. The Qin unification of China was actually "a unified territory with disparate institutions." Under Qin rule, state power did not reach directly into the vast rural and border areas, in accordance with the principle that "Imperial power does not reach down to the county; imperial power does not extend to the border areas." With the help of the revolution, the PRC extended direct state power to the county and below and to the border areas. This involved the basic institutional framework of prefectures and counties, with its long history, ensuring that state power extended to the base level and border areas. A modern national system was thus established rapidly.

Historical complications and setbacks after the establishment of the PRC did not end the development of China but inspired the governing party and the Chinese people to rethink the Chinese development road. In particular, core rural reform involving decentralization and economic invigoration encouraged people to undertake a courageous and insightful exploration of China's Road. The most distinctive feature of rural reform was the reestablishment of the independent status of household operations in a way that recognized and absorbed the positive elements in the historical family system. The abolition of people's communes freed hundreds of millions of peasants from the old system and the land, greatly raising their morale. Rural reform not only brought rapid economic development but also prompted the governing party to explore China's Road of development and develop the idea of socialism with Chinese characteristics. The main feature of the road was going one's own way without blindly copying foreign models; this required following a way that accorded with national conditions, including carrying on China's fine historical tradition. This interlocking with historical continuity was an innovative continuation.

Reform and opening up was the key to China's fate and a node in the formation of the socialist road with Chinese characteristics. The process was one of unprecedented breadth and depth. In particular, the establishment of the socialist market economy activated the positive factors in China's long history and promoted the country's economic and social development. China's reform and opening up was a great achievement that cannot be separated from the ground and undercoat of its long history.

Firstly, China's reform and opening up was an active and predominantly domestic movement, one that was closely related to the autonomy of the population and unity of the nation over its long history. In modern times, individual autonomy was raised to the national level and became national autonomy. The ancient system of prefectures and counties provided formal conditions for a modern country, enabling national unity to be achieved rapidly after 1949. China's autonomy and unity offered basic historical conditions for reform and opening up, making possible the free choice of contents and forms. Priorities for reform and opening up were based on the national interest and aimed at developing the productive forces.

Secondly, it was China's subjective agency and self-awareness that enabled reform and opening up to bring together all positive elements conducive to development and create the miracle of China's rapid economic growth. From the perspective of the world's largest agrarian civilization, this was undoubtedly unique in world history. The elements that created the miracle were positive historical factors such as open markets, active governments and hard work, all of which played an important role in economic development and had historical antecedents. The "Chinese miracle" superimposed the advantages of industrial civilization on those of agrarian civilization, further proving that not all factors in China's 5000 years of history displayed inertia; some were positive and dynamic, albeit somewhat repressed by negative institutions. Once they were reformed, the dynamic factors that had previously been repressed would be released with explosive energy.

Thirdly, the achievements of reform and opening up gave the governing party confidence in its own choice of road, enabling it to adjust its governance thinking and tactics in accordance with changed conditions to govern this massive country effectively in times of change. For example, when the development of the market economy conflicted with the Party's intrinsic ideology, it proposed the thought of the "Three Representatives," emphasizing that the governing party should advance with the times. When economic and social development were unbalanced, the Party put forward the "scientific outlook on development," taking the road of coordinated development. When China became a world economic power with not a few associated problems, the governing party put forward the idea of promoting the modernization of the state governance system and governance capacity, thus deepening and progressing the road of socialism with Chinese characteristics.

China's Road did not come ex nihilo; the country had a strong historical foundation, making its development sustainable rather than subject to rupture. The positive elements in the long history of China's Road not only played a positive role in contemporary development but also, imbued with the innovative meaning of the times, ensured at the same time that Chinese characteristics had universal world significance.

Firstly, man is the creator of civilization, and can only be fully inspired to be creative if he is autonomous. The heart of China's Road centers on people, giving full play to their initiative and creativity. World history is the history of man's liberation; freed from bondage and oppression, he created splendid world civilizations. The ancient Chinese were the first to be freed from narrow regional communities, creating the world's most brilliant agrarian civilization. The revolutions and reforms of the last hundred odd years once more freed the population from oppression, as "the people's position is the fundamental political position of the Chinese Communist Party." This generated a tremendous popular force, creating the miracle of China's development and China's Road. In terms of popular autonomy and creativity, the historical value of China's Road is universal.

Secondly, the sign of a population's entry into civilization is the emergence of the state. Once the state came into being, it had coercive powers, generating powers beyond the reach of any individual. Only those powers born of endogenous social demand and benefiting the human race were sustainable. Conversely, however strong a tyranny might be, its powers were unsustainable if it did not respond to social demand. The Chinese state emerged from public demand, so its public role endured. Revolutions and reforms over the last hundred odd years further endowed the state with responsibility for public functions, requiring it to ceaselessly meet public demands and advance the modernization of the national governance system and governance capacity in order to achieve unprecedented government capacity and the rapid development of China's economy and society. In terms of governmental capacity born of endogenous public needs, the historical value of China's Road is universal.

Thirdly, human society is a process of constant change. Only governance based on adjusting to change can maintain the orderly development of society. No society is unchanging, and similarly there is no unchanging mode of governance. Ideal governance is that which can promote development under different conditions. Since the time when "the great Yu combated the flood," the Chinese state has always adapted its mode of governance, thought he adaptations have varied with differences in scope, degree and nature. Even the Chinese revolutions and reforms of the last century and more have been included in the content and tactics used by the state in adapting to changing times in accordance with changing demands and historical conditions. In terms of adaptive governance, the historical value of China's Road is universal.

CHAPTER 3

China's Path to Modernization (1949–2014)

Hu Angang

In 1949, the People's Republic of China (PRC) was established and the Chinese People's Political Consultative Conference was convened to formulate the "Common Program" and elect the Central People's Government Committee of the People's Republic of China. Mao Zedong then declared the PRC to be founded. He said, "China's history has opened a new era from now on."[1] *He predicted that "as the high tide of the economic construction arrives, the cultural construction will also usher in its high tide.* The era under which Chinese were considered uncivilized has passed and we will appear in the world as a nation with a highly-developed culture."[2] This signifies China's formal entry into its era of modernization. For many Western countries this process has took hundreds of years and for Japan it took 70–80 years after the Meiji Restoration. How then should China start its industri-

[1] Mao Zedong, *Cheer for the Great Union of Chinese People* (September 30, 1949), collected in *Selected Works of Mao Zedong*, Vol. 5, Beijing: People's Publishing House, 1996, p. 347.

[2] Mao Zedong, *Chinese People Stand Up from Now On* (September 21, 1949), collected in *Selected Works of Mao Zedong*, Vol. 5, Beijing: People's Publishing House, 1996, p. 345.

H. Angang (✉)
Institute for Contemporary China Studies, Tsinghua University, Beijing, China
e-mail: anganghu@tsinghua.edu.cn

H. Men (ed.), *On China's Road*,
https://doi.org/10.1007/978-981-13-7880-5_3

alization and modernization? How should it chase after its forerunners? Is it possible for China to become a modernization transcender and inventor?

Today, a very modernized, powerful, and open socialist China towers in the East. Looking back, we can clearly see that China created a great era after 1949, an era for China's industrialization, modernization, and socialism, and an era for the Chinese nation to realize its great rejuvenation.

Since 1949, the aim of New China has always been achieving socialist modernization. This is the grand objective pursued by successive Chinese leaders. At the same time, they have always faced several fundamental problems: What is modernization? What is the proper historical point to start industrialization and modernization? What is China's socialist modernization? How do we design the strategic objective of socialist modernization? How do we achieve the strategic socialist modernization objectives at different stages?

It should be noted, regarding the above problems, that China's leaders did not immediately obtain a profound and comprehensive understanding of which path to follow. Rather, it has been an iterative process that involved continuous practice and understanding, followed by continuous practice and understanding again and again. It is also a process of accuracy and mistakes, success and failure, and ease and difficulties. Thus, it is a socialist modernization path with Chinese characteristics that has been continually explored and innovated.

Taking China's modernization path as the main theme, the text consists of following sections: (1) Definition and Implications of Modernization; (2) How Leaders Recognize China's Modernization; (3) Historical Transition and Stages of China's Modernization; (4) Three Indexes to Measure China's Modernization Progress; (5) China's Path and Three Factors and Advantages; (6) China's Modernization Contributions to World Development; (7) Conclusion: From a Lagger Playing Catch-up to China's Success and Role as a Contributor.

1 Definition and Implications of Modernization

In view of the history of modernization development worldwide, since the first industrial revolution in England, two fundamentally different kinds of modern economic growth paths have emerged. The first path belongs to countries that are leaders in modernization, or technology or science. Economists generally consider these countries in terms of endogenous growth, and their technology improvement is rooted in internal operations rather than significant external technology breakthroughs. Technology improvements enhance the economic growth rate and realize "modern economic growth" where the per capita income or per capita GDP growth rate is more than 1%. The second path belongs to countries that are considered laggards and backward in terms of modernization. Rather than endogenous growth, these countries experience catch-up growth. The technology that facilitates the growth is developed outside these countries rather than within them.[3] Obviously, China displays the typical characteristics of a country that was once backward and a laggard, and has since become a modernization catch-up country.

What is modernization? How does China's socialist modernization occur and develop? As a lagger and latecomer to modernization, is it possible for China to create its own path to modernization? Can it catch up and surpass the modernization of Western countries? These questions are relevant to the basic modernization theories and practices of China's modernization.

Based on Zhang Peigang's definition of industrialization (1949 and 1991),[4] I define modernization as follows: "modernization is a course of continuous breakthrough changes or revolutions within a series of modern factors and a combination of forms, changing from low level to high level worldwide standards."[5]

China's modernization practice is one that has involved the world's largest population and is the most successful to date. It has surpassed Western modernization and has extremely rich implications. How can we understand the meaning of modernization? What enlightenment and

[3] Jeffrey D. Sachs, *The Age of Sustainable Development*, Columbia University Press, March 3, 2015.

[4] In 1949, Zhang Peigang defined industrialization as "a process whereby a series of fundamental production functions undergo continual changes" (Zhang Peigang, *Agriculture and Industrialization: Primary Study on Industrialization Problems in an Agricultural Country*, Wuhan: Publishing House of Huazhong Institute of Technology, 1984, p. 70). Later, Zhang Peigang defined industrialization as "a process whereby a series of fundamental production functions (or a combination of various forms of the production elements) undergo breakthrough changes (reforms) from a low level to a high level in the national economy" (Zhang Peigang, *General Introduction to Development Economy, Vol. 1: Industrial Problems in an Agricultural Country*, p. 190, Changsha: Hunan Publishing House, 1991). This represents the original contribution of Chinese scholars to industrialization theories.

[5] Hu Angang, *China's Road and China's Dream, Hangzhou*: Zhejiang People's Publishing House, 2013.

guidance will it bring to China's modernization? Below, I categorize the meanings into five aspects.

First, modernization must be a historical and development concept. Thus, modernization is not a fixed or immutable concept, but a concept that continually enriches, improves, and changes along with people's modernization progress and cognitive development. It also means that modernization has no fixed mode or unique path. Modernization does not equate with Westernization. Different countries have different modernization roads. For instance, China's modernization path is not an imitation or duplication of Western modernization. Rather, China simply learns from the experiences of others and uses such learning as references. From there, China innovates and surpasses.

Second, modernization should be modernization within the entire society in two main ways: (1) modernization includes not only economic modernization, which is the basis of modernization within the entire society, but also modernization regarding society, politics, culture, the people, the construction of an ecological civilization, and national defense and military. Therefore, "modernization" is not "singular" and is not equivalent to only economic modernization, but it is a "complex" process that affects many facets. (2) Modernization is not only for a select few but for the entire population. Furthermore, it is not only urban modernization but also rural modernization; it is not only modernization in coastal regions but also modernization in central and western regions. Modernization focuses not only on the Han People but also on all minorities within China. In this sense, Chinese modernization must be socialist modernization. Whether it is an education system, a cultural system, a social safeguard system, a basic political system, or a democratic voting system, it should apply to all populations within China, and all people should join in, accept it, and share it.

Third, modernization refers to modern factors and multiple modes involving land, resources, energy, capital, labor, education, science, technology, culture, information, knowledge, system, and laws. Different factors have different modes. Some factors need to use a market mechanism and others need to be provided by using governmental mechanism, or by two or more diversified mechanisms or social cooperative mechanisms.

Fourth, modernization is a process of continual accumulative development and construction. It starts with low-level development, followed by intermediate-level and finally high-level development. Similarly, it starts with quantitative change followed by partial qualitative change, followed by quantitative change and then partial qualitative change, and finally qualitative change. It shows the stage and qualitative change characteristics of modernization development. For instance, in the past 30 years, China has transitioned from absolute poverty, to solving the problem of feeding and clothing its entire population.[6] Furthermore, it has achieved a moderate level of wealth, and created a moderately well-off society.[7] Meanwhile, modernization in China is an unceasing process of accumulation. We should, however, avoid any damage and interruption, namely, "do not be afraid of being slow but instead avoid stagnation and interruption." In this view, the degree of modernization is a function of time.

Fifth, modernization is an all-round revolution process that includes revolutions in terms of, for example, concept, economic system, social system, and culture system. In essence, it is the construction of a modern national system and system reform.

Chinese modernization is reflected in the above five aspects and continues to occur, develop, evolve, transition, and grow. The definition and meaning of the modernization mentioned above provides a theoretical basis for us to understand and analyze Chinese modernization.

2 How Leaders Recognize China's Modernization

Since the founding of New China, China's leaders have always upheld socialist industrialization and modernization as the grand objective, and they consider it as the path to "enrich the nation and strengthen the country." How then do they understand Chinese modernization and design

[6] The report presented at the 14th National Congress of the CPC in 1992 pointed out that China's problem of feeding and clothing 1.1 billion people had been solved and China was marching toward becoming a moderately well-off society. See Jiang Zemin, Accelerate Reform and Opening-up and Modernization Construction Pace, as well as Seize Bigger Victory of Socialist Cause with Chinese Characteristics—Report at the 14th National Congress of CPC, October 12, 1992.

[7] The report presented at the 16th National Congress of the CPC in 2002 revealed that the people's standard of living had reached a moderately well-off level overall. However, the moderately well-off level reached at that time was still at a low level, and represented weak and imbalanced development. The report proposed that in the first 20 years of the century, we must gather all our power to construct a moderately well-off society, in all aspects, of a higher level. See Jiang Zemin, Construct a Moderately Well-off Society in All-round Aspects and Create New Layout of the Socialist Cause with Chinese Characteristics—Report at the 16th National Congress of CPC, November 18, 2002.

the objectives? This has occurred through a repetitive process (practice—understanding—more practice—more understanding) and a multi-cycle cognition process from the realm of necessity to the realm of freedom. Furthermore, it is a historical process of more than 60 years.

In 1953, the Central Committee of the Communist Party of China (CPC) proposed its national industrialization objective:

> The general line and general mission of the CPC is to, over a rather long period, gradually realize national socialist industrialization and complete national socialist reform in the agriculture, handicraft and capitalist industries and to commence this step by step. ... To turn existing non-socialist industries into socialist industries, turn China from a country with underdeveloped industry and backward agriculture into a country with advanced industry, and to make the socialist industry the leading power with a decisive role in the whole national economic development of China.[8]

Following this announcement, China successfully started its national industrialization and easily met the main objectives stated in the first Five-Year Plan. The path to industrialization that the Central Committee of the CPC followed at that time was the same as that undertaken by the Soviet Union.[9]

In 1956, at the 8th National Congress of the CPC, the CPC Constitution first put forward the "Four Modernizations" objective, namely, China would one day possess a powerful modernized industry, modernized agriculture, modernized traffic and transportation system, and modernized national defense.[10] This is the main line of the 8th

[8] *Fight for Mobilizing All Powers to Turn Our Country Into a Great Socialist Country—Study and Publicity Outline of CPC on General Line for Transition Period* (Made and Released by the Propaganda Department of CPC Central Committee in December 1953 and approved by the CPC Central Committee), collected in *Selected Important Documents since the Founding of the PRC*, Vol. 4, Beijing: Central Party Literature Press, 2011, pp. 602–603.

[9] "The road that the Soviet Union followed (the industrialization of the country) in the past is exactly the example that we should learn from." *Fight for Mobilizing All Powers to Turn Our Country into a Great Socialist Country—Study and Publicity Outline of CPC on General Line for Transition Period* (Made and Released by the Propaganda Department of the Central Committee in December 1953 and approved by the CPC Central Committee), collected in *Selected Important Documents since the Founding of PRC*, Vol. 4, Beijing: Central Party Literature Press, 2011, p. 607.

[10] *The Constitution of the CPC* was passed at the 8th National Congress of the CPC. It stated that *the mission of the CPC is to carefully develop the national economy, make all efforts to systematically realize rapid national industrialization and to carry out the technological*

National Congress of the CPC. In the preparatory meeting of the 8th National Congress, Mao Zedong also proposed the objective whereby China would spend 50 years (up till 2006) to catch up to the United States and a further 10 (referring to 2016) to surpass it.[11] Two years later, Mao Zedong started the "Great Leap Forward" without careful consideration and this seriously set back China's modernization process.

By the end of 1964, the first session of the 3rd National Congress of the CPC proposed a new set of "Four Modernizations." The aim was to realize modernization in agriculture, industry, national defense, and science and technology in all aspects within the century.[12] In 1966, one year later, Mao Zedong started and led "the Great Cultural Revolution," again setting back China's modernization.

In January 1975, the first session of the 4th National Congress of the CPC reiterated the "Four Modernizations" to ensure that the Chinese economy ranked first in world.[13] In November of the same year, Mao Zedong set forth his "Anti-Rightist Tendency to Reverse Past Verdicts" and China's development was temporarily interrupted again. Despite these challenges, the CPC's main objective has always been to achieve modernization. In 1977, the 11th National Congress of the CPC once again included the "Four Modernizations" into the CPC Constitution.[14]

reform of the national economy step by step, so that China may have a strong modernized industry, modernized agriculture, modernized traffic and transportation, and modernized national defense. See *Constitution of CPC* (passed in the 8th National Congress of the CPC—September 26, 1956).

[11] Mao Zedong said that "The United States was founded 180 years ago. It had only 4 million tons of steel 60 years ago. We fell behind more than 60 years. *If given 50 or 60 years, we should surpass the United States. This is a kind of responsibility. China has a big population, a large piece of land, rich resources, and followed superior socialism. If China cannot surpass the United States after 50 or 60 years of development, how would the world see China? Then China would be fired from the world! Thus, it was not only probable but absolutely necessary and essential that we surpass the United States.*" See *Selected Works of Mao Zedong*, Vol. 7, Beijing: People's Publishing House, 1999, p. 89.

[12] Zhou Enlai, *Major Tasks to Develop National Economy* (December 21, 1964), collected in *Selected Works of Zhou Enlai*, Vol. 2, Beijing: People's Publishing House, 1984, p. 439.

[13] Zhou Enlai, *March Towards to Grand Objective of Four Modernizations* (January 13, 1975), collected in *Selected Works of Zhou Enlai*, Vol. 2, Beijing: People's Publishing House, 1984, p. 479.

[14] *Constitution of CPC* (General Principles) pointed out that "*within the century, the Party should lead the people to build China into a great socialist power with agricultural modernization, industrial modernization, national defense modernization, and scientific modernization.*" See *Constitution of CPC* (passed in the 11th National Congress of the CPC on August 18, 1977).

After China's reform and opening-up, China's leaders once again had a good understanding of the national conditions. They realistically noted that they would be unable to achieve the "Four Modernizations" by the end of the twentieth century and proposed a modernization objective and roadmap suitable to Chinese conditions.

In December 1978, the central theme of the third session of the 11th National Congress of the CPC was to shift the key emphasis of the work of the CPC to the socialist modernization construction, to carry out the main aim of the 8th National Congress of the CPC, and to start China's reform and opening-up.

At the 12th National Congress of the CPC in 1982, the CPC Constitution considered the realization of the "Four Modernizations" as the key task,[15] and abandoned the idea of achieving the objective by the end of the century. The report presented at the 12th National Congress of the CPC proposed a new objective to be achieved by the end of the century: to quadruple the total value of national industrial and agricultural output. The total national income and the output of the major industrial and agricultural products would rank top in the world. The modernization process of the whole national economy would enjoy significant growth, and the income of China's urban and rural people would double and then redouble. Furthermore, people's material and cultural lives would reach the moderately well-off level.[16] Deng Xiaoping defiantly told the nation at the opening ceremony of the 1982 National Congress to "Go on your own path and build socialism with Chinese characteristics."[17]

In 1987, the report presented at the 13th National Congress of the CPC stated that China's socialist transformation from the private ownership of productive materials (as it had been in the 1950s) was basically complete. Furthermore, it was noted that a further 100 years were required to realize China's socialist modernization and that the nation was

[15] This was proposed in the *Constitution of the CPC* at the 12th National Congress of the CPC: the general task of the Chinese Communist Party was to unite all nations, motivate one's self, work hard, and *gradually modernize industry, agriculture, national defense, and science and technology, and turn China into a socialist country with highly developed civilization and democracy.* See *Constitution of CPC* (passed on September 6, 1982, in the 12th National Congress of the CPC).

[16] Hu Yaobang, *Create a New Socialist Modernization Construction Situation in All Aspects—Report at the 12th National Congress of the CPC*, September 8, 1982.

[17] Deng Xiaoping, *Opening Speech on the 12th National Congress of the CPC* (September 1, 1982), collected in *Selected Works of Deng Xiaoping*, Vol. 3, Beijing: People's Publishing House, 1993, p. 3.

currently in a primary stage of socialism. *Hence, a strategic plan for Chinese economic construction was created: the "Three-step" idea, whereby the catch-up objective was to reach middle-developed countries and the core objective was to achieve overall modernization.*[18]

At the 14th National Congress of the CPC in 1992 and at the 15th National Congress in 1997, modernization, as understood by China's leaders, still focused on economic and socialist modernization, with economic construction being the priority.

After entering the twenty-first century, as the social practice of Chinese modernization deepened the understanding of international modernization, China's leaders have continued to extend the understanding of Chinese modernization and have gradually formed the general layout of China's "five-in-one" modernization process. In 2002, the amendment of the CPC Constitution at the 16th National Congress of the CPC resulted in some new modernization objectives: "in the new century and new stage, the strategic economic and social development objective is to consolidate and develop the essentially obtained moderately well-off level; to build a moderately well-off society of a higher level that benefits 1.3 billion people by the time of the CPC's 100-year anniversary; and China's per capita GNP will equal that of middle-developed countries and we will basically achieve complete modernization before the PRC's 100-year anniversary."[19] Meanwhile, the report presented at the 16th National Congress of the CPC proposed a "three-in-one" layout, including economic construction and economic system reform, political construction and political system reform, and cultural construction and cultural system reform.[20] The 2007 report at the 17th National Congress of the CPC

[18] The report presented at the 13th National Congress of the CPC stated that the strategic deployment of Chinese economic construction was generally divided into three steps: the first step was to double the 1980 GNP rate and to have enough food and clothing. This task has been basically completed. The second step was to achieve, by the end of the century, the doubling of GNP and to improve people's living standards to a moderately well-off level. *By the middle of the next century, the third step was to be achieved: to realize per capita GNP equal to that of middle-developed country*, for people to lead a rich life, and for modernization to be completed. From there, China was to continually march forward on this basis. See Zhao Ziyang, *March Forward Along Socialist Road with Chinese Characteristics—Report at the 13th National Congress of the CPC*, October 25, 1987.

[19] *Constitution of CPC* (partially revised on the 16th National Congress of the CPC and passed on November 14, 2002).

[20] Jiang Zemin, *Build a Moderately Well-off Society and Create New Socialist Cause Situation with Chinese Characteristics in All Aspects—Report at the 16th National Congress of the CPC*, November 8, 2002.

proposed a "four-in-one" layout for economic construction, political construction, cultural construction, and social construction.[21]

In 2012, the report presented at the 18th National Congress of the CPC proposed a "five-in-one" layout for economic construction, political construction, cultural construction, social construction, and ecological civilization construction.[22] The amendment of the CPC Constitution at the 18th National Congress focused on the modernization objective to achieve "a rich, strong, democratic, civilized and harmonious socialist modernized country."[23] In 2013, the third session of the 18th National Congress of the CPC stated that "the general objective of deepening the reform in all aspects is to improve and develop the socialist system with Chinese characteristics and facilitate modernizing the national governance system and capacity."[24]

In this way, the Central Committee of the CPC basically completed the general plan for Chinese socialist modernization in the first 50 years of the twenty-first century (2000–2050). This shows that Chinese modernization includes two main aspects: the first is national modernization construction. The various aspects of China's modernization have become more and more comprehensive and coordinative. This can be seen in the development of the aims: from national industrialization, to the Four Modernizations, to achieving a moderately well-off level, to becoming a moderately well-off society and then the "five-in-one" objective. *The second is national governance modernization.* From the construction of a modernized national system (New China), to the reform, opening-up, and rebuilding of modernized national systems, to continuous reform and

[21] *Decision of the 17th National Congress of the CPC on the 16th Central Committee Report* (passed on the 17th National Congress of the CPC on October 21, 2007).

[22] Hu Jintao, *Unswervingly Adhere to the Socialist Road with Chinese Characteristics While Marching Forward and Strive for Building a Moderately Well-off Society in All Aspects—Report on the 18th National Congress of the CPC*, November 8, 2012.

[23] *Constitution of the CPC* (General Principles), "The basic line of the CPC at the primary stage of socialism is: to lead and unite the Chinese nation to focus on economic construction, adhere to four basic principles, insist on reform and opening-up, motivate itself, work hard to start a business, and *strive to turn China into a rich, powerful, democratic, civilized, and harmonious socialist modernized country*." See *Constitution of CPC* (partially revised in the 18th National Congress of the CPC and passed on November 14, 2012).

[24] *Decision of the Central Committee of the CPC on Several Important Problems in Deepening and Reforming in All Aspects* (passed in the third session of the 18th National Congress of the CPC on November 12, 2013).

the improvement of national systems, and finally to the modernization of China's national governance system and capacity, these two aspects are mutually affiliated, affected, and facilitated. Thus, they constitute a modernization path with Chinese characteristics.

Based on the above, it is clear that the general layout of China's modernization has been formed not once but many times. It has been designed and developed numerous times, and it has gradually become comprehensive by way of much iteration of understanding, continual improvement and practice, and exploration and innovation spanning more than 60 years (first starting in 1953). It can be said that it has transitioned from economic modernization to overall modernization and entailed the coordination of various modernizations in all aspects so as to enable China to facilitate the comprehensive coordination of its modernizations when entering the twenty-first century. From this perspective, China's "five-in-one" modernization strategy has surpassed Western modernization symbolized by economic and material modernization, and it has provided an important experience for Southern countries to innovate and achieve complete modernization.[25] Therefore, the definition and objective of Chinese modernization has, to a great extent, directly influenced the basic features and historical process of Chinese modernization.

3 Historical Transition and Stages of Chinese Modernization

When analyzing the process of Chinese modernization, I adopt the national development lifecycle theory, namely, the "Four-phase Theory" of the national development lifecycle, as the theoretical framework to analyze and explain the road to modernization in China.[26]

Because the world is composed and guided or ruled by many countries rather than just one, especially under the competitive layout designed by big countries, international competition between country A and country B may be formed like market competition between product A and product B. From this the "Four-phase Theory" arrives, generated by the development and competition of two countries. Here, the ratio of the economic

[25] Hu Angang, *China's Road and China's Dream*, Hangzhou: Zhejiang People's Publishing House, 2013, pp. 89–90.

[26] Hu Angang, *National Life Cycle and China's Rising*, collected in *Teaching and Studies*, Issue 1, 2006, pp. 7–17.

power or comprehensive power of one country to the world can be expressed with vertical coordinates to reflect the relative changes in the outcome of competition between country A and country B (Fig. 3.1).

The development lifecycle of modern China is generally composed of two periods: *the first is the period of decline of the traditional country. In the middle of the nineteenth century, China began to follow Western modernization and started to decline. This steered China away from its Chinese development path and further changed Chinese society.* As Mao Zedong pointed out, the capitalist invasion brought two results: the first saw China gradually turn into a semi-colonial and semi-feudal society and the second forced a key change within Chinese society. Capitalism played a significant decomposition role in Chinese economic society. On the one hand, it damaged people's self-sufficiency and destroyed the urban handicraft and rural home craft industries; on the other hand, it facilitated the development of China's urban and rural commodity economy. Therefore, some modernization factors resulted from the capitalist invasion.[27] China was in decline during the Qing Dynasty as were ancient agricultural and farming practices.

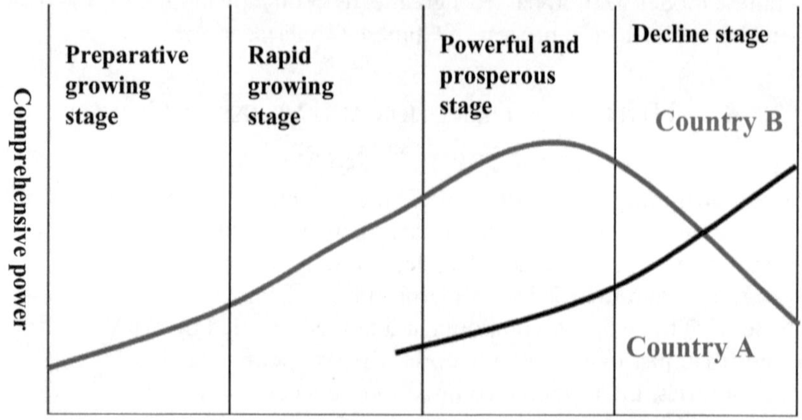

Fig. 3.1 "Four-stage theory" of the national development lifecycle. Data source: Angang Hu, *National Lifecycle and China's Rising*, in Teaching and Studies, Issue 1, 2006, pp. 7–17

[27] See Mao Zedong, *China's Revolution and Chinese Communist Party* (December 1939), collected in *Selected Works of Mao Zedong*, Vol. 2, Beijing: People's Publishing House, 1991, pp. 626–627.

In 1840, China was a closed, rigid and aging "big empire."[28] Britain, with a GDP less than one/third of China's (according to the international dollar price in 1990) defeated China. Then in 1870, China's percentage of GDP to the world's GDP rapidly fell to just 17%. In 1913, when the Qing Dynasty was overthrown as a result of the 1911 Revolution, the percentage dropped even further to 8.8%. The Beiyang government and the government of the Republic of China were unable to save China from its rapid decline and the percentage reduced further to 7.4% in 1929. China's GDP in 1950 was only 4.5%,[29] reaching the lowest point in its history. In addition, China was the poorest country in the world at that time and its per capita GDP was USD 448, far lower than the 1820 rate of USD 600.[30] In 1950, China's generating capacity (a current modernization factor) equaled only 1.2% of the United States' electricity generation. Thus, China represented a country in "poverty and stagnating."

In the second period, China began a new national development lifecycle after 1949, symbolized with a modern economy, ruling party, and national system. Thus, China had entered into the first stage of this period: the preparative growth stage.

The founding of the PRC helped China to finally build a highly unified and independent modern country.[31] Therefore, the People's government under the leadership of the CPC was able to begin its processes of industrialization, urbanization, and modernization on a large scale. This was from the starting point as a historical laggard. From here, modern China entered an era of modern economic development in a true sense, where its annual growth rate of per capita income or per capita GDP now exceeds 1%. China also chose the socialist development path to *become the biggest socialist country in the world and has made full use of the socialist system advantages that gathers all the necessary forces for great events.* Although China was once seriously set back and influenced by the Great Leap

[28] Mao Zedong said, *in the past, China was always described by people as a "big empire," the "sick man of the East," and with a laggard economy, laggard culture, and bad sanitation, and as a country with poor sporting ability, women with small feet, men with braids, and eunuchs.* Mao Zedong, *Strengthen Party's Union and Inherit Party's Tradition* (August 30, 1956), collected in *Selected Works of Mao Zedong*, Vol. 7, Beijing: People's Publishing House, 1999, p. 87.

[29] Angus Maddison, *Historical Statistics of the World Economy: 1–2008 AD.*

[30] Angus Maddison, *Historical Statistics of the World Economy: 1–2008 AD.*

[31] [America] Authored by R.R. Pairner, Joel Colton, and Lloyd Kramer. Sun Fusheng et al., trans., *A History of the Modern World—to 1870 (10e)*, Beijing: World Publishing Corporation, 2010, p. 8.

Forward and the Cultural Revolution, by the end of the 1970s China had achieved industrialization and created independent and relatively complete industrial and national economic systems. Furthermore, a scientific and technological system had been established, as had various social businesses, and primary and secondary school education had been made more accessible. Illiteracy was eliminated and semi-illiteracy rates were down, and this was accompanied by publicly funded healthcare and rural cooperative medical systems. Obvious improvements were also made to the main education, health, and human development indexes.

This laid the foundation for China's material capital, human capital, and system capital to enter the second stage of the national development lifecycle in the era of reform and opening-up: economic take-off and rapid growth. In view of exploring the road to socialist modernization, this stage still comprises experimental exploration and the accumulation of experience.

In 1978, China entered the second stage of its national development lifecycle: rapid growth and modern economic take-off. China will remain in this stage for some time and accelerate its development while pursuing socialist modernization.

According to the historical course of "China's Road," huge economic social changes have occurred in China through its modernization development spanning more than 60 years. These changes are explained below.

From a "country in famine" to the largest agricultural production country in the world: when New China was founded in 1949, its national grain yield was only 1035 kg per hectare, and the per capita grain distribution was only 210 kg. From the foundation of New China to the 1960s, China was a net grain exporter. After the 1960s, China (at certain times) both imported and exported grain, with grain imports exceeding exports. Since the reform and opening-up in the late 1970s, the ratio of imported grain to the grain produced in China has declined: 3.2% in 1978–1984, 1.2% in 1985–1990, and 0.4% in 1991–1995. To date, China has experienced the biggest increase in total grain output, main economic crops, agricultural and livestock products, and agricultural added value. Among the 19 key agricultural products worldwide, China ranks first in the world for 12, second place for 2 products, and third for the remaining 4.

From a country with lagging industries to one with powerful industries: the industrial basis of New China was initially extremely weak. From 1861 to 1949, during which time China attempted to follow Western development, China's total industrial accumulative fixed assets was approximately CNY 10 billion (price at 1952) and its per capita fixed assets close to CNY 20. China's net industrial value was only CNY 4.5 billion, accounting for 12.6% of the national income. The total industrial output was low: China's highest output occurred in 1936, but the United States' steel output was 117 times that of China in the same year, and its electricity generation was 39 times that of China. Various industrial sectors were incomplete and only comprised mining, textile, and simple manufacturing industries. Many products could not be produced independently and China was completely dependent on imports. Now, however, China has built a powerful industrial system with complete industries covering 39 major categories, 191 intermediate categories, and 525 subcategories. According to industrial development and mobilization reports of the UN and international standard industry classifications, among the 22 major categories, China ranks first in 7 manufacturing industries and in the top three in 15 major categories. In 2007, 172 Chinese manufacturing products ranked first and, in 2010, China became the largest manufacture country in the world, producing 19.8% of the world's goods and surpassing the United States (19.4%).[32]

From a country with a backward infrastructure to a country with a modernized infrastructure: in 1949 there was just 80,700 km of highway in China and only 40% was paved. Similarly, there was 21,800 km of railway and the only engines were steam locomotives. China had just 12 small planes, 12 short-distance airlines, and approximately 30 basic airports only suitable for small planes. As of 2014, however, China's railway network measures 111,800 km (surpassing Russia) and ranks the second in the world. Its high-speed railway now covers 16,726 km, giving it a first place world ranking and representing half of the world's high-speed tracks. China's highways total 4,463,900 km, making it second in the world, and its high-speed highways cover 111,900 km. Thus, China has surpassed the United States (92,000 km) and now ranks first in the world. Furthermore, China's inland waterways are now 126,300 km,[33] representing another first place ranking. For eight successive years, China's container throughput at its ports has been the highest in the world. In 2014, the throughput of six Chinese ports made the world's top ten (first: Ningbo-Zhoushan Port; second: Shanghai Port; fourth: Port of Tianjin; sixth: Port of Guangzhou; eight: Port of Qingdao; tenth: Port of Dalian). Five other

[32] Report of HIS Global Insight, American Economic Consulting Organization, March 14, 2011.

[33] Edited by the National Bureau of Statistics of China, *China Statistical Abstract 2015*, Beijing: China Statistics Press, 2015, p. 126.

ports also reached the top ten (first: Shanghai Port; fifth: Ningbo-Zhoushan Port; seventh: Port of Qingdao; eighth: Port of Guangzhou; tenth: Port of Tianjin).

In the early years of the PRC, China's communication capability was extremely outdated and underdeveloped. In the more than 60 years since the foundation of New China, China's communication capacity has rapidly improved, and its network scale and capacity and technological and service levels have experienced significant improvements. Thus, China has created a modern postal service network to connect urban and rural areas. This covers the whole country and links China to the world. It is fast becoming one of the largest postal service networks in the world. China's telecommunication industry now includes a public telecommunication network, and this includes optical fiber, digital microwave communication, satellite, program-controlled switching, mobile telecommunication, and data communication. China's network covers the whole country and links the world. The Chinese telephone network is the largest in the world and China has the most internet users. China has become the largest informatization society in the world and is the biggest producer, consumer, and exporter of ICT technology.

From the world's largest traditional rural society to the world's largest modern urban society: in 1949, there were only 132 cities in China and its urban population was just 39.49 million (7.3% of the entire population). Only ten Chinese cities had a population exceeding 1 million, accounting for 7.6% of the total population. By 2011, China had 657 national cities, including 14 cities with a population of more than 4 million, 31 cities with a population of 2–4 million, 82 cities with a population of 1–2 million, 114 cities with a population of 0.5–1 million, 150 cities with a population of 0.2–0.5 million, and 266 cities with a population of less than 0.2 million. Furthermore, in 2014 the total urban population was 749 million,[34] 2.39 times that of the total population of the United States (2013 data). China's urban infrastructure has also been improved. In 2013, running water was available to 97.6% of the urban population and natural gas was available to 94.3%. Furthermore, as of 2014, 90.2% of the urban population could access sewage treatment and 35.9% of urban areas were green spaces. China is demonstrating remarkable growth in its

[34] Edited by the National Bureau of Statistics of China, *China Statistical Abstract 2015*, Beijing: China Statistics Press, 2015, p. 16.

urbanization strategic layout and has gradually produced three world-class urban agglomerations: the Circum-Bohai-Sea region, Pearl River Delta, and Yangtze River Delta.

From a "country with high illiteracy" to a "country with powerful human resources": in 1949, there were just 116,500 university students and 1.27 million secondary school students, and 80% of the population was illiterate and semi-illiterate. Between 1912 and 1948, just 210,000 students graduated from university.[35] On average, people received only one year of schooling. In 1949, just 0.034% (185,000) of the total population had a university degree. However, by 2010, more than 96% of all adults were considered literate, and the average length of schooling for those aged or above 15 years old had increased to ten years or more. This rate is ten times greater than the 1949 rate, and clearly exceeds the world average (7.76 years). Furthermore, in 2014, China had 25.477 billion students at university or studying higher education, giving it a first place global ranking. Furthermore, the gross entry rate of higher education (18–22 years old) reached 37.5%.[36] In 2014, 150 million Chinese had a university or higher degree, which is 810 times higher than the 1949 rate.

From the "sick man of Asia" to a "healthy China": before 1949, the average life expectancy of Chinese was approximately 35 years; for the rest of the world it was 49 years (in 1950). In 1950, China's infant mortality rate was 200%, which was higher than the average level (175%) for underdeveloped countries. In the early years of the new nation, there were around 20 million drug abusers, representing 3.7% of the total population. After the founding of New China, China introduced its first nationwide health reforms and basically controlled and eliminated serious infectious and parasitic diseases. China created a basic medical care system for both urban and rural populations and now provides medical care services via a commonly available public service. In 2014, life expectancy in China reached 76 years. In 2013, the infant mortality rate declined to just 9.5% and the mortality rate of children under five years fell to 12.0%; the maternal mortality rate declined to 23.2/100,000. These improved indexes are among the highest of developing countries and there is no longer a significant gap between China and developed countries. The incidence of Chinese infectious diseases is lower than the world average and that of most developing countries.

[35] Edited by the National Bureau of Statistics of China, *First Fifty Years of New China (1949–1999)*, Beijing: China Statistics Press, 1999, p. 9.

[36] Edited by the National Bureau of Statistics of China, *China Statistical Abstract 2015*, Beijing: China Statistics Press, 2015, p. 156.

From a country with a "large population living in poverty" to a "moderately well-off society": when New China was founded in 1949, China had the world's largest population living in poverty. The per capita disposable income of urban residents was less than CNY 100 and the per capita income of rural residents was CNY 44. The Engel coefficient of urban households was estimated to be higher than 70% and for rural households it was estimated at more than 80%. In 2014, China's per capita GDP was approximately USD 7380 (and ranked 96th of 214 countries or regions).[37] However, the Engel coefficient of urban residents decreased to 30.0% in 2014 and this population has now entered a richer level. The Engel coefficient of rural residents has decreased to below 33.6%,[38] and they have entered the rich level. In 2012, the per capita construction area of urban and rural residents was 32.9 m^2 and 37.1 m^2, respectively.[39] The human development index improved from an extremely low level of 0.125 (in 1950) to 0.456 in 1980, reaching 0.719 in 2013; this ranked China 91st among 187 other countries or regions. China has entered a level of high human development and enjoyed the fastest increase of all countries in the past 40 years.

From a country with "sedentary science and technology" to a "creative country": at the beginning of the foundation of the PRC, there were no more than 30 specialist institutes and just 50,000 scientists and technicians, representing 0.028% of China's labor force. Those devoted to scientific research totaled no more than 500. As of 2011, China's population of national scientific and technological employees reached 58 million (1160 times higher than in 1949). Furthermore, 20 million people hold a bachelor degree or higher, and this is higher than in the United States (17 million). In 2014, China's full-time employees devoted to research and experimental development reached 3.937 million,[40] far exceeding that in the United States (1.4 million, data for 2000–2006), the EU (1.2981 million, data for 2000–2006), and Japan (780,500, data for 2000–2006). China has become the second largest knowledge-producing country in the world, the first in patent applications, and the third in international patent applications. Furthermore, China exports the highest number of high-tech products.

[37] Database of the World Bank, http://data.worldbank.org.cn/.

[38] Edited by the National Bureau of Statistics of China, *China Statistical Abstract 2015*, Beijing: China Statistics Press, 2015, p. 58.

[39] Ibid., p. 60.

[40] Ibid., p. 150.

From a closed and semi-closed society to an open society in all aspects: in 1950, China's imports and exports totaled USD 1.1 billion, accounting for 0.9% of the world's total trade volume and representing just 5.5% of that of the United States and 23.4% of Germany (West Germany). In 1978, this amount increased to USD 21.1 billion, accounting for 0.8% of the world total and equivalent to 6.4% of the United States' trade volume and 8% of Germany's.

Now, according to 2014 values, China is the biggest exporter, accounting for 12.37% of the world's total exports. Furthermore, it is the world's second largest importer, accounting for 10.30% of total imports worldwide.[41] China is the biggest importer and exporter of goods (29th in 1978), the 5th largest service exporter, and the 2nd largest service importer in the word. China's foreign exchange earnings from international tourism ranked it fifth in the world. From 1979 to 2014, China's total foreign direct investment exceeded USD 1513.3 billion[42] and its total foreign capital value ranked it second in the world.

Thus, the modernization progress achieved by New China in the past 60 years represents a real historical transition: China was once characterized by its poverty and stagnation, and it was often described as "big but weak" and as a "big empire." Similarly, it was noted for its traditional agricultural economy and society. However, all that changed when China underwent a remarkable transformation and emerged as a country with an increasingly modernized economy and society. Thus, it is now an increasingly powerful socialist country. The CPC has become the core power to lead the cause of socialist modernization.

4 Four Indexes to Measure China's Modernization Progress

How can we balance China's modernization process? What indexes can be used to fairly and correctly measure the modernization process? Does China's modernization process follow the same trends as other big countries such as, for instance, the United States, or does it have different features? First, a distinction needs to be made between two types of indexes: the first com-

[41] Data source: WTO Database, quoting from an edition by the National Bureau of Statistics of China, *China Statistical Abstract 2015*, Beijing: China Statistics Press, 2015, p. 176.

[42] Edited by National Bureau of Statistics of China, *China Statistical Abstract 2015*, Beijing: China Statistics Press, 2015, p. 96.

pares national modernization progress and therefore a gross index is generally adopted; the other compares national modernization levels and a per capita index is generally adopted. Here I mainly compare the gross development of China and the United States and adopt four indexes:

- *The first is a GDP index relevant to economic growth.* GDP is used to balance the value of a country's total economic output and the value of all final products and labor service outputs in the economy of a particular country. The advent of GDP is one of the greatest developments of the twentieth century, whereby, for the first time, a system of national accounts could be used to measure the material wealth and national economic power of individual countries and the world.
- *The second is generating capacity relevant to modernization factors. Generating capacity* is a physical quantity index to measure the modernization factors of individual countries, and it the most important innovation to come out of the industrial revolution so far. It is also the most popular example of technology in the world. Here we suppose that modernization cannot occur without generating capacity[43] and modernization factors exist only when generating capacity is realized. This measure is applied to both countries and families.
- *The third is indexes that can symbolize scientific and technological development capacity*, for instance, the *application and granting of patents.* These indexes are a kind of capacity that measures a country's scientific and creative power during its modernization process and influences human development and people's life quality.
- *The fourth is an index of international market competitive capacity*, which measures, for instance, exports. It is an index that measures a country's competitive capacity in the international market during its modernization process and the country's contributive capacity to global transaction growth.

To conduct my international comparisons and to measure China's degree of modernization I use China's index scores relative to those of

[43] According to the estimate of International Energy Agency, over 20% of the world's population has no access to electricity and most of them live in Sub-Saharan Africa, India, and in villages of other developing countries in Asia. International Energy Agency, September 21, 2010.

the United States. Thus, I use the United States, the world's most developed and powerful country, as the catch-up reference number and take its values as 100% to implement a relative and dynamic measurement. For the sake of simplification and convenience, I use four indexes (see Table 3.1): the first is GDP (purchasing power parity [PPP], international dollar in 1990). It is the best index for carrying out long-term historical comparisons. I also consider short-term international comparisons and use and refer to GDP looking at both PPP (current dollar price) and the exchange rate method (current dollar price). The second is exports and the third is generating capacity. The fourth index is the number of patent applications. The latter three indexes can be used for both long- and short-term comparisons.

Table 3.1 Comparison of main Chinese and US indexes (1950–2014)

Year	*GDP (PPP, 1990/ USD)*[a]	*GDP (PPP, current USD price)*[b]	*GDP (exchange rate law; current USD)*[c]	*Amount of exports (current USD price)*[d]	*Generating capacity*[e]	*Application amount of invention patent*[f]
1950	16.8			14.7	1.2	
1960	21.6		11.4	9.2 (1961)	6.8	
1970	20.7		8.5	5.3	6.7	
1980	24.6		6.6	8.0	12.1	
1990	36.6	19.1	6.0	15.8	19.5	5.9
2000	41.0	35.1	11.6	31.9	34.0	17.5
2010	104.1	81.0	39.6	123.4	97.2	79.8
2012	117.1	91.0	50.7	132.4	116.0	120.3
2013	123.5	96.2	55.0	140.0	126.5	144.0
2014	126.6	103.5	59.5	144.3	131.5	

[a]Data for 1950–2008 from Angus Maddison: Historical Statistics of the World Economy: 1–2008 AD; data for 2010–2014 was calculated by the author

[b]Data for 1990–2014: World Bank, World Development Indicator 2015; IMF: World Economic Outlook, April 2015, p. 149

[c]Data for 1960–2014: World Bank, World Development Indicator 2015

[d]Commodity export data: data in 1950 was sourced from Angus Maddison; *Bicentennial Review of World Economy*, Chinese Edition, Beijing: Reform Publishing House, 1997, pp. 162–163; export data for 1960–2014 is sourced from the database of World Trade Organization and World Bank, http://data.worldbank.org.cn

[e]Generating capacity data for 1950–1985: New Palgrave World History Statistics; data for 1990–2014 sourced from BP Statistical Review of World Energy 2015

[f]Database of the World Intellectual Property Organization (WIPO), 2014

According to the GDP (PPP, international dollar in 1990) index, China first experienced a decrease and then an increase relative to the US level. During 1900–1950, the index dropped continually from 68.9% to 16.8%; it then increased after 1950 until it reached 24.6% in 1980.[44] The index clearly increased after 1980, more so after 2000, and surpassed the United States in 2010. The index reached 126.6% in 2014 (see Table 3.1).

Since 1950, China's international GDP status has shown a constant increase: in 1950, China ranked fifth in terms of GDP, sitting behind the United States, the Soviet Union, Britain, and Germany. In 1961, Japan passed China, pushing it to the sixth place. However, in 1966, China's GDP was close to that of Britain (they both ranked fifth) after the United States, the Soviet Union, Japan, and Germany. In 1967, China was again in sixth place. However, by 1970 China ranked fifth after the United States, the Soviet Union, Japan, and Germany. By 1982, China was still in fourth position but surpassed Germany (following the United States, the Soviet Union, and Japan). China surpassed the Soviet Union in 1990 and sat in third place after the United States and Japan. China moved to the second place in 1992 (surpassing Japan), and to the first place in 2010.

According to the GDP index using the PPP method (current dollar price), China's GDP in 1990 was equivalent to 19.1% of the US rate and exceeded the United States' GDP, equivalent to 103.5% of the US rate (see Table 3.1).

According to the GDP exchange rate method (calculation according to current dollar price), in 1990 China's GDP was equivalent to 6.0% of the GDP of the United States and increased to 59.5% in 2014 (see Table 3.1). According to the growth trend, China will surpass the United States around 2020. This will likely represent the last remaining key index in which China has yet to surpass the United States.

Regarding generating capacity, China's modernization factors continue to increase, and its total has surpassed that of the United States. In 1900, China's generating capacity was equivalent to only 0.01% that of the United States. Thus, the United States' generating capacity was about 10,000 times greater than China's and it can be said that China was essentially engaged in non-modernization. In 1950, half a century later, China's generating capacity was only 1.2% that of the United States. Thus, China's degree of modernization was at the levels of "poverty and stagnation"; the United States' modernization factors were 83 times greater than China's.

[44] Angus Maddison, *Historical Statistics of the World Economy: 1–2008 AD.*

After the industrialization and modernization achieved in Mao Zedong's era, by 1980 China's generating capacity equaled 12.1% of the US generating capacity, meaning that China's modernization factors had increased tenfold and the gap between the United States and China had been reduced 8.26 times. After 1980, China's generating capacity increased continually relative to the US level and reached 34% in 2000. It exceeded the United States in 2011. In 2014, China's generating capacity was 131.5% that of the United States.

In 1950, China's generating ratio represented just 0.48% of the world total. However, by 1980, China's generating capacity far exceeded that of Britain. Furthermore, by 1986, China's generating capacity exceeded that of Germany and then surpassed Russia in 1994, Japan in 1995, and the United States in 2011. As of 2014, China's generating capacity represented 24% of the world's total (see Fig. 3.2). Thus, China's modernization factors have exceeded those of the United States.

Sixty-five years ago, China had an essentially non-existent electricity network and just a small proportion of the population had access to electricity. Over the last 60 years, China has managed to provide "total electricity coverage" to the entire population. According to the 12th Five-Year

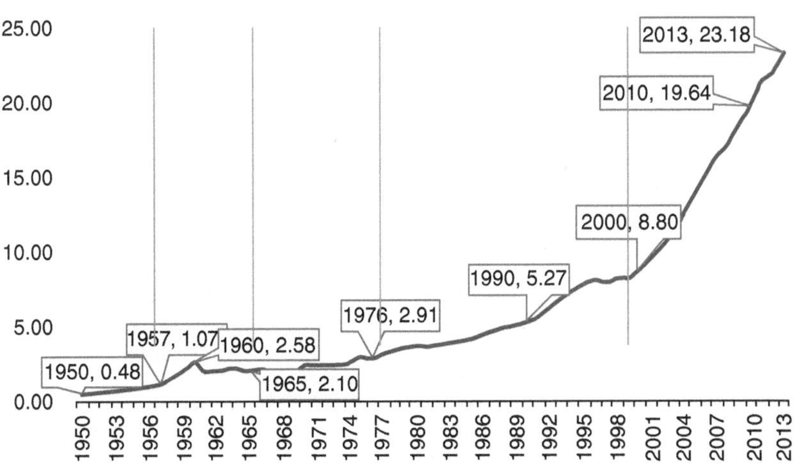

Fig. 3.2 Ratio of China's generating capacity to the world (1950–2013, %). Data for 1950–1992 sourced from *New Palgrave World History Statistics*; data for 1992–2013 sourced from *BP Statistical Review of World Energy 2014*; data for 2020–2030 calculated by the author

Plan on national energy, China will achieve the objective that "all administrative villages will have an electricity supply and people in regions without electricity will obtain electricity."[45] This means that all Chinese will experience the modernization factor "total coverage," with China being the first of all developing countries to realize this objective.[46]

Regarding patents, China has significantly narrowed the gap between itself and the United States. In 2013, China became the country with the largest number of patent applications and was ranked second in terms of the number of successful applications.

Regarding the drafting and issuing of patent laws and regulations, China is a follower[47] in that it first began to do so some 200 years after Britain. However, China has also had great success in catching up and transcending other countries. In 1624, Britain passed the Statute of Monopoly; in 1790, America enacted its first patent law, with France following in 1791. In 1877, Germany followed suit and Japan introduced its patent law in 1899. In 1968, the number of patent applications filed in Japan surpassed that of the United States and, in 1978, the Patent Cooperation Treaty came into effect.

Historically, China had always had a scarcity of technological patents. During the 32 years from 1912 to 1944, just 692 patents were approved.[48] It

[45] *Energy Development the "12th Five-year Plan,"* http://www.gov.cn/zwgk/2013-01/23/content_2318554.htm, January 1, 2013.

[46] According to the estimates of the World Bank, at present, approximately 1.2 billion of the world's population does not have access to electricity, accounting for 17% of the world's total population (7.09 billion). The largest proportion of these people live in *India, namely, 306.2 million people (representing 25% of the global population without electricity and 25% of the Indian population)*. Populations without electricity—Nigeria: 82.40 million; Bangladesh: 63.90 million; Congo: 55.90 million; Tanzania: 38.20 million; Kenya: 31.20 billion; Sudan: 30.90 million; Uganda: 28.50 million; Burma: 24.6 million; Mozambique: 19.9 million; Afghanistan: 18.5 million; North Korea: 19 million; Madagascar: 17.8 million; the Philippines: 15.6 million; and Pakistan: 15 million (Website of the Ministry of Commerce, June 7, 2013).

[47] In May 1898, the Qing Regime issued China's first regulation about patents—*Revitalization Technology Reward Regulation*. The regulation states that the invention would be protected by the patent for 50, 30, or 10 years, depending on the invention. *However, at its essence is an exclusive right and this differs from the meaning of an existing patent right. The regulation was abolished two months later*. In 1912, the government of the Republic of China introduced the *Award Craft Temporary Regulation*. In 1944, the Kuomintang government enacted the Law of Patent. *Chinese Patent History (II)*, Website of State Intellectual Property Office, July 14, 2005.

[48] *Chinese Patent History (II)*, Website of State Intellectual Property Office, July 14, 2005.

was not until May 1, 1985, that China enacted its first patent law. China is not only a successor of already established modern intellectual property systems but also a country with a largely non-existent patent history. However, China has played catch-up and transcended the established players in the world of patent applications. For example, regarding China's global status for the number of patent applications, China surpassed France in 1993, Britain in 1998, Germany in 2001, Japan in 2010, and the United States in 2011.

In 1985, the number of patent applications filed by China equaled just 7.4% of the United States; however, this increased to 17.5% by 2000. China then entered an accelerated catch-up stage and surpassed the United States in 2011. In 2013, the number of Chinese applications was 1.44 times that of the United States (see Table 3.1).

In 1950, China's exports totaled just 1.7% of the world's exports and this decreased to 0.69% in 1977, the lowest point in China's history. In 1978, Chinese exports were ranked 28th in the world. After this point, China began to experience considerable growth, reaching 3.83% in 2000 and 9.51% in 2009. Thus, China became the largest exporter worldwide. In 2014, China's exports represented 12.37% of the world's total.

In 1950, Chinese exports matched just 14.7% of those from the United States, and this figure declined to 5.3% in 1970. After the reform and opening-up, Chinese exports in 1978 were equivalent to 6.8% of the United States' exports, increasing to 36.5% by 2001. After China joined the World Trade Organization (WTO), China's catch-up to the United States was accelerated. In 2014, China surpassed the United States, exporting the equivalent of 144.3% of the United States' output. China's total goods transactions exceeded those of the United States (1.067 times greater), ending the United States' historical run in first place since its passing of Britain in 1913. The change in China's main indexes, relative to US levels, reflects that China, as a modernization lagger, is also a catcher and will be a transcender. In terms of national development lifecycle theory, China first experienced an initial growth period (1949–1977) followed by a period of rapid growth (1978–), and this period has not yet ended.

In the four core indexes relative to US levels, China has successively experienced three phases: the preliminary chase, a fast chase, and overtaking. China realized the various industrialization and modernization stages within a much shorter time period than the United States—it took the United States more than 200 years to achieve such development. While China has surpassed the United States in the above four indexes, a considerable gap remains in terms of per capita values. Thus, it will take more

Table 3.2 China's main per capita indexes relative to US levels (1950–2014)

Year	*Per capita GDP (PPP, international dollar in 1990)*[a]	*Per capita invention patent application quantity (piece)*[b]	*Per capita good exports (dollar)*[c]	*Per capital generating capacity (kWh)*[d]
1950	4.7			0.3
1960	5.8		2.6 (1961)	1.4
1970	5.2		1.3	1.5
1980	5.7	1.7 (1985)	1.9	2.7
1990	8.1	1.3	3.5	4.1
2000	11.7	3.9	7.1	7.6
2010	25.6	18.5	28.5	20.7
2014	29.4	33.5 (2013)	32.6	30.6

[a]Data for 1950–2008: Angus Maddison: Historical Statistics of the World Economy: 1–2008 AD; the data for 2010–2014 was calculated by the author

[b]Data source: Database of WIPO, 2014

[c]Data on commodity exports: data for 1950 was calculated by Angus Maddison; Bicentennial Review of World Economy, Chinese Edition, Beijing, Reform Publishing House, 1997, pp. 162–163; export data for 1960–2014 was sourced from the database of WTO and World Bank, http://data.worldbank.org.cn

[d]Generating capacity data for 1950–1985: New Palgrave World History Statistics; data for 1990–2014: BP Statistical Review of World Energy 2015

time to reduce this gap. China must follow two strategies to reach the level of US modernization. The first strategy is to chase after and surpass the United States in the main indexes and China has essentially spent more than 60 years (1949–2014) doing so; the second strategy is to chase after and surpass the United States in terms of per capita values within the main indexes and this will require further decades to achieve. Thus, we have entered a new chase phase.

China's creative capacity influences China's national development life-cycle and determines that not only China can successfully chase after the United States but it will also successfully surpass it (Table 3.2).

5 China's Path and Three Factors and Advantages

How was China able to change from a poverty-stricken and barren country into the most powerful socialist modernized country in the world? In regard to this point, Mao Zedong had a plan and much foresight as well. In 1954, at the opening ceremony of the first session of the 1st National

Congress of the CPC, Mao Zedong proposed to "build China into an industrialized and great country with highly modern civilization." He also announced a fundamental system plan for realizing that objective: "the core power of leading our advancement is the CPC."[49] Looking back now, it can be seen that the latter was not able to exist without the former. Nevertheless, the latter carries the Chinese socialist modernization mission as well as the task of rejuvenating China into a great nation. The most important point is that it created China's Path.

Chinese biggest innovation is "China's Road," namely, *socialist modernization path with Chinese characteristics.* In the beginning of the reform, China's leaders noticed that "what we have seized is great. It is absolutely wrong to neglect the great achievement." Similarly, they were aware that "The path that we have experienced is not flat. We have experienced not only relatively smooth development but also serious setbacks. Compared to the hard work and effort of the Chinese people, plus the superiority of the socialist system, our achievements are insufficient."[50] *However, China's leaders did not abandon the quest for socialism in light of these setbacks and failures; instead, they resolutely proposed that China's reform objective still needed to adhere to the path of socialism*, but one that differed from socialism under the Soviet Union. *From the very beginning of the reform, China's leaders consciously proposed "China's Path," namely, followed the objective of building a socialist modernization path with Chinese characteristics.* In April 1979, Li Xiannian raised a significant problem: how should China implement its modernization? In response, he answered on behalf of the Political Bureau of the Central Committee of the CPC and the State Council: "we must start from the actual conditions of our country and walk a Chinese-style path that realizes modernization under a socialist system."[51]

This is the earliest expression of "China's Road," and included three basic factors: the first is the modernization factor and at that time it referred to "Four Modernizations"; the second is the socialist factor, refer-

[49] Mao Zedong, *Fight for Building a Great Socialist Country*, collected in *Selected Works of Mao Zedong*, Vol. 6, People's Publishing House, 1999, p. 350.

[50] Ye Jianying, *Speech on Celebrating the 30th Anniversary of the Foundation of the People's Republic of China* (September 29, 1979), collected in *Decisions and Determinations of the Reports and Bulletins of the Congress of Party Representatives and Plenary Session of the Central Committee Since the 3rd Session of the 11th National Congress of the CPC*, Beijing: China Fangzheng Press, 2008, p. 52.

[51] Li Xiannian, *Speech on Central Working Meeting* (April 5, 1979), collected in *Selected Works of Li Xiannian (1935–1988)*, Beijing: People's Publishing House, 1989, pp. 356 and 358.

ring to a fundamental political socialist system and a fundamental economic system, and this the most important factor emphasized by Mao Zedong; and the third is the factor of Chinese culture—a basic factor that provides a valuable historical source.

5.1 Three Factors of China's Road

(1) *Continually increase its modernization factors*: enlarge production, create wealth, and make full use of modern elements such as land, resources, energy, capital, labor, education, science, technology, culture, information, knowledge, systems, and laws. Regarding the modern elements already possessed by developed countries, China should also possess these but reach a much higher level. Regarding those modern elements not yet possessed by developed countries, China needs to work hard to obtain these.
(2) *Continually increase the socialist factors*: China needs to realize common development, common sharing, and common prosperity, develop the political advantages of the socialist system, and solve the extremely serious problems that were unable to be solved in the past while following capitalist modernization (e.g., economic crises, financial crises, and the polarization between the rich and poor).
(3) *Continually increase China's cultural factors*: China needs to engage in significant innovation in building an ideal society with Chinese characteristics such as a moderately well-off society, a harmonious society, a learning society, and a content society. China needs to walk a path of peaceful development and build a harmonious world.

If the first factor of China's modernization path is basically the same as that of the United States, then the second and third factors represent the biggest difference between China and the United States. Thus, China's Road is unique and it also displays unique advantages.

5.2 Three Advantages of China's Road

(1) *Late-mover advantage*: this means that China's catch-up (as a backward country) in terms of economic growth may be much faster than the endogenous economic growth a newer country. For instance, while

the annual growth rate of the former's per capita GDP is 1–2%, the latter exceeds China and a rapid chase begins.[52] China is the most successful chaser in the world to date. Although China is still far from the threshold (i.e., USD 2000; international dollar in 1990) for per capita GDP (PPP) to realize modern economic growth and take-off[53] (e.g., China's per capita GDP in 1950 was only USD 448), China experienced its first significant economic growth period in 1950–1957 and its annual GDP growth reached 9.2%. Furthermore, China's percentage of GDP in the world total improved from 4.6% to 5.5%.[54] Even at the beginning of the reform and opening-up in 1978, China's per capita GDP was only USD 978. However, China then entered a period of economic growth lasting more than 30 years. China's economic growth rate was around 10% and this substantially narrowed the relative gap with the United States. It is undeniable that China has indeed has made full use of its late-mover advantage to achieve catch-up economic growth through opening-up, attracting foreign capital, and via the large-scale importing of advanced technologies. Thus, in many technological innovative fields, the gap between China and the world's most advanced technological level continues to narrow. The entire society becomes richer and the entire country becomes more developed. Thus, China faces two choices. The first is to continually implement its traditional catch-up strategy, to introduce and purchase new technologies, to learn from and copy developed countries, stick to this path, lock self, imitate at every step, and to forever be a follower. The second, however, is to implement an innovation-driven strategy, introduce new innovations, including assembly and system innovations, while continually introducing advanced technologies and strengthening independent innovation. Within this pathway, China will transform from a learner to a transcender, from a copier to an innovator, and from a follower to a leader. Similarly, China will change from a manufacturer to a creator, and from a technology importer to a technology exporter. The most important requirement is to study and surpass the modernization mode of developed countries, learn from their experiences, avoid their pitfalls,

[52] Jeffrey D. Sachs, *The Age of Sustainable Development*, Columbia University Press, March 3, 2015.

[53] Jeffrey D. Sachs, *The Age of Sustainable Development*, Columbia University Press, March 3, 2015.

[54] Angus Maddison, *Historical Statistics of the World Economy: 1–2008 AD.*

and create green industrialization, urbanization, and modernization from a higher, newer, and greener starting point. China must further realize the transition from modernization chaser to modernization innovator and leader, and provide experiences for Southern countries to advance and realize modernization of their own.

(2) *Socialist advantage*: as a country with delayed modernization, to change from an underdeveloped poverty-stricken country to a developed country, China has always had the choice of two different paths: the first was to closely copy Western countries, to walk the capitalist path, and to change an Eastern country into a Western country and then ultimately become a developed country. This was the choice China made in the first half of the twentieth century. However, Western teachers have always bullied the Chinese student and failed to help China experience real modernization. Between 1913 and 1950, China's generating capacity only increased from 0.26% to 1.2% (as a percentage equivalent to that of the United States). The proportion of China's GDP to the world's declined from 8.8% in 1913 to 4.6% in 1950. This approach failed to make China rich. Furthermore, China's GDP declined from USD 552 in 1913 to USD 448 in 1950.[55] The second choice was to choose a special path, to create a special system, and to form a special political advantage. Only in this way can China accelerate its catch-up to Western countries, especially the United States. It was for this reason that China's leaders chose the path of socialism and created a socialist system. Historical facts proved that it was reasonable and feasible and exceptionally unique. The road to modernization in China is an innovation of the socialist path instead of simply reenacting the capitalist path. This represents the biggest difference to all developed countries and explains why China has emerged as an economic wonder. Geoffrey Sax described China as a unique example of a fast economic growth miracle. In any case, China's economic growth is second to none and, now, anything that China does, with its population of 1.3 billion, will shock the world. Since 1978, as a fast-growing economic entity, China's GDP has experienced an annual increase of 10%.[56]

(3) *China's cultural advantages*: China has a unique culture that has evolved for more than 5000 years. It is a culture that is rich in historical and cultural resources. China's rich history of culture not only lends nourishment to China's modernization but also facilitates it to be more

[55] Angus Maddison, *Historical Statistics of the World Economy: 1–2008 AD.*

[56] Jeffrey D. Sachs, *The Age of Sustainable Development*, Columbia University Press, March 3, 2015.

open and tolerant. By studying other cultures from around the world and by learning, communicating, and engaging, Chinese culture will become a huge cultural advantage that leads to modernization with Chinese characteristics.[57]

China's Road consists of a main path and a branch path. The main path is the socialist modernization path with Chinese characteristics. What then is the socialist modernization path with Chinese characteristics? In his speech celebrating the 90th anniversary of the foundation of the CPC, Hu Jintao provided a classic definition: *the path of socialism with Chinese characteristics is the unavoidable path to realize socialist modernization and it is the only path to create a beautiful path for the people.*[58]

On November 8, 2012, Hu Jintao further concluded in the report presented at the 18th National Congress of CPC that

> the path of socialism with Chinese characteristics, under the leadership of the CPC and based on national conditions, is to focus on economic construction as the core, adhere to the four fundamental principles, insist on reform and opening-up, release and develop social productivity, and to build a socialist market economy, socialist democratic politics, socialist advanced culture, socialist harmonious society, and socialist ecological civilization, and facilitate human development in all aspects. It is to gradually realize the common enrichment of all people and build a rich, democratic, civilized and harmonious socialist modern country.[59]

[57] Xi Jinping commented at the closing ceremony of the first session of the 12th National Congress of the CPC on March 17, 2013: The Chinese nation is a nation with extraordinary creative power. We have created a great Chinese civilization and we can also continually expand and well walk the development road in compliance with Chinese conditions. All nationalities should strengthen their confidence in the socialist theory, socialist road, and socialist system with Chinese characteristics and unswervingly adhere to the correct Chinese road.

[58] Comrade Hu Jintao concluded with a description of the "socialist road with Chinese characteristics": "it means to, under the leadership of the CPC, be rooted in basic national conditions, concentrate on economic construction, uphold the four fundamental principles, adhere to the reform and openness, liberate and develop social productivity, consolidate and improve the socialist system, build a socialist market economy, socialist democratic politics, socialist advanced culture, socialist harmonious society and establish a rich, powerful, democratic, civilized and harmonious socialist modernized country." See Hu Jintao, *Speech on Celebrating the 90th Anniversary of the Foundation of the CPC*, July 1, 2011.

[59] The underlining is added for emphasis. Hu Jintao, *Unswervingly Adhere to Socialist Road with Chinese Characteristics and Fight for Establishing Moderately Well-off Society in All Aspects—Report on the 18th National Congress of the CPC*, November 8, 2012.

This description fully reflects the "five-in-one" modernization factors, socialist factors, and Chinese cultural factors. The adding of the following sentence, "develop socialist ecological civilization, facilitate human development in all aspects and gradually realize common enrichment of all people," clearly expresses China's Road in a clear and comprehensive manner. *It also reflects the three steps and three stages of China's Road: the "some are rich first" stage (1978–2001); the "common rich theory" stage (2002–2030); and "everyone is rich" (2030–).*

The detailed path includes an agricultural modernization path with Chinese characteristics,[60] a new industrialization path with Chinese characteristics,[61]

[60] Comrade Hu Jintao pointed out that "to follow the agricultural modernization road with Chinese characteristics is a necessary choice in following the common agricultural development rules of the world but rooted in Chinese conditions. It is the inevitable requirement of planning urban and rural development and coordinating and facilitating industrialization and urbanization, and it is the unavoidable road to building a new socialist society and advancing agricultural sustainable development. … [T]he general idea to facilitate the rural reform and development is to consider the construction of the new socialist society as a strategic task, to follow the agricultural modernization road with Chinese characteristics as the basic direction, and to make the acceleration of forming a new integrated layout of the urban and rural economy a fundamental requirement. It is to insist that industry re-feeds agriculture, the city supports the village and gives more, takes less, and we liberate the countryside and push forward for the sound and rapid development of the agricultural economic society." See Xinhua Agency, Beijing, January 24, 2009.

[61] The report presented at the 16th National Congress of the CPC pointed out that "it remains China's arduous historical task during the modernization process to *follow a new industrialization road*, implement a strategy to rejuvenate the country through science and education, and to realize industrialization. Informatization is an inevitable choice for China to accelerate and realize its industrialization and modernization. Please insist on using informatization to drive industrialization, use industrialization to drive informatization, and walk a new industrialization road with significant science and technology content, good economic benefits, low resource consumption, reduced environmental pollution, and human resource advantages." See Jiang Zemin, *Construction Moderately Well-off Society in All Aspects and Create New Socialist Cause with Chinese Characteristics*, November 2003.

Comrade Hu Jintao pointed out that China should master scientific development, focus on the main task to make changes to China's economic development, follow the industrialization laws, and adapt to the changing market requirements. It is also necessary to *positively develop a modern industrial system with an optimized development structure, advanced technology, strong safety mechanisms, high value, and with powerful employment capacity according to the new scientific and technological improvement trends. Furthermore, we must enhance the industrial development quality and benefits, strive to transition from a big industrial country to a powerful industrial country*, and establish a solid material foundation for building an all-round moderately well-off society and accelerate the advancement of socialist modernization. See Hu Jintao, *Speech on Firmly Following New-type Industrialization Road with Chinese*

new urbanization path with Chinese characteristics,[62] an independent and innovative path with Chinese characteristics,[63] socialist democratic political development with Chinese characteristics,[64] socialist ecological civilization path,[65] and a military–civilian integration development path with Chinese

Characteristics in Political Bureau of the CPC Central Committee and Accelerating Economic Structure Strategic Adjustment in the 33rd Group Study, May 29, 2012.

[62] We must uphold the great socialist flag with Chinese characteristics and follow Deng Xiaoping's theory. Furthermore, we must look to the "Three Representatives" and scientific development strategy for guidance, *focus on enhancing the urbanization quality, and accelerate the transition of urbanization development. Furthermore, we must facilitate the urbanization of the agricultural population with human urbanization as the core. It is also important to advance the coordinative development of big cities, middle-sized cities, and small cities via urban agglomeration, promote urban sustainable development via a comprehensive carrying capacity strategy, and realize the potential for urbanization development through system reform innovation. China's new urbanization road with Chinese characteristics must be followed with its human orientation, synchronization of the four modernizations, optimized design, ecological civilization and cultural inheritance.* We must also advance the economic transition as well as improve social harmony and establish a solid foundation for China's dream of building a moderately well-off society, accelerating socialist modernization, and realizing the great rejuvenation of the Chinese nation. See *National New-type Urbanization Plan (2014–2020).*

[63] Comrade Hu Jintao pointed out that China should implement its scientific development strategy and properly develop the country through science and education. The country should also be strengthened through talents and sustainable strategies, and China needs to seek *independence and innovation, maintain its important scope, support development, and lead the future.* It is also important to improve China's independent creative capacity as the strategic basis to develop science and technology as well as to adjust the industrial structure and implement changes to the development form. We must consider the construction of a creative country as the significant strategic choice for the future and consciously and firmly stick to the independent and creative road with Chinese characteristics. See Hu Jingtao, *Speech on the Opening Ceremony of the 14th Congress of Academicians of the Chinese Academy of Sciences and the 9th Congress of Academicians of the Chinese Academy of Engineering*, June 23, 2008.

[64] Xi Jinping emphasized, "in China, the key to developing socialist democratic politics, guaranteeing people's autonomy of their own affairs, guaranteeing a political life with vitality, stability and order is to adhere to the Party's leadership, the people's autonomy in their own affairs and to rule the country by laws and to carry out organic unity. Thus, the system of the people's congress is a fundamental system. To insist on and improve the system of people's congress, we must unswervingly insist on the leadership of the CPC, guarantee and develop the people's autonomy of their own affairs, facilitate governance by law in all aspects and stick to democratic centralism." See Xi Jinping, *Speech on Celebrating the 60th Anniversary of the National People's Congress*, The Xinhua News Agency, Beijing, September 5.

[65] Xi Jinping points out that, to facilitate the construction of an ecological civilization, we must implement and carry out the spirit of the 18th National Congress of the CPC in all aspects, follow Deng Xiaoping's theory, the important idea of the "Three Representatives,"

characteristics.[66] *The general path decides the detailed path and the detailed path reflects the general path. They are mutually affiliated, supported, and influenced.*

6 China's Modernization Contributions to World Development

Early in 1956, Mao Zedong predicted that "in 40 or 50 years, *namely the year of 2001, entering the twenty-first century, China will undergo a big change. China will turn into a powerful socialist industrial country.* This will happen because China is a country with an area of 9.6 million square meters and with a population of 600 million. *China will make a great contribution to human beings.*"[67] Sixty years later, Mao Zedong's prediction has been proven correct.

China's modernization represents modernization that has affected the largest population and influenced the largest population in the world. When New China was founded, China had the largest rural population, the largest population living in poverty, and the highest illiteracy and semi-illiteracy rates in the world. *The success of China's modernization itself has made great contributions to world development, while also having a significant overflow effect on the outside world*—we call this the "Chinese contribution." Some effects can be calculated and quantitative, while some cannot. Therefore, we need to evaluate such contributions fairly and objectively.

and have a scientific outlook on development. We must also *establish an ecological civilization strategy whereby we respect nature, follow nature and protect nature, and adhere to the basic policy of saving resources and protecting the environment. We must insist on saving, protecting and recovering, and make great efforts to establish an ecological strategy, improve the ecological system, and maintain ecological safety. We must optimize the ecological environment and further form a spatial layout, industrial structure, and productive methods and ways of living to reduce resources and protect the environment.* See Xi Jinping, *Speech at the Sixth Group Study on Ecological Civilization Construction Facilitated by Political Bureau of the Central Committee of the CPC*, May 24, 2013.

[66] Comrade Hu Jintao points out that we must plan the economic construction and national defense construction as a whole and follow the military and civilian integration development road with Chinese characteristics to unite the country's enrichment and military strengthening during the comprehensive construction of a moderately well-off society. See Hu Jintao, *Speech on Celebrating the 90th Anniversary of the Foundation of the CPC*, July 1, 2011.

[67] Mao Zedong, *Memory of Mr. SunYat-sen* (November 12, 1956), collected in *Selected Works of Mao Zedong*, Vol. 7, Beijing: People's Publishing House, 1996, p. 156.

Since the reform and opening-up, China has made a growing contribution, and it has contributed to increasing trade and reducing poverty worldwide.

First, China made the greatest contribution to reduce the number of people living in poverty. In 1981, China had both the largest population and the largest number of people living in poverty. According to data provided by the World Bank, calculated based on the international low-income level whereby per capita consumption expenditure is less than USD 1.25 a day,[68] 835.1 million people were living in poverty in China in 1981. The poverty rate was 84.0%, accounting for 43.6% of absolute poverty in the world. In 2010, these figures declined to 157.1 million, 11.8%, and 12.9% (a decrease of 678.0 million, 72.2%, and 30.7%, respectively). At the same time, the number of people living in absolute poverty reduced from 1.9134 billion in 1981 to 1.215 billion in 2010, representing a decrease of 698.4 million. Thus, the decrease in the number of Chinese living in poverty accounted for 97.1% of the total decrease in poverty worldwide.[69]

Second, China's contribution to the world's economic growth continues to grow. Data provided by a World Bank database, calculated according to PPP, shows that between 1993 and 2007, 19.50% of global economic growth came from China, and this is higher than the US contribution at 15.71%. Calculated using the exchange rate method, 9.90% of global economic growth came from China and was lower than 23.93% of the U.S. During 2007–2012, looking at both PPP and the exchange rate method, China's contribution to world economic growth was 26.46% and 31.73%, respectively, clearly exceeding that of the United States at 13.32% and 10.20%, respectively.[70] China with its continual and rapid economic growth is worthy of the title as the world's largest "engine" of the global economy.

Third, China's contribution to the world's trade growth continues to grow and ranks first in the world. During 1993–2000, China's contribution to global export transactions growth was 2.73% and the US contribution at the same time was 14.72%. Between 2000 and 2007, China's contribution

[68] Database of the World Bank, http://data.worldbank.org.cn/.

[69] Calculating data source: Shaohua Chen and Martin Ravallion, "The developing world is poorer than we thought, but no less successful in the fight against poverty," *Policy Research Working Paper Series 4703*, The World Bank. http://econ.worldbank.org/povcalnet; World Bank and IMF, *Global Monitoring Report 2001: Improving the Odds of Achieving the MDGs*, The World Bank. http://econ.worldbank.org/povcalNet, 2008.

[70] Calculating Data Source: Data for 1978–2007: World Development Indicator 2013; data for 2007–2012: use IMF data.

increased to 10.05% and the US contribution fell to 7.99%. Furthermore, between 2007 and 2011, China's contribution to global export transactions growth increased again to 19.48% while the US contribution fell further to 7.31%. It should be noted that the United States became the largest importer and exporter in the world after 1913. However, in 2013, 100 years later, China took first place ahead of the United States. It is expected that China will continue to make greater contributions to global transaction growth and will do so for decades to come.

In the future, China will continue to make important contributions to the world in the following three aspects:

First, scientific and technological contributions: according to the data provided by WIPO, during 2000–2012 China's contribution to the number of patent applications worldwide increased from 3.8% to 27.8%. At the same time, the number of US patent applications increased from 22.4% to 23.1%. Similarly, China's contribution to the growth in the world's patent numbers was 61.95% whereas the US rate was 25.46%. In 2013, China has become the third largest WIPO after the United States and Japan. China has the potential to surpass these two countries. In 2013, it ranked second behind the United States in terms of papers published in international academic journals; thus, the relative gap is narrowing rapidly. Before long, China will surpass the United States and publish the largest number of papers in international academic journals worldwide. By the end of the first half of the twenty-first century, China will have the largest scientific and technological innovation center in the world and make significant scientific and technological contributions.

Second, cultural contribution: China has a history of civilization that goes back more than 5000 years. This is the most precious resource for China's cultural modernization. China's ancient culture is unique and at its spiritual core is the concept of harmony. This is the genetic code of Chinese culture as well as the fundamental driving force of Chinese culture to continually create and develop, to continually advance to achieve historical improvements, and to continually contribute ideas and intelligence to humankind. It also results in a huge overflow and has many positive externalities, as well as its own unique vitality and innovative power. When dealing with the different cultures among nations and countries, the notion of harmony emphasizes the importance to seek common points while preserving differences, mutual respect, and to realize harmonious coexistence, compatibility, and tolerance. When dealing with the relationship between one country and the world, the notion of harmony emphasizes the "great support for just causes," highlights the need for friendly relations, mutual benefits, and win-win outcomes. It is also important to "make oneself agreeable to everybody" and to avoid hegemonism and power politics. Similarly, we must adhere to equality between countries, and respect the right of other countries to independently choose their own development paths. Therefore, China's Road provides a unique and very effective form of development to the world. However, as a member of the world's civilization and ecology, China has provided referential ideas and cultural philosophies to other countries, helping them to solve various conflicts and this has resulted in numerous positive externalities.[71]

Third, green contribution: Since the eighteenth century, the capitalist expansion of Northern countries has created unprecedented development. However, it has also created an unequal world pattern and unparalleled ecological crises. The future of humankind depends on whether Southern countries such as China can create a green development path. China is involved in a significant historical mission that is relevant to the long-term development of humankind in the twenty-first century. This mission involves creating a green development path, initiating a green industrial revolution, and realizing green modernization. It should also comprise building a green world and making the largest green contributions to the development of humankind. China will lead the green growth and open an unprecedented "golden growing period" in the green economic development history of the world. China will become the biggest engine for global green transactions and the largest exporter of green products. Furthermore, China will join and lead the way in global green governance and become a world leader in global green development.

In addition, China's modernization has changed the global pattern of basic modernization with the North as the center, the West as the standard, and with United States and its hegemony. First, Chinese modernization has driven the rise of Southern countries and initiated a change in the 200-year-old "big divergence" pattern between the North and South. A new "convergence" pattern between the North and the South will soon appear and it will reflect that the ratio of the main economic indexes of the Southern countries to the world is higher than that of the Northern countries. Second, the road to China's modernization has provided new experiences

[71] Hu Anbang and Liu Tao, *The Essence of National Great Rejuvenation Is Cultural Rejuvenation—Discuss the Uniqueness of Chinese Modern Culture*, collected in *People's Forum: Academic Frontier*, Issue 14, 2012, pp. 6–12.

and enlightenment to the modernization of those Southern countries that wish to develop according to their own conditions. It has also changed the political understanding after the Second World War whereby Southern countries imitated and copied Northern countries (e.g., the Washington Consensus). There will be a more diversified development path, and diversified systems, civilizations, and cultures. Third, if China surpasses the United States and becomes the most powerful country in the world, it will gradually change the long-term world pattern led by hegemonism and power politics, and also enable the world to develop in a direction of equality, mutual trust, balance, peace, and safety.

In a word, although China's modernization path is nowhere complete, it has shown considerable positive externalities and demonstrated that it will continue to make even greater contributions to the development of humankind.

7 Conclusion: From a Lagger Playing Catch-up to China's Success and Role as a Contributor

Considering the world's pathway to modernization before 1949, China was always marginalized, a laggard, and even beaten and a loser.[72] However, for a while China emerged as a victor; that was until the Anti-Japanese War, after which China slipped in its standing in the world (in terms of the main indexes) and its relative gap with the United States grew significantly.

Since 1949, China has strongly established itself on the path to modernization. For the first time, China's modern economic growth, namely, the per capita GDP growth rate, has remained consistently at 1.0%. As a modernization chaser, this is the core national objective with which a country can achieve modernization. So far, China's modernization process (1949–2014) has achieved rapid and forward-leaping development.

[72] Gilbert Rozman and others consider that "in the 19th century, China, as top dog, obviously held a kind of onlooker attitude about the changes in the world around it. The Chinese government looked corrupt and incapable in front of the challenges from relatively modernized countries. In the first half of the 20th century, although China started its reform and attempted to build a stable government that could facilitate scientific and technological development, advance economic growth, and realize the social integration, it lagged behind." See [America] edited by Gilbert Rozman in chief and trans., "Comparison of Modernization," *Task of the National Social Science Fund of China: Modernization of China*, Nanjing: Jiangsu People's Publishing House, 1988.

China's position in the world in terms of the main indexes continues to rise and the relative gap with the United States has been considerably narrowed. China has surpassed the United States in many aspects and has transformed from a chaser to a transcender.

In view of the history of the modern world, New China can be crowned the modernization winner. Joe Colton and Lloyd Kramer, commentators on modern world history, have stated that China has set a glorious example for the great economic development and modernization of the world in the last decades of the twentieth century. China has become a main influencing power in the "history of the modern world" of which they have no doubts.[73]

China's success in modernization may generate positive externalities that will influence both world and human development. Thus, China will make huge contributions to humankind around the world. In return, world development and human advances may create "proper time" and "geographical advantages" for China's modernization.

China's Road is the only way to realize socialist modernization in all aspects and it is the necessary path to achieve the great rejuvenation of the Chinese nation. Only by adhering to the path of socialism with Chinese characteristics can we guarantee the people's subjectivity in the great rejuvenation of the Chinese nation and guarantee that all Chinese will create and share the fruits of national rejuvenation. Furthermore, only by adhering to the path of socialism with Chinese characteristics can we guarantee the adaptability and flexibility of the Chinese political system to the national conditions and the competition and superiority to the Western systems. We can therefore guarantee the steady progress of the national modernization process.

The road to modernization in China is not only very special in China's history but it is also very unique in the world. *China did not follow the well-trod Western path but explored a new path one step at a time. China did not copy the Western system and blindly take the "baton"*; instead, China created a special path, opened its own way, innovated its own system, and mastered its own fate. In this way, China has successfully

[73] [America] Authored by R.R. Pairner, Joel Colton, and Lloyd Kramer. Sun Fusheng et al., trans., *A History of the Modern World—To 1870 (10e)*, Beijing: World Publishing Corporation, 2010, pp. 8–9.

chased after and ultimately surpassed developed countries (especially the United States).

China's Path continues to validate the predictions of both Mao Zedong[74] and Deng Xiaoping.[75] This is why China's Path is superior to the "Western path," and as Xi Jinping said, "we walk our own path with incomparable undetermined stages, incomparable historical heritage, and with an extremely powerful willpower."[76]

[74] "Mao Zedong's Prediction", Mao Zedong once pointed out at the 7000 Cadres Conference in 1962: "capitalist development has occurred over hundreds of years and the 16th century should not be the starting point. It began in the middle ages. From the 17th century to now, it has been more than 360 years. In our country, I thought we needed more than 100 years to build a powerful socialist economy." He also pointed out: "compared with capitalism, socialism is superior in many ways. The economic development of our country will be faster than for a capitalist country. It takes more than 300 years to build a capitalist economy. What was wrong with building powerful socialist economy within 50 to 100 years?" See Selected Works of Mao Zedong, Vol. 8, Beijing: People's Publishing House, pp. 301–302.

[75] "Deng Xiaoping's Prediction", Deng Xiaoping once stated in a conversation with foreign guests in 1987: "what we should do now is to accelerate our development productivity through reform, adhere to a socialist road, use our practices to prove the socialist superiority, and we need to realize the objective through the efforts of two generations, three generations, or even four generations. By that time, we can really say that socialism is superior to capitalism with facts." See *Selected Works of Deng Xiaoping*, Vol. 3, People's Publishing House, 1993, p. 256.

[76] Xi Jinping, *Speech at the Symposium Commemorating the 120th Birthday of Comrade Mao Zedong*, December 26, 2013.

PART III

Domestic Foundations of China's Road

CHAPTER 4

China's Five-Year Plan and Transformation of China's Governance Modernization

Yan Yilong and Jiang Jiaying

1 Preface

The 3rd Plenary Session of the 18th National Congress of the Communist Party of China (CPC) proposed the general objective of modernizing the national governance system and governance capacity. Comrade Xi Jinping pointed out that the national governance system and governance capacity are the concentrated embodiment of a country's system and institutional executive capacity, which supplement each other. The modernization of the national governance system and national governance capacity does not involve evolution toward a certain preset mode, but a self-improvement process of the institutional system.

After the 3rd Plenary Session, national governance has become a topic of hot debate in academic circles. Researchers have explained national governance from different angles and the studies can be considered to fall into two viewpoints or perspectives as a whole. The first perspective

Y. Yilong (✉)
School of Public Policy and Management, Tsinghua University, Beijing, China

Institute for Contemporary China Studies, Tsinghua University, Beijing, China
e-mail: yangzs06@mails.tsinghua.edu.cn

J. Jiaying
School of Public Policy and Management, Tsinghua University, Beijing, China

H. Men (ed.), *On China's Road*,
https://doi.org/10.1007/978-981-13-7880-5_4

explains national governance modernization as an aspect of system exogeneity, referring to the governance systems of the western developed countries and understanding China's national governance modernization as "modernization" increasing in national governance system. This perspective emphasizes that China should strengthen the common features of the western developed countries' national governance systems—such as democratic politics, market economies, the rule of law, and citizen society—as basic conditions for national governance. Meanwhile, the transformation of the governance form from "regulation" to "governance" forms the model of the diversified-subject shared governance.[1] Therefore, the essence of governance modernization is to safeguard the citizens' subjectivity in the governance system via various institutional arrangements.[2]

The second perspective considers national governance modernization as involving unification with modern western systems, emphasizing the system generality and exogeneity, but ignoring the individuality and endogeneity of the system at the same time. As a construction course of political legitimacy, national capacity, subject, and structure, national governance modernization should be understood as a process of endogenous evolution, shaped by specific national conditions.[3] From this perspective, national governance modernization should not refer to westernization but to gradual reform and self-improvement of the national system. Meanwhile, some effective explorations formed during the tentative reforms process over the past 30 years or more are finalized in the system way.[4]

[1] Li Jingpeng, *About Boosting the Modernization of National Governance System and Governance Capacity—The "Fifth Modernization" after Four Modernizations*, collected in *Tianjin Social Sciences*, Issue 2, 2014; Sang Yucheng, *Discussion on Constructing Modern National Governance System*, collected in *Thoughts and Theories Education*, Issue 1, 2014.

[2] Lan Zhiyong and Wei Ming, *Modern National Governance System: Top-level Design, Practice and Complexity*, collected in *Journal of Public Management*, Issue 1, 2014; Ren Jiantao, *Construction of Modern National Governance System: Evaluation Based on Recent Top-level Design*, collected in *Journal of Renmin University of China*, Issue 2, 2015.

[3] Zheng Yan and Li Meng, *Facilitate the Modernization of National Governance System and National Governance Capacity*, collected in *Jilin University Journal Social Sciences*, Issue 3, 2014.

[4] Hu Angang and others, *Modernization of Chinese National Governance*, Beijing: People's Publishing House, 2014; Ding Zhigang, *How to Understand National Governance and National Governance System*, collected in *Academics*, Issue 2, 2014; Tang Mei and Bu Fan, *Discussion on the Governmental Power Allocation and Operation in National Governance System*, collected in *Probe*, Issue 1, 2014.

The two exogenous and endogenous research perspectives reflect that China is a latecomer to governance modernization and, thus, its institutional evolution is based both on solving the endlessly emerging problems in the country and on the study and imitation of the preemerging countries. The exogenous and endogenous factors involve not only internal tensions but also fundamental conflicts.

China's planning system of five-year plans has evolved based on these factors. China has undertaken five-year plans since the foundation of the People's Republic of China, and such plans are an the important component of the Chinese national governance system. The system involves constant self-adjustment and gradual improvements to further progress governance efficiency. It is the result of the common effect of the two powers. China has learned from the Soviet Union since it founded and established the five-year plan system. During the course of developing its own plans, China has constantly attempted to break from the Soviet Union mode of a planned economy and to form a system of planning with Chinese characteristics, based on a "general plan and individual freedom". After its reform and opening-up, the Chinese economic system has gradually transformed from a planned economy to a socialist market economy. The system of five-year plans has also undergone gradual adjustments. However, in contrast to developed countries, China has not abolished its planning system.

At present, China is about to enter into the period of its 13th Five-Year Plan and it has reached a turning point. The Party Central Committee proposed four comprehensive general strategic layouts. Therefore, we need to reconsider the orientation of the five-year plan in the modern national governance system and what role the five-year plan should play in the course of modernizing the national governance system and the national governance capacity.

Currently, there are no existing studies that examine the orientation of the five-year plan in the modern national governance system in depth. Given that the state gives great weight to facilitating the modernization of the national governance system and governance capacity and to establishing a modern national governance system, it is important from both the theoretical and the practical perspective to correctly understand the role of the five-year plan in the modern national governance system.

Based on our discussion of the role of the five-year plan in the national governance modernization process, we can see that, during the process of system transformation, China's capacity to achieve its national goals has been strengthened rather than being weakened. After the reform and opening-up, the completion rate index for the five-year plan has become higher than in the Mao Zedong Era. The fundamental reason for this is that, based on its modernization and transformation, China's government system has become neither a traditional monocentric system controlled by the nation nor a polycentric system featuring marketization and separation of powers. Instead, its government system is a combination of these two systems. A new type of governance mechanism, combining bottom-top and top-bottom reforms, has been formed. We refer to this as the "*N*+1" central governance mode, where "*N*" indicates that diversified subjects, such as different departments, local governments, enterprises, and citizens, join in the national governance system together, and "+1" means that there is always a core leading power.

The word "polycentric" was first proposed by Jewish British physical chemist and philosopher Michael Polanyi.[5] The "polycentric" governance concept was developed by the Austrian School, based on criticism of the socialist economic system, and it was later introduced into the public governance field by the Ostroms. They proposed a third plan between market and society, namely self-governance or polycentric governance. As well as mutually independent central decisions, polycentric governance emphasizes diversification. Thus, the polycentric governance theory considers that the unified authority mainly provides the first impetus for the legal framework and the macroscopic system framework. Once the frameworks are established, this authority may have a coordinative function and there is no need to establish a unified authority above them to coordinate.

A key feature is that the polycentric governance is dispersed as well. Polycentric governance is effective for small-scale or regional public governance up to a certain size region, but it may face problems in large-scale, national governance and even global public product supply owing to a lack of effective integration. Furthermore, the integration involved is not a once-and-for-all form, such as occurs in a system framework; instead, it is necessary to unceasingly adjust the integrated framework according to the changing situation. The five-year plan simply provides an integration framework based on integrated knowledge[6] and then further forms an "N+1" governance mode.

[5] Polanyi, *Society, Economy and Philosophy—Collective Works of Polanyi*, Beijing: The Commercial Press, 2006, pp. 207–224.

[6] Yan Yilong, *Objective Governance: Visible Hand of the Five-Year Plan*, Beijing: China Renmin University Press, 2013.

Table 4.1 Comparison of different governance forms

	Monocentric governance	*Polycentric governance*	*"N+1" governance*
Plan and market	Planned control	Market mechanism	Plan and market complementarity
Decision-making form	Top-down centralized decision-making	Bottom-up democratic	Brainstorming decision-making, combining top and bottom
Central government and local government	Centralization	Highly decentralized	Combination of decentralization and central guidance

Regarding the relationship between the plan and market, the market is a dispersed and diversified mechanism, whereas the plan, as the macroscopic integration mechanism, can plan the public resource allocation and guide the social resource allocation. Thus, it supplements the market mechanism. In the plan, a brainstorming decision-making form that combines top and bottom has been formed. It collects and absorbs the dispersed information and forms a consensus decision. With regard to the relationship between the central and local governments, although highly decentralized decisions have been made, the central government has the capacity to guide local governments to ensure general compatibility between the central and the local incentives (Table 4.1).

2 Five-Year Plan and National Goal Realization Capacity

State capacity refers to the capacity of the state (the central government) to turn its own desires and objectives into reality. The objectives made in the five-year plan are the state objectives for the following five years. The objectives made in the Chinese five-year plan are generally realized, which is a striking contrast to the objectives of western governments, which tend only to be visions.

It can be shown that the objectives established in China's five-year plans have often been realized in recent times, after learning from some less successful plans early on. The "1st Five-Year Plan" was one of the best-performing plans with regard to completion in the planned economy, with a completion rate as high as 84.4%. Most indexes outperformed the planning.

However, the "2nd Five-Year Plan" was an "impossible" plan, with an average completion rate of only 21%. About half of the indexes had completion rates of less than 10%. In the first year of the "3rd Five-Year Plan", the Cultural Revolution occurred, with adverse effects on the plan implementation, such that the final completion rate was barely satisfactory, at 46.9%. From the "4th Five-Year Plan" onwards, lessons were learned from the earlier plans and much more moderate indexes were established. However, the effects of the Great Cultural Revolution meant that the completion rate of the "4th Five-Year Plan" was very poor, at only 34.6%. In particular, many of the industrial productivity indexes could not be completed. The "5th Five-Year Plan", the "Great Leap Forward", was a relatively imprudent plan and its completion rate was also poor, at 31.3%, although the total industrial output value was 92% of that planned.

The "6th Five-Year Plan" was the second plan that was successfully completed after the "1st Five-Year Plan", with almost all indexes completed or outperformed. The overall completion rate was 84.8%. The "7th Five-Year Plan" realized its proposed strategic objective and its completion rate was 71.4%. The "8th Five-Year Plan" had the best completion conditions of all the five-year plans, with the completion rate reaching 92.6%. The "9th Five-Year Plan", which contained some unrealistic ideals, had a completion rate of 75.0%. The basic completion reached up to 93.8%. Completion of the "10th Five-Year Plan" was generally good and the completion rate was 64.3%. The basic completion rate was 73.2%. The average completion rate was 104%. The main objectives of the "11th Five-Year Plan" have been basically and comprehensively completed and various objectives were implemented smoothly. The completion rate was as high as 90.9%. It was one of the five-year plans with the best completion conditions. Based on the data estimates for the period 2011–2014, only two of the 28 indexes for the "12th Five-Year Plan" were obviously lagging. There may be difficulty in completing these indexes, but the completion rate for the objectives of the "12th Five-Year Plan" are expected to be up to 91.7%, very close to the historical record of the 8th Five-Year Plan (Table 4.2).

In contrast, the western countries have proposed grand visions, but their realization is far from ideal. For instance, in the United States, many of the goals that President Obama established in his presidential messages were not smoothly realized. In the last state message during his first term of office, he commented that the whole of Washington has been trapped in a dilemma of fragmentation and accomplishing nothing. The European Union has also failed to realize its goals. It proposed the Lisbon Strategy

Table 4.2 Completion condition of all five-year plans

Period	*Index quantity (set)*	*Ratio of the completed indexes*	*Completion percentage mean*
1st Five-Year Plan	32	84.4	136
2nd Five-Year Plan	21	0.0	21
3rd Five-Year Plan	51	46.9	101.3
4th Five-Year Plan	52	34.6	88
5th Five-Year Plan	16	31.3	90
6th Five-Year Plan	33	84.8	178
7th Five-Year Plan	28	71.4	119
8th Five-Year Plan	27	92.6	267
9th Five-Year Plan	16	75.0	144
10th Five-Year Plan	45	64.3	104
11th Five-Year Plan	22	90.9	132
12th Five-Year Plan	29	93–100	–

in 2000 for the first decade of the new century, but three of the proposed objectives were not met: although the strategy aimed at annual economic growth of 3%, in reality growth was only 1.42%; the ratio of the R&D capital to gross domestic product (GDP) was only 2%, below the 3% target in the strategy, and the average employment rate was only 65.3% in 2007, below the goal of 70%.

3 Public Affairs Governance Plan for Remedying Market Failures

With the transformation of the Chinese economic system to a market economy, decision-makers were faced with the problem of how to deal with the planned system. China did not commit the mistakes that former socialist countries, such as Russia and Eastern European countries did, of "pouring the baby out with the bath water". Instead, China adjusted the planned system pragmatically and rationally. Gradually, it has realized a mutual combination of a planned economy and a market economy, in which the two systems complement each other.

At the beginning of the reform and opening-up process, China relaxed the economic plan and control function and carried out a guided plan in some cases, or allowed absolutely free market adjustment for key important economic activities, according to the different conditions for each product or activity. At the beginning of the twentieth century, China established the reform objective of the socialist market system. It did not cancel the plan but included the definition of the planning. Since the 14th CPC National Congress, all reform decisions have clearly defined the development plan as the macro-control orientation.

Planning as a tool to facilitate economic growth has remained in place, regardless of whether the plans were similar to those implemented by a traditional socialist planned economy, or a guideline plan implemented under market economy conditions, such as had been applied in some capitalist countries, including France, or a plan made by the developing countries in East Asia for facilitating economic growth. However, in China, the degree of control on the economic activities is different to that under a traditional socialist planned economy. Thus, the state announced that it would inevitably quit from the historical stage. However, this has not occurred.

The fundamental reason for the prosperity and increasing activation of the Chinese state plan is that, over the last 30 years, the Chinese five-year plan has been transformed into a new state plan. We refer to it as the public affairs governance plan. It no longer focuses on the microscopic details of activity, but instead is concerned with the broader issue of public affairs governance. Hence, the state plan can be mutually compatible with a market economy and become an effective means of supplementing market failures.

The present five-year plan differs greatly from those made before the reform and opening-up of China. First, regarding the breadth of coverage, the plan is much more integrated and comprehensive. It relates not only to economic development but also to social development and it focuses not only on public-ownership units but also on nonpublic ownership units. Second, the objects to be adjusted in the plan are much more macroscopic and strategic, mainly focusing on structural issues, such as industry, region, city and village, land use, social service, and economic environment protection. With regard to these objects, the plan emphasizes the orientation, task, and corresponding development strategy and measures of economic and social development. It does not attempt to carry out microscopic activities that may influence the enterprises. Third, the key points of the plan have been gradually transformed from economic construction to public affairs governance. The economic indexes accounted for 60% of the "6th Five-Year Plan", but only 12.5% of the "12th Five-Year Plan". Most indexes are governance indexes of public affairs, such as education, science, and technology, resources and the environment, and people's living standards and well-being (Table 4.3).

Table 4.3 Proportion of quantitative indexes in different five-year plans (planning) (%)

	6th Five-Year Plan	*7th Five-Year Plan*	*8th Five-Year Plan*	*9th Five-Year Plan*	*10th Five-Year Plan*	*11th Five-Year Plan*	*12th Five-Year Plan*
Economic growth	15.2	21.4	26.9	23.5	10	9.1	4.2
Economic structure	45.5	35.7	30.8	23.5	23.3	13.6	8.3
Total of economic indexes	60.7	57.1	57.7	47	33.3	22.7	12.5
Education and science and technology	15.2	7.1	3.8	11.8	23.3	9.1	16.7
Resources and environment	3	3.6	7.7	11.8	20	27.2	33.3
People's living standards and well-being	21.2	32.1	30.8	29.4	23.3	41	37.5
Total for public governance indexes	39.3	42.9	42.3	53	67.7	77.3	87.5

"The market part should be governed by the market and the plan part should be governed by planning". The five-year plan as resource allocation means that mutually separate work with market mechanism. The market mechanism plays a decisive role with regard to the resource allocation at the microscopic level and with regard to private products. The plan only guides the resource allocation at the macroscopic level and with regard to public affairs governance. The plan complements the market and supplements failures of the market mechanism in two ways. First, it compensates for the blindness of the market mechanism at the macroscopic layer. The market-based micro-equilibrium based on dispersed information cannot achieve macroscopic coordination, whereas the plan may make use of the overall knowledge at the macroscopic layer and provide the general orientation for state development. Second, the plan makes up for market failures in the allocation of products and resources that are not pure private products and resources, and enhances the overall efficiency of resource allocation for society.

The five-year public affairs governance plan consciously uses the overall knowledge, makes a state plan, and guides resource allocation to facilitate the realization of the plan's objectives. First, it is a kind of state governance form. In contrast to the simple top-down instruction and administration of the planned economy, it involves public affairs governance and the participation of multiple entities, with central and local governments, enterprises, and citizens working together via channels such as administrative forums, social networks, and the market mechanism. Second, it is a kind of governance mode that makes use of overall knowledge to provide public goods. The five-year plan mechanism is able to effectively generate and adopt this overall knowledge, whereas the market mechanism is not. Third, it is a form of governance that guides resource allocation through centralized planning. Decisions based on the overall knowledge are implemented in a concentrated way. This does not mean that other parties are forbidden to join in the decision-making, but the central authority needs to make a concentrated arrangement and plan for public affairs. The centralized plan becomes the important means to guide the resource allocation. It coordinates the behaviors of dispersed subjects through direct orders and indirect guidance and directs resource allocation to facilitate the realization of the state objectives.

The development plan for public affairs governance is not only applied to the supply of public products. The information provided by the planning is public and, therefore, it can be applied to private and mixed products. According to the different applied forms of overall knowledge, it can be divided into predictive planning, oriented planning, and restrictive planning. Regarding private products, the state's predictive planning can provide signals to investors and producers and reduce the uncertainty that they otherwise face. In the mixed product field, the government and market can both play roles simultaneously and the oriented plan can be referred to for guidance in conducting daily policies and market activities. The provision of public products is mainly the responsibility of the government and it involves restrictive planning, with upper-class governments issuing orders to lower-class governments. Restricted planning provides the goals and indicators that governments need to allocate resources to ensure the objectives and indexes are realized (Table 4.4).

Table 4.4 Different functions of development planning

	Predictive planning	*Oriented planning*	*Restrictive planning*
Application type	Private product	Mixed product	Public product
Planned function	Provide expected macroscopic signals	Play a guiding role in industrial development, etc.	Guarantee the realization of the supply objective of public products

4 Brainstorming During Decision-Making

The establishment of Chinese five-year plans occurs through various means, including debates and exchanges of opinion on many aspects of the plan and several demonstrations. It reflects the special Chinese democratic decision-making method of brainstorming, which has its roots in Chinese traditional wisdom. In addition, it is reflective of the "democratic centralism" of new China as well as of decades of achievements in constructing the Chinese planning system.

China's five-year planning process has undergone four generations of decision-making modes. For the "1st Five-Year Plan" and the early period of the "2nd Five-Year Plan", decision-making occurred through an internal governmental group that negotiates broadly and made collective decisions. This mode of decision-making was abolished with the start of the Great Leap Forward. During the later period of the "2nd Five-Year Plan" until the "4th Five-Year Plan", Chinese decision-making was made by only one person, rather than by a decision-making system. During the "5th Five-Year Plan" and "the 6th Five-Year Plan", the internal group decision-making system was rebuilt. From the time of the "7th Five-Year Plan", members of society, such as experts and scholars, began to be involved, such that the five-year plan became a process of consultative decision-making. From the "10th Five-Year Plan", decision-making became a process of brainstorming, symbolized by public participation in the planning. Although it has gone through many twists and turns, it can be seen that the democratic decision-making mode for the five-year plan has continually improved. Since "the 10th Five-Year Plan", the innovation and improvements have continued.

"Great Wisdom Makes A Country Stronger, When Based on Brainstorming". The recent "13th Five-Year Plan" has undergone four stages: mid-stage assessment (2013), basic thought research (2014), compilation of the *Proposal* of the Party Central Committee (January–October 2015), and formal compilation of the *Outline* (October 2015–March 2016). Each stage has involved five rounds of "brainstorming", as follows: (1) gather advice from the public: mobilize the people to provide advice at an early stage of establishing the plan; (2) collect public ideas: the draft team analyzes and absorbs the opinions gathered and drafts the staged policy; (3) listen to different voices: collect opinions and revisions from all parties and form a policy draft based on the staged policy; (4) negotiate and decide together: discuss and decide collectively based on formal conferences at different decision-making layers and form a formal policy document; (5) declare to all: send the formal policy documents to all and implement the policy. The simple model reflects the "democratic first, concentrated later, democratic again and concentrated finally" decision-making logics of the Chinese five-year plan.[7]

The "12th Five-Year Plan" involved three stages, namely basic thought research, compilation of the *Proposal* of the Party Central Committee, and official preparation of the *Outline*. Each stage involved the five rounds of brainstorming noted above, and the completion of each stage provides the foundation for the next stage. Of course, the five rounds are not clearly separated. The decision-making process is also a course of soliciting opinions. At the stage of gathering ideas, there will be feedback from various parties (Table 4.5).

It has taken as long as three years to make a national five-year plan *Outline* after going through the first four stages above, repeatedly "putting heads together". The decisions made in Chinese five-year plans not only are democratic but also have the following outstanding features compared with the decisions of other countries.

First, the plans involve investigation and study. An emphasis on investigation is one of the most significant features of the Chinese government's decision-making in the establishment of the five-year plans. All Chinese five-year plans are established after carrying out systematic, specialized investigations and research. For instance, in the "12th Five-Year Plan", China has undertaken multiple investigations at the various levels involved in the decision-making, including the supreme decision-makers, the plan draft team, the National People's Congress (NPC), the Chinese People's Political Consultative Conference (CPPCC), and the think tanks. It is this broad, wide-ranging investigation that enables the decision-makers to master the firsthand information and to develop a practical and realistic five-year plan.

The investigation underlying the "13th Five-Year Plan" was innovative. In the previous plan, the "12th Five-Year Plan", several regional meetings were held, with regional forums divided according to the east, west, northeast, and center of China. However, all the meetings were hosted by relevant persons-in-charge of the National Development and Reform Commission. In compiling the "13th Five-Year Plan", however, Comrade Xi Jinping has convened forums and directly exchanged opinions with the officials of the different provinces and regions in Zhejiang, Guizhou, and Jilin. This is the first time that this has occurred in the history of compiling national plans.

[7] Wang Shaoguang and Yan Yilong, *Great Wisdom Makes a Country Stronger—Making of Chinese Five-Year Plan*, Beijing: China Renmin University Press, 2015.

Table 4.5 The "brainstorming" mechanism at different stages of establishing the five-year plan

	Gather advice from the public	*Collect public ideas*	*Listen to different voices*	*Negotiate and decide together*	*Declare to all*
Compilation of Basic Thought	Study subjects and thought of department and local governments, conduct seminars	Draft basic thought	Regional meeting and expert committee meeting	State Council and Standing Committee of Political Bureau	Investigation and ministerial and provincial-level study class
Compilation of *Proposal*	Study subjects and themes of departments, suggestions and advice of NPC and CPPCC, investigation of draft team	Listen to reports, learn together, collect opinions, research and discuss and draft	Internal opinion collection and seven large-scale opinion collections	Standing Committee Meeting of political bureau and meeting of central committee of the CPC	Teach-in, central committee meeting of the Communist Party of all departments, propaganda and mobilization
Compilation of *Outline*	Public advice and suggestions, investigation and seminars	Draft and internal discussion	Premier's Forum, Vice Premier's Forum, Expert Committee Meeting, Opinion Collection of Local Departments	Routine meeting of the State Council, plenary session of the State Council, meeting of the Standing Committee of the Political Bureau, conference of NPC	Publicity and mobilization

Data Source: Filed by the author

The second outstanding feature of the Chinese national planning process is the extensive consultations that occur. The plan is compiled gradually on the basis of repeated exchanges, comparisons, and consultations. It is a course of residing sciences in democracy, including brainstorming and draft formation during the early stages, repeated internal discussions during the compilation stage, and continual opinion collection from many parties after the formation of the *Basic Thought*, the *Proposal*, draft of the *Outline*, and the collective opinion draft of the *Outline*. Such repeated consultations are a vivid illustration of Chinese negotiations and democratic practice. The governmental internal group consultations and plan release must be carried out on the basis of repeated discussions, reviews, and many decision-making meetings at different levels. The NPC and CPPCC play important advisory roles. There is significant participation by experts and scholars, and the general public also provides opinions.

The third feature of Chinese national planning is public participation. The compilation of the five-year plan involves gathering public opinions, which is a different process to political participation. It demands decision-makers at different levels to reach out to the general public and, meanwhile, encourages the general public to express their opinions sufficiently. A key feature of China's decision-making process is "reverse" participation, where as well as offering advice and suggestions to society, the decision-maker listens to and absorbs public opinion through the process of carrying out investigations and convening forums. Thus, public opinions are expressed via formal and informal channels.

During the compilation of the "13th Five-Year Plan", a new channel for early public participation was established. In June 2014, the National Development and Reform Commission and the local governments established the WeChat public advice platform to gather and adopt public suggestions for the "13th Five-Year Plan".

The fourth feature of Chinese national planning is democratic concentration. Through a combination of sufficient democratic inputs and high-level concentrated decision-making, decision-makers can gather massive amounts of dispersed and incomplete information and determine the benefits to the diverse participants in the planning process. The brainstorming process gathers the dispersed information and overcomes information asymmetry through the mechanism of "gathering advice from the public". Then, the decision-makers reach political consensus through the mechanism of "negotiating and deciding together" and overcome individual one-sidedness and subjectivity in making decisions through the mechanism of the "General Remarks". As this decision-making mode emphasizes sufficient prior consultation with diverse decision-making subjects, it is likely to effectively result in policy consensus and, thus, it can avoid handicaps and delays while making decisions and reduce the difficulties experienced when the policy is implemented.

5 Incentive Compatibility of Central and Local Governments

In the period of the planned economy, China was trapped in a dilemma whereby "China became unified and then died; once dead and then released; once released and then became chaos". When the concentrated planning system allocated the resources, there was a serious problem of information asymmetry. It is very hard to collect and balance information during the process of formulating a five-year plan. Even just the communication of information between the coordinative plan department and various parts and places is a huge project. Owing to this information asymmetry, a central plan is always divorced from local realities and results in many problems for local governments implementing the plan. However, as the economic scale enlarges, the information cost rises gradually as well. In the later 1950s, to ease the problems associated with information asymmetry, China began to decentralize power and allow local governments to become the center of plan coordination. However, the release of excessive power meant that the local governments developed unrealistic plans that were not balanced by the state's macroscopic views, which caused further chaos.

Since the reforms and opening-up of China, during the process of transitioning from a planned to a market system, the autonomous rights to develop the local five-year plans have been enhanced. The method of compiling a local plan according to the controls transmitted by the center, which occurred under the planned economy period, has gradually changed. From the time of the "9th Five-Year Plan", the central government canceled the mandatory index and did not transmit control indexes to the local governments. Thus, China's model of five-year plan compilation essentially involves "hierarchical decision-making, parallel compilation and vertical guidance". The formulation of the goals of the five-year plan for the central and local governments is a vertical democracy course, and is generally implemented in an authorized manner. It complies with the central expectation in that the local government formulates the local development objectives and the central government gives instructions to achieve the local objective.

Although it has decentralized governance, the central government has retained its macroscopic guidance of politics. The central government ensures that its intentions are sufficiently reflected in local policies through certain decision-making mechanisms and arrangements. First, the central and local governments exchange information early in the process of the plan compilation. Thus, the local five-year plan is made to reflect not only the local realities but also the central requirements and it must obtain central government support. Second, the local five-year plan needs to be linked with the plan of the state, and the outline must be reported to the National Development and Reform Commission to ensure connection.

Such institutional arrangements enable China to decentralize the formulation and implementation of the five-year plan yet also retain the provision of effective central government political guidance to local governments. The central and local objectives gradually become compatible through this process. Since the reform and opening-up, the local and central objective functions have generally been in accordance. The ratio indicating the consistency of the local indexes with the central indexes was 64.7% for the "6th Five-Year Plan". By the "8th Five-Year Plan", it had increased to 77.9%, but then fell to 43.2% for the "9th Five-Year Plan". It then rose again after the "10th Five-Year Plan", reaching levels of 83.2% and 74.9% in the "11th Five-Year Plan" and the "12th Five-Year Plan", respectively (Table 4.6).

On the other hand, the political guidance of the central government cannot sufficiently restrict local impulsion to maximize self-investment, fiscal income, and economic growth objectives. The layered code-building mechanism for the formulation of indicators did not change the historical tradition of upgrading the economic growth rate objectives since the 1950s, especially since the "Great Leap Forward". The central objective basically establishes the baseline nationwide. Then, the problem is that the provincial goal is set higher than central one; the prefecture-level goal is higher than the provincial one; and the county-level objective is higher than the prefecture-level one. As a result, the objective becomes higher and higher at every level. This mechanism has failed to change fundamentally. Calculations based on the "11th Five-Year Plan" at the state, provincial, prefectural, and county levels reveal that that the phenomenon of increasing level-by-level objectives does indeed exist. For instance, the GDP growth rate objective made in the national "11th Five-Year Plan" was 7.5%, whereas it was 10.1% on average in the plans made by 31 prov-

Table 4.6 Ratio of consistency indexes of local five-year plans and the national five-year plan

	6th Five-Year Plan	*7th Five-Year Plan*	*8th Five-Year Plan*	*9th Five-Year Plan*	*10th Five-Year Plan*	*11th Five-Year Plan*	*12th Five-Year Plan*
All indexes	64.7	77.5	77.9	43.2 (42.1)	53.2 (46.6)	83.2 (89.3)	74.9 (76.9)
Economic index	56.4	81.0	79.2	27.1	25.3	59.9	34
Noneconomic index	89.3	70.7	76.0	62.8	66.4	95.5	86.7

Notes:

1. The economic index refers to economic growth and economic structure indexes; the noneconomic index refers to those indexes that go beyond economic measures, including measurements of people's well-being, resources and the environment, education, science and technology, and the public service
2. The indexes consistent with the central indexes include the same indexes to central indexes and indexes that can express central indexes. Other indexes are made by local government independently
3. The data for the "6th Five-Year Plan" to the "8th Five-Year Plan" are based on the average values calculated according to the five-year plans of Zhejiang Province, Jilin Province, and Qinghai Province. The data for the "9th Five-Year Plan" to the "11th Five-Year Plan" are based on the average values calculated according to the five-year plans of 31 provinces and regions
4. To provide a consistent comparison, the calculated average values of Zhejiang Province, Jilin Province, and Qinghai Province are shown in parentheses for the "9th Five-Year Plan" to the "12th Five-Year Plan"

inces, cities, and regions. One local plan even aimed at a 13% growth rate for GDP. Local government has a strong motivation to maximize the investment and fiscal income objectives. After the "9th Five-Year Plan", the state began to formally cancel the fiscal and investment index. However, local government did not make a corresponding reform, preferring to set high objectives to attract business and promote investment. In the "9th Five-Year Plan" and the "15th Five-Year Plan", more than two-thirds of the provinces established fiscal and investment indexes. There was a small reduction in the "11th Five-Year Plan", in the number of the provinces that made investment indexes. The state did not make fiscal indexes in the "11th Five-Year Plan", but 24 provinces, cities, and regions made local fiscal income growth indexes. The "12th Five-Year Plan" involved some greater reforms in this regard, as the number of provinces that made fiscal and investment indexes decreased to 21 and 15, respectively.

6 Conclusion and Discussion

The modernization of the national governance system and governance capacity in China is not an evolution to a certain preset mode but a process of self-improvement of the institutional system while drawing on other forms of governance.

Since its reform and opening-up, the Chinese economic system has gradually transformed from a planned economy to a socialist market economy. Meanwhile, adaptive transformation is occurring in relation to the five-year plan system. The five-year plan has become an important form of modern state governance. Instead of becoming weakened, the objective realization capacity has strengthened during the transformation course of the five-year plan. The reason may be that it preserves the core leadership at the same time as there is a process of power decentralization and the formation of the "N+1" governance. As the integration mechanism at the macroscopic level, the plan's function is to organize the public resource allocation and guide the social resource allocation. Furthermore, it plays a role in supplementing the market mechanism; it involves a collective brainstorming decision process that combines top and bottom decision-makers and collects and absorbs the dispersed information to reach a decision consensus. While the plan results in the decentralization of decision-making to local government, it maintains the central leadership and ensures that the overall incentives of the central and local governments are compatible.

Of course, the modern governance transformation of the five-year plan is still in progress. According to the 3rd Plenary Session of the 18th CPC National Congress, the market must play a decisive role in resource allocation. The plan can be used as a means of effective resource allocation and it requires much clearer border definition from the market. With the proposal that the country should be comprehensively governing according to law, the similarities and differences between the plan and the law should be further clarified. During the planning and decision-making process, the public participation is insufficient and the plan compilation procedure lacks legal references. The function of binding local economic development impetus is not enough. All of these issues should be solved during the next stage of national planning governance modernization.

CHAPTER 5

Tradition, Cultural Modernization and Soft Power: China's Anxiety and Options

Sun Yingchun

Modernization is a worldwide historical phenomenon. The global expansion of Western culture, as a universal force, has promoted the ubiquitous shift of different traditional societies towards modernity. Along with changes in such aspects as production modes, economic patterns, social organization and political systems come the increasingly acute conflicts and contradictions between local traditions and modernity. These two competing forces are vying for control of the general public's cultural consumption, lifestyle and values, while impacting on their attitudes and choices.

China's rapid economic growth in recent years has not necessarily enhanced people's cultural confidence to the desired extent. Anxiety permeates every dimension of contemporary Chinese culture, and the requirement for cultural modernization has raised a range of difficult questions for us to consider: for example, how can we define our own cultural tradition and understand and interpret local value systems, ideological frameworks, and discourse systems? How should we handle the relationship between tradition and modernity and respond to the dilemma resulting from the tension between modernity and post-modernity? How can we

S. Yingchun (✉)
Institute of International Relations, Communication University of China, Beijing, China

H. Men (ed.), *On China's Road*,
https://doi.org/10.1007/978-981-13-7880-5_5

find the subtle connecting point between tradition and modernity, in order to promote the convergence and fusion of local and global societies? What is the future direction of Chinese culture when taking into account the course of human history as well as people's modern aspirations to freedom, equality and rationality? Will Chinese culture be able to provide universal values for mankind's virtuous life? And what are the global ramifications of its modernization?

1 Tradition and Modernity

The sophisticated juxtaposition of tradition and modernity is at the core of modernization theory, which is often criticized and challenged. Regarding the procedure-based social activities and sustainable cultural development that modernity seeks to achieve, modernization theory from different periods presents varied assessments and options with respect to tradition and modernity. Relevant theoretical progress and conceptual changes have become part of the worldwide ideological trend of cultural consciousness, requiring Chinese scholars to rethink their approach.

Since the 1950s, Western modernization studies and related theoretical schools have changed profoundly, affecting a wide range of areas including economics, politics, history and sociology. Given the evolution from the classic modernization theory represented by Talcott Parsons to the new modernization theory represented by Cyril Black, the historical trend and humanistic concerns of modernization studies have gradually been recognized and enhanced. Tradition is no longer regarded as the opposite of modernization, and following in Western footsteps is no longer viewed as being the only way towards modernity. Correspondingly, non-Western countries tend to hold a more rational attitude towards tradition and modernity, expecting more from tradition in their exploration of national development and future modernization. The East Asian academic community attributed the success of modernization in countries such as Japan and South Korea to the support and application of traditional elements, and believed that this success proved the possibilities of co-existence and intergrowth of modern systems and traditions, as well as the positive significance of traditional ideas and behaviours, for modernization. The global mainstream ideological community has also gradually reached more consensus: modernization is a progressive process in both practice and perception and there is more than one model, so each nation must look to what suits its own unique situation. Given that the nature of modernity is stipulated by cultural patterns rooted in different traditions, in the West and beyond, the existence of tradition in modernity has almost become a law whereby all cultures and countries can find certain traditional resources contributing to modernity.

Chinese tradition consists of a widespread cultural heritage with a set of systems containing a mixture of diverse elements that are distilled and selected over generations. Despite the rise and fall of China in history, its cultural bloodline has been carried on to the present day. In this process, cultural tradition in the sense of Chinese community, which results from its diversified yet integrated ethnic structure, has nurtured the mentality and moral fibre of the nation while creating a leading social civilization in East Asia and the rest of the world for a considerably long period of time. Yet, the predominance of Western culture and the superiority of its politics, economy and military affairs since modern times dictate that China's social modernization, from its infancy, is unavoidably entangled between its own cultural tradition and Western modernity, with ongoing debate between the radical and the conservative, the liberal and the conservative, the traditional and the modern. Beginning with Yan Fu's idea of "learning from others and then competing with them", ceaseless efforts have been made to address this entanglement: the cultural integration theory proposed by the Liang Qichao-led group, that is, creating a new culture system that mixes elements from the East and the West; the idea of "absorbing new knowledge" on the grounds of "advocating the national essence" as the most effective way to build new culture by the conservative Xueheng School represented by Wu Mi; the conceptual shift of Chen Duxiu and other early Communists to relying on Marxism for solving China's problems, and the "cultural pluralism" by Liang Shuming to oppose the monism of "indiscriminate Westernization", and so on. All this mirrors the collective anxiety of Chinese society about this subject.

After its foundation the People's Republic of China, a country that achieved its cultural autonomy through revolution, totally ruled out the option of entering the modern global system established by Western countries. The ideological stranglehold it imposed resulted in a highly unified social culture, an imbalance between cultural mentality and social structure, and an ever-marginalizing tradition on the brink of discontinuity. Consequently, the country's cultural life was gripped by bigotry and extremism. Under this influence, the pro-West and anti-West contradiction continued to exist in Chinese society after forty years of reform and opening up, and a conflicting sense of inferiority and arrogance towards international society persists. Meanwhile, China in the twenty-first century, together with other non-Western countries, is faced with the same challenges posed by the global diffusion of Western culture. Modernity and post-modernity, in particular consumerism culture and ideology, have jointly dominated the overall transformation of the cultural and spiritual systems. Such domination caused psychological perplexity and anxiety in the cultural choices of society as a whole, including the intellectual elite.

Compared with over a hundred years ago, the nature of China's current options has not changed much: rejecting modernity and modern culture would deprive it of access to the advanced world civilization, while renouncing the tradition would destabilize the very identity of its own civilization. In academic discussions in China in recent years, some scholars have inherited the anti-tradition attitude towards and radical opinions of indiscriminate Westernization from liberalists like Yan Fu, Hu Shi and Chen Xujing who sought to rebuild Chinese culture within the Western modern framework. However, such an indiscriminate Westernization concept is unconvincing because this approach fails to combine China's social reality and domestic issues. Liu Junning commented that the absence of a well-established master plan to integrate Confucianism and literalism revealed that studies in this area "have failed to expound the modernization of a Confucian society at the height of Eastern and Western civilizations", and the right answers to many questions can only be found through the endeavours of more scholars who carry out long-term research, observation and exchange of ideas.[1]

The camp of cultural conservatism is relatively more influential than liberalism; the cultural conservative stands for, but does not stand on, traditional values, and regards the relationship between tradition and modernity as a complementary union of opposites. Amongst the cultural conservatives, Mou Zongsan emphasized that as Confucianism was at the heart of Chinese culture, the only path towards modernization lay in uncovering its essence appropriately, because "Confucianism is not in conflict with modernity and it should play an active role in modernization instead of passively adapting to it".[2] Tu Weiming, a proponent of this camp, held that modernization was pluralistic and that neither tradition nor modernity should be viewed as a linear process. We should accurately

[1] Liu Junning, Liberalism and Confucian Society, www.21ccom.net, January 2010.

[2] Mou Zongsan and Zheng Jiadong, *Reestablishment of Moral Idealism*, Beijing: China Radio Film & TV Press, 1992, p. 4.

grasp the interactive relationship between tradition and modernity, Eastern culture and Western culture, mass culture and elite culture, and globalization and localization, rather than simply using modernity to deny tradition. In regard to the development of Confucian culture and Chinese culture, Tu Weiming hoped that the former could adhere to the principle of rationality in communication while the latter could realize modernization and globalization.[3] Yet, according to Yu Yingshi, due to divergence and disorder in the intellectual world in the last century, the basic values of Chinese culture did not have a chance to be organized and modernized in a systematic and conscious manner, with rational thinking replaced by sentimental wavering that saw people "either propose to use Western culture to defeat Chinese tradition, or the other way around". In his view, China's value system would not collapse due to modernization and real life was not isolated from local culture but embodied it, so the renewal of Chinese culture depends on "how to adjust and transform the basic values and core notions of Chinese tradition as required by modernization".[4]

According to Clifford Geertz's concept of "local knowledge", culture is a system of diverse special meaning. In different cultures the order of life is still determined by local traditions. In recent years, an increasing number of Chinese scholars have combined this view with the post-modern critique of meta-narratives and the critique of Western cultural hegemony by post-colonialism. They believe that local knowledge is not only justified as being on an equal footing with the Western knowledge system, worshipped as the standard for a long period of time, but also has an irreplaceable advantage for the potential of human understanding. Even in modern times, the moral life, spiritual life and communication with the inner self that people need are primarily based on local traditions. The everlasting binding effect of the moral and emotional content carried by tradition, that is, local knowledge, cannot be ignored and abandoned easily. More importantly, the status and influence of tradition in China cannot be simply equated with the situation of any other country or nation. It is precisely this difference that reflects the unique value, role and significance of Chinese tradition. As the "spiritual chain" of the Chinese people generation by generation, Chinese tradition boasts a longer history and more distinctive evolutionary logic compared with that of other major coun-

[3] Tu Weiming, "Relentless Statement for Development of Confucianism," *Dushu*, Vol. 10, 1995.

[4] Yu Yingshi, Modern Interpretation of Traditional Chinese Ideology, pp. 45 and 52.

tries. If broken to the point of being irreparable, it would inevitably push the entire civilization system of China to the brink of deconstruction. If this were the case, this drastic change would lead to unimaginable turbulence, misery and sacrifice.

What cannot be ignored is that, despite the ups and downs, the pursuit of modernity has been the basic theme of Chinese culture since modern times, and contemporary Chinese society has also had the value orientation and ideological framework of modern culture in place. Led by the intellectual elite, in particular, the notion of rationality, which has not been highlighted in the Chinese tradition, has gained an important momentum in modern and contemporary culture. The traditional resources explored by generations of intellectuals are also, consciously or unconsciously, aligned with the modern spirits of science and democracy, at least without the explicit rejection of the merits of modern culture, whereas certain traditional content that runs counter to the modern spirit is neglected, criticized or rarely promoted at different periods. Li Xianghai states that "In terms of the basic value orientation, Chinese culture has basically completed the transformation from pre-modern to modern, with modern spirits such as science, democracy and freedom already internalized into the inherent requirements of Chinese culture". He also emphasized an important issue: the rise of post-modernism and its practical impact has made the position of Chinese culture very complicated in modern times. To be specific, there is a temporal gap between the contemporary development of Chinese culture and Western culture, in the sense that while Chinese culture has not yet enjoyed the achievement of modernization to the full extent, the West has already made comprehensive and sharp criticisms about its drawbacks. "In contrast to their diachronic occurrence in the West, pre-modern, modern and post-modern cultural phenomena in contemporary China, to a large extent, have been compressed into one single synchronic dimension, which inevitably overshadows the future development of Chinese culture with difficulties and severe challenges".[5]

Of similar importance is that although the status of Chinese tradition as a whole has declined in the process of modernization, it does not mean that it has stopped playing its role in reality. In particular, the secular traditions passed down among the people, though incomplete, still own a large

[5] Li Xianghai, "Philosophical Reflection on the Modernization Process of Chinese Culture," *Social Sciences in China*, Vol. 6, 2002.

number of guardians and defenders with different mentalities. In other words, the results of the game between tradition and modernity show wins and losses on both sides that fuse and interact with each other in different situations and in different regions. Just as Raymond Firth claimed, the importance of traditional influences cannot be overlooked. People's lifestyles and thoughts might have changed fundamentally after a long period of exposure to foreign culture, but "they will still recover old habits or revive some of the traditional customs in their new way of life".[6]

After a field study in 1996 on the modernization of China's rural society, Cao Jinqing pointed out that the evolutionary process of the Chinese society was reflected in two aspects: firstly, in concept, that is, the change in the perception of intellectuals influenced by Western knowledge and ordinary people; and, secondly, in reality, that is, what actually happened in the world, including the evolution of urban and rural, coastland and inland areas. Judging from the concepts of intellectuals, and life in the cities and coastal areas, China seemed to have been "almost modernised", but from the viewpoint of ordinary people and the backwardness of the mainland and countryside, "China was not far from its starting point".[7]

Many studies have also noted that although Chinese society has undergone major changes at different levels since the 1950s, people's daily lives and methods of interpersonal communication, especially the social relations and core concepts of those in the vast rural and mid-western regions, have not had any structural changes and have even signalled a tendency towards accelerated regression in recent years. During his visit to Western China in 1988, Arthur Barnett wrote that the far western area was a huge "mixture of old and new", "the influence of modern civilization is gradually and firmly infiltrating and changing previously undeveloped areas" and that the area, "in spite of all its tremendous changes, is still bound and influenced by deep-rooted traditional ideas as if a modern island has been solidly built on past tradition. While most people's living standard is rising significantly, there is still a small number of people living a very poor life".[8] The study by Ma Chunhua et al. (2010) noted that families across China had their own unique values and lifestyles. Even though China's overall social development follows the path of industrialization and urbanization

[6] Raymond Firth, Human Types, p. 159.

[7] Cao Jinqing, *China along the Yellow River*, Shanghai Wenyi Press, 2000, pp. 757 and 763–764.

[8] Arthur Barnett, *China's Far West: Four Decades of Change*, Sun Yingchun et al., trans. Beijing: The Eastern Publishing, 1998, pp. 326 and 247.

in the West, family changes in different regions of China still show both their distinctive trends and modern family patterns, as a result of the combined influence of the overall social changes and tradition, as well as the struggle between tradition and modernity.[9]

Cultural modernization, as a solemn and sacred movement, serves both the past and the future of China. It is not about merely saving Chinese tradition from peril but also about catapulting China's historical culture into a higher and better-established position.[10] With such a cultural stance and in order to carry forward Chinese tradition, it is essential to deal with the pressure of resolving the conflict between Chinese and foreign cultures, between different political and cultural values in China, and between mainstream culture and subcultures. From this point of view, the modern transformation of the Confucian tradition is a conundrum. It cannot be denied that Confucianism, having been revised through the ages, can be regarded as the dominant tradition in Chinese culture, as it controls the basic cultural mentality and value orientation of the Chinese nation while constraining and influencing people's secular behaviours in every corner of daily life. The East Asian modernization miracle, which has lasted from the 1970s to today, indicates a co-existent and even complementary relationship between Confucian tradition and modernization. More of the intellectual elite have acknowledged that China's modernization can be fulfilled without destroying the Confucian tradition, a tradition that is not necessarily a fundamental obstacle to modernity. In this sense, the endeavour to disseminate the spirit of Chinese culture worldwide through a reinterpretation and reconstruction of Confucianism is essential for China to position itself in the diversified landscape of global society and to also provide the main cultural resource for the Chinese intellectual elite to engage in with the West. Tu Weiming has an ideal proposition to enhance what can be the fundamentally and universally significant cultural contributions of Confucianism: adapting the key concepts of Confucianism to empower it with an ability to communicate with other cultures. In other words, in order to enrich and reinforce ideology, Confucianism must be exported from China and the Chinese-speaking countries in East Asia to harmonize with foreign cultures and "absorb more nutrients".[11]

[9] Ma Chunhua, Shi Jinqun et al., "Trend of China's Urban Family Change and Latest Discovery," *Sociology Study*, Vol. 2, 2011.

[10] Jin Yaoji, *From Tradition to Modern Times*, Beijing: China Renmin University Press, 1999, p. 3.

[11] Tu Weiming, *The East-Asian Values and Pluralistic Modernity*, Beijing: China Social Sciences Press, 2001, p. 214.

It is for certain that the contemporary value of Confucianism must be critically assessed and not overrated. Many researchers have pointed out that although Confucianism is instrumental in the discussion of ethics, philosophy of life and the like, it features much less prominently in other areas such as the exploration of nature, the development of science, the unbiased construction of political systems, the pursuit of an infinite ideal, and the awe and aspiration for God, the transcendent being. Cao Jinqing also put forward a pertinent view: "the contemporary value of the Confucian tradition can be discovered not in the interpretation of the Confucian classics, but in the evolution of the family and the nation of China in the past twenty, fifty or a hundred years".[12] According to him, family and nation are in constant flux, and with their shifts from ethical to contractual, the Confucian ethics will lose their practical significance. Furthermore, given the historical lessons and the realistic gap between China and Western countries, one cannot overemphasize the significance of Confucianism as the only source for the construction of modern Chinese culture. Chinese tradition, as a pluralistic unity since ancient times, has been enriched from different angles and to different extents by not only Confucianism, but also Taoism and Buddhism, the cultural traditions of different ethnic groups, and it also constitutes an important resource for the construction of today's social and cultural community in China. The twenty-first century is an era of multiculturalism, and Confucianism will not dominate the world or become the only mainstream culture in China.

For a period of time, China's mainstream ideology has focused on the goal of achieving the great rejuvenation of the Chinese nation for cultural modernization, demonstrating an emphasis on cultural traditions and local ideological resources. However, one problem such an ideology may entail is an overemphasis on the future-proof nature and the practical issue-specific traits of this ancient concept, and a conviction that the ancient Chinese philosophy contains a factual basis for solving practical issues, such as the belief that "harmony between man and nature" can help save mankind, and so on.[13] Based on the modern experience of other non-Western countries, the contemporary value of local traditions should not be exaggerated to the extreme as a rival against globalization. Otherwise,

[12] Cao Jinqing, *China along the Yellow River*, Shanghai Wenyi Press, 2000, p. 757.

[13] Zhao Jianying and Gan Chunsong, "Modernity and the Cultural Identity Risk and Restructuring of the Chinese Since Modern Times," *Academic Monthly*, Vol. 1, 2005.

it may cause the vicious expansion of nationalism and exert many negative effects. Wang Ning and other scholars stressed that in a global landscape it was not ideal to employ a localization strategy with a strong nationalist sentiment, because it "may intensify the current regional conflicts and then trigger political and cultural confrontation between the East and the West".[14]

In this regard, in order to properly handle the relationship between tradition and modernity, it is necessary to draw upon the Confucian wisdom of "Middle Way" and take an unbiased approach to avoid both overestimation and underestimation. Meanwhile, it is crucial to emphasize that the advocacy for tradition does not mean succumbing to a rigid local cultural structure. The excessive defence of tradition is prone to descend towards romanticism and reminiscence imbued with certain religious feelings, which prevent tradition from making a constructive contribution to the complicated process of modernization in practice, for it is merely a temporary ostrich strategy.

2 Soft Power and "Discourse Trap"

Ever since the concept of soft power was proposed by Joseph Nye, it has continuously drawn the attention of Chinese scholars and government departments, with its importance extending from academic discussion to social practice. They "have interpreted soft power differently based on the existing cultural resources and ideology"[15] and applied it to China's foreign and domestic cultural policies, seeking the support of developing countries on the one hand while promoting China's culture-related national interests through ideological and commercial means on the other.

According to Shi Yinhong, China's philosophy in foreign activities is to "rely on peaceful international exchanges indisputably and resort to soft power in its broad sense, especially peaceful trade, international negotiation and smile diplomacy in most occasions", and it is characterized by "nonviolence, gradual accumulation, extensive diffusion and a large degree of mutual benefits, a nearly unstoppable force that incurs the least

[14] Wang Ning, "Cultural Dispute and Dialogue in Age of Globalization," *Oriental Culture*, Vol. 4, 1999.

[15] Shi Zhiyu and Shao Xuanlei, "Global 'Self-Care': Practice of Cultural Resources of Responsible Stakeholders," *Chinese Journal of Strategic Studies, Series 1*, Men Honghua ed., Beijing: People's Publishing House, 2013, p. 87.

resistance and costs, and relatively most acceptable results".[16] When it comes to domestic practices, China's approach is to depend on the conscious selection of national policy-makers for strategies that facilitate large-scale cultural industry development and cultural product promotion so as to channel cultural influence into soft power. Since 2011, the Chinese government has made a strategic plan for "building a country with cultural strength". It encourages the cultivation of competitive cultural industries by improving the market access system; increases input into cultural industries; promotes emerging cultural industries such as cultural innovation, animation and games; motivates the generation of cultural content; enhances the establishment of cultural brands; and facilitates the direct launch of cultural products in international markets. In contrast to other countries, China has adopted soft power construction as an important part of its economic restructuring and upgrading, hoping for a balance between culture and economic and social development. In short, discussions about soft power continue to intensify in all walks of life in China, causing the rise and fall of enthusiasm and confidence among different groups of people.

Among Nye's constantly revised explanations of soft power, the latest divides a country's soft power into three dimensions: a culture that is attractive to other countries in different aspects; political values that are observed and practised in domestic and foreign affairs; and a justified foreign policy that is morally authoritative.[17] Based on this concept, some Chinese scholars put forward the idea of "cultural soft power", which is described in many works as the charm and influence that are shared by traditional and modern cultures and which embody distinctive characteristics of the national spirit. These involve political and value systems, technical and educational strength, cultural heritage and products, and quality and morality, as well as such factors as creativity in knowledge and institutions, and wisdom and practices in decision-making and diplomacy, and so on. According to these scholars, as the way and means for a country to participate in international competition, cultural soft power will inevitably contain the country's mainstream ideology and basic value orienta-

[16] Shi Yinhong, "Achievement and Challenge: China's Peaceful Development, Harmonious World Ideology and Situation of Foreign Policies," *Contemporary World & Socialism*, Vol. 2, 2008.

[17] Joseph Nye and Wang Jisi, "The Rise of China's Soft Power and Its Implications for the United States," *World Economics and Politics*, Vol. 6, 2009.

tion, signal a distinctive "conquest" message in a subtle manner, and facilitate the participation of its country in international competition with its specific spiritual charm, summarized as mainstream ideology, basic value orientation and the conquest message.[18] In recent discussions, some scholars and institutions have also linked cultural soft power with cultural security. Their principal concern was to protect mainstream ideology and the socialist core value system from the influence of internal or external forces, thus ensuring a full and complete cultural sovereignty and safeguarding the cultural, ethnic and national identity of the Chinese people.

For countries that have started late in the modernization process, they should be alert to the discourse trap set up by the political system and social formation of the Western discourse on world order and soft power, and they should prudently analyse the context of soft power construction and its application. China should instigate an independent and feasible theoretical discourse according to the overall strategic planning of the country and the cultural value orientation and benchmarks that support its national conditions and its long-term interests. In particular, the discourse should be consistent with the actual internal and external goal of rejuvenating Chinese culture rather than focusing on expanding its influence. Although Nye's position on soft power has changed, there is a solid foundation: a country has a set of core values that it firmly believes in and is persuasive to others, that can be placed in the arena of international competition in a specific context, and that can serve as a means to compete and exert influence. Based on the competitive logic of soft power, China needs to find something unique in order to draw the attention of the international community and gain the so-called influence. However, in terms of its recent national conditions, China should give priority to solving obvious domestic problems, including economic inequality, infrastructure problems, political transition pressures and social instability, instead of paying too much attention to its soft power performance in the world. After all, it calls for long-term efforts for Chinese culture to transform itself from local knowledge to global knowledge with truly global influence. Furthermore, as far as China's cultural construction is concerned, culture is not only a kind of soft power or a means to pursue national wealth and influence, but also a realistic choice based on the actual life experiences of individuals and groups, a choice that is closely associated with their personal interests, dreams and lifestyles.

[18] Huo Guihuan, "Philosophical Reflection on Cultural Soft Power," *Academic Research*, Vol. 3, 2011.

Historical experience also shows that cultural and national identity, as promoted by the power of the regime or ideology of a national state, is likely to enable the entire society to withstand the influence of modernization and to delay the process of transformation in various ways, including the rupture between traditional and modern cultures, the state's strong control of society and the loss of autonomy of folk traditions, and the collapse of traditional social structures and meaning systems. As indicated by China's history, from its founding to its reform and opening up, the suppression and elimination of historical tradition-focused local knowledge made it impossible for the top-down cultural system to correspond with reality and effectively infiltrate the everyday life of the grassroots and the general public.

The Chinese intellectual community makes a point that the large-scale construction of soft power at present needs to be geared towards the future with institutional and cultural planning for society in the long run. It cannot be simply regarded as a way to join the international political game; it should be measured and strategized based on the long-term interests of the country and the people instead. It is undeniable that after being implemented at various levels, the strategic arrangements for "building a country with cultural strength" made by the Chinese government in 2011, following other fronts in economic and social development, also slid into a developmentalism that values GDP growth impulsion and performance demands. In 2012, I wrote an article that addressed the general concerns of the Chinese intellectual community: as it is a gradual process of accumulation, the development of the cultural industry needs time, tolerance and diversity, and will not necessarily be motivated by the guidance and interference of governments or related authorities. It needs be free from short-sightedness and utilitarianism and will not necessarily bear fruit due to the market-oriented approach of certain cultural institutions and commercial sectors.[19] Moreover, the rise and the decline of cultural soft power have a direct bearing on the attitudes and reality of the society as a whole. The statistics of the cultural industry scale, which continue to skyrocket, do not necessarily indicate a real increase in the impact of Chinese culture on the international community. If it single-mindedly seeks the expansion of the cultural industry and the production of consumer culture, it may expose traditional culture to the impact of a new round of commoditization, thrust controversies related to modernity and

[19] Sun Yingchun, "The Basis of Cultural Prosperity is Tolerance," *Study Times*, May 18, 2012.

tradition into new chaos, and may trigger a lasting ideological civil war with various cultural ideas being influenced by politics and vested interests.

In addition, it must be observed that China, as a not-so-wealthy country, has undertaken a great number of international aid obligations in recent years, and its own development has also provided important opportunities for the world. However, extensive growth and export-oriented development strategies have intensified the competition for global resources and markets, changed the structure of benefit distributions, and also affected the interests of certain countries and communities. As a result, China has won acclaim in some developing countries, but with little moral charisma, while its image and influence continue to decline in Western countries. For a vast country with a very complicated history and reality, there are many disadvantages to simply relying on state acts to improve cultural soft power, such as a lack of room for manoeuvrability and persuasion, and the tendency to misunderstand its covert purpose as hegemony. Shi Zhiyu pointed out that "the strength of China's soft power depends on whether it can co-exist peacefully with other countries without making them feel threatened despite huge differences in lifestyles, language and values, through the cultivation of social relations and selfless compromise in policies".[20]

More importantly, the true test of cultural development for any country consists in its attitude towards itself. Sacrificing its long-term interests to cater to the outside world is not consistent with the essence of soft power construction, that is, seeking trust, understanding and respect from the outside world, and working for the well-being of its people, of which the latter is fundamental. Modernization is not a perfect process in which all parties can benefit. The cultural soft power of the major countries in the international community is a trade-off and needs to be viewed dispassionately. The reality of China will by no means meet the expectations of all countries and groups in the world. The response of the outside world should be taken into account to a certain extent, but what is more important is to make China's growth consistent with its people's will and its social reality. In September 2013, Li Keqiang demonstrated this new stance in his speech at the opening ceremony of the Davos Forum, which could be seen as a new starting point for China on the subject of soft power, that is, China has a long, challenging way ahead

[20] Shi Zhiyu and Shao Xuanlei, "Global 'Self-Care,'" *Chinese Journal of Strategic Studies, Series 1*, Men Honghua ed., p. 69.

towards modernization, and the international responsibilities and obligations it undertakes can only be adapted to the requirements of its own level of development.

3 Local Society and Global Society

No country is isolated in our rapidly changing global society. It is impossible for us to observe the world and solve our own problems without setting the local context within the global field. We need to develop an open and global vision to understand our local society and the world we live in. According to the experiences of other countries, the evaluation of local traditions on which modernization goals are based must not go against the developmental laws of history and society, to hinder cultural development and changes. Otherwise, it will inevitably lead to the loss of freedom and the ossification of culture. Given the urgency of all aspects of social development in China, we must not lose sight of the historical stage nor abandon the main content of modern culture and the global society.

In terms of the goal of China's cultural modernization and soft power enhancement, the pressure of globalization in human society will inevitably require the establishment of a new framework to reconsider the complex structures of the local and external worlds. As mentioned above, it is impossible to understand the outside world from a narrow perspective, which would only lead to self-righteousness. Compared to previous periods, Chinese society is experiencing a complicated and ever-changing period of historical transition, with the advent of critical social differentiation and internal ethical crises. Some intellectual elite, with sceptical and critical attitudes, are also seeking weapons of criticism from Western culture, and are focusing on whether indigenous materials and spiritual resources can be used to maintain the sustainability of modernization. From this point of view, China is mainly faced with choices about what kind of mentality it should adopt in order to respond to the multicultural trend of local and global societies. Should it become involved in the global society or remain self-focused? Would it become lost in the conflict between tradition and modernity, or would it rejuvenate a hybrid culture that is embedded in a national cultural identity? At the same time, it must also be realized that the reason Western culture can become a globally dominant cultural system based on its political and economic power lies in its comprehensive strength on the one hand and its modernity and cultural dialogue strategy on the other. Not only can it effectively legitimate unbalanced development and power relations, but it also has a magnetic influence that attracts all societies to follow its practice. What is more important to see is that, in the face of diversified global cultural markets, Western culture will continue to proffer diversified cultural and commercial designs, and a kind of hybrid culture may come into being eventually, no matter what steps other cultures may take to resist this.

Faced with these major trends, we cannot simply expect to realize our cultural dreams based on invariable traditions. Rather, we need to carefully consider the cost of social progress, and gradually establish a reasonable and flexible structure so that traditions can be fully embedded in all aspects of social life through institutional arrangements. The experiences of Japan, South Korea and other countries are particularly useful for people in embracing a modern lifestyle embedded in traditions. This means that China's cultural modernization must take a unique approach. Instead of a move towards further Westernization or an indiscriminate return to and extension of traditions, it should stay focused on the diversified development of spiritual life and cultural awareness, enabling the traditions to be embedded in modern elements. Such embedded traditions can be seen as a local framework for different Chinese cultural groups to observe the world, helping people to inherit local traditions without preventing them from knowing the outside world. This is also a re-production process after a fracturing of traditions. It does not merely inherit what is available, but produces culture through institutional arrangements and incorporates the progress of contemporary society's understanding of traditions.

Modernization is a process in which the institutional structure is constantly reformed, the success of which hinges on the transformation of institutions and systems, and the establishment of a modern ideology that expands social and individual freedom. Its philosophy and wisdom lie in the integration of technical and moral methods to solve problems rather than them operating in isolation. The same is true with the further enhancement of soft power, which requires both cultural and institutional responses. Needless to say, ignoring the intrinsic connection between institution and culture is a mistake that has not yet been fully corrected in the process of China's modernization. Addressing the conflict between the institutional systems based on Western culture, and local and national cultures, means that there is an urgent need for the transformation of culturally relevant systems and institutions. This institutional change has a bearing on the reconstruction of China's state and social relations, and needs to take into account all of the following: the investigation of social and cultural development, and social costs; the formation of civil society; the growth of civil autonomy; the impact of income concentration; social stratification and social structural disruption and social moral systems; social control mechanisms; and the process of the rule of law.

The reality for Chinese society is that the relationship between modern culture and the country is still quite a new issue. The contemporary social transformation driven by modernization in China is a very complicated and juxtaposed process, comprising two concurrent transitions, one from tradition to modernity and the other from modernity to tradition. In other words, China is not only transitioning from pre-modernity to modernity, but also from an old-style modernity to a new-type modernity. This undoubtedly represents a profound social movement where China's policy-makers and intellectuals are required to be patient and pragmatic in facing the concepts and various propositions of modernity by following Confucianism's "Middle Way" philosophy, such as "being moderate and keeping integrity" and "adapting to the changing times" and grasping any opportunities that can transform tradition for the benefit of the contemporary era. It is imperative that we obtain the values of balance and the ethical resources from both the cultural heritage and modern culture so as to avoid further social structural differentiation and division of the value system, and to protect society as a whole from irreversible secularization and vulgarization. This is a major issue that we must work hard to address in this era. Confronted with the inflexible historical inertia of civilization and cultural development, we should push forward this institutional reform based on facts, knowledge and open-mindedness and implement a truly prudent and stable overall cultural policy that can address the "rigidity" and ineffectiveness of political and economic institutions and the social order in regulating multiculturalism. Such institutional change also means that there is a need for further agreement between China's cultural traditions and its comprehensive national political system, and that the Chinese government has the ability to formulate various policies to regulate the quality and characteristics of its contemporary culture, as well as to stop and prohibit various practices that seriously damage its cultural traditions and diversity.

It also means that over an extended period of time, efforts should be made to coordinate these two relationships. The first step is to coordinate cultural traditions and diversified development. The large-scale changes in Chinese society have led to the irreversible diversification of beliefs and behaviours. Indiscriminate Westernization and "going back to the ancient times" are too unrealistic to provide a suitable platform for the local society to coordinate its hybrid and diversified cultures. A key point in such coordination is to properly deal with the relationship between the minor traditions of different regions and ethnic groups in China and the major traditions that represent national ideology, laws and regulations, and elite culture. Its value lies not only in protecting the diversity of China's own culture, but also in retaining the foundation for its future development. The second step is to balance the relationship between the local and the global society. Modernization is closely related to openness and dialogue among cultures. The future for the modernization of Chinese culture and the enhancement of its soft power is determined by whether or not it can be a reference for the existence and development of global culture. Chinese culture should be able to respond to developmental trends and changes in world culture; this requires it to look for useful ideological resources and to value feedback from different cultural systems in the world and to rebuild a new consensus on the universal value of Western countries. The universal value cannot be simply viewed as a tool to safeguard hegemony and monopolize cultural power, or as a reactionary ideology that conflicts with the value of Chinese society, which would undermine China's political stability and the Communist Party's authority.[21]

Furthermore, in terms of China's current national conditions, it is necessary to rethink the contemporary lifestyle, cultural trends and value systems in greater depth so that the will of the state and traditional resources can be mobilized through effective institutional arrangements. This does not mean revisiting a compromise scheme that is similar to the Westernization of Chinese style, but an endeavour to establish a new cultural system based on China's diversified traditions that can not only effectively respond to today's major problems in the process of China's development, but also reflect and absorb shared human values and ethics. In the 1980s, based on the fundamental conflicts in economy, politics and culture, and the severe fracture between social structure and culture in the West, especially in the United States, Daniel Bell proposed the assumption that societies should "return to a certain religious concept" so as to rebuild morality and culture from its roots, as well as building the connection

[21] On September 24, 2013, Wang Sanyun, Secretary of the Gansu Provincial Party Committee, delivered a speech at the Provincial Propaganda and Ideological Work Conference, saying: We must take a clear-cut stand against counter-reactionary trends such as Western universal values, and boycott non-Marxist and negative things.

between traditions and modernity.[22] From today's perspective, this kind of thought, though a unique concept in a Western cultural context, can indeed help inspire more open and rational thinking. According to my article in 2010, an urgent task for the development of Chinese culture in the twenty-first century is to promote a globally recognized value system that not only fits into China's reality but also may have a positive impact on the world. This value system is also a cultural ideal called the "China Dream".[23] This "China Dream" shares some similarities with the "Chinese Dream" proposed by the Chinese government in 2012, but at the same time it also means something different. It depicts a homeland aspired to by modern Chinese people, a blueprint for how humans live together in the future world, and also a kind of "dream" where the exotic "others" are willing to be involved. This dream has to be open to the world for global recognition, rather than ending up as China's one-man show.

According to this reflection on the soft power theory and China's experience gained in practising its soft power in different areas, China should further adjust its traditional security thinking, attaching more importance to the cultural dimension of national security, and regarding cultural security as an important part in its achievement of the overall security goal and many strategic objectives. To this end, we should fully consider the political system and cultural ecology of Chinese society by constructing a cultural soft power that is centred around cultural traditions, modern-day socialist core values and global ethics, in combination with the actual and future development goals of China's historical and cultural resources, and by building a future-oriented new cultural security concept featuring "pragmatism, confidence, open-mindedness and diversity".[24] This is not only an objective requirement for dealing with foreign cultural influences and maintaining cultural independence, but also a basic measure for creating a good international environment for future development.

To be specific, "pragmatism" here means seeking truth from facts and objectively assessing the numerous challenges and choices faced by Chinese culture, especially the subversive influences brought about by the development of modernity as well as social and cultural changes, for the purpose

[22] Daniel Bell, *Capitalism Cultural Contradictions*, Beijing: Sanlian Bookstore, 1989, p. 17 of the Introduction of the Chinese translation.

[23] Sun Yingchun, "Cultural Construction of China's National Image," *Teaching and Research*, Vol. 11, 2010.

[24] Sun Yingchun and Wang Yi, "Rethinking the Theory of Soft Power and China's 'Cultural Security Viewpoint,'" *International Security Research*, Vol. 2, 2014.

of making precise and well-targeted cultural policy-making and project designs. "Confidence" refers to the fact that with the economic and social development of China, there has been an ongoing transformation in the accustomed attack-and-defence relationship between Chinese and Western cultures. Now China has the ability to advocate a cultural independence based on its traditions, that is, demonstrating a kind of contemporary cultural subjectivity with unique Chinese characteristics. Furthermore, we should embrace an open-minded cultural ideal. It is fair to say that the reason why Chinese traditions were destroyed or disrupted in the context of modernization and globalization is partly because its isolationism could not provide valued resources and consumer satisfaction to match the modern world. The reason why Western culture has been invincible in modern times is not only due to its military power but also because, as an open system, it embodies modern values and ethics with universal significance. In this sense, in response to modernity and global social changes, it is reasonable for developing countries to make an objective evaluation of the position and value of Chinese and Western cultures, and to embrace global ethics that are conducive to cross-cultural communication and the common interests of human beings. The assessment of China's traditions, modernization and soft power improvement requires an understanding of global ethics and the common values and interests of mankind. In other words, Chinese culture must seek resonance with other cultures in dimensions such as values, emotions, aesthetics and ethics, for the enhancement of its reputation and influence. At the same time, it must select from its own traditions the ethics and values that are widely accepted in the global ethical system, blaze a trail for Chinese culture to contribute to the common interests of mankind, and gradually strike a cultural and ecological equilibrium in which China can actively interact with the world, seeking the global society's trust in a sustainable manner, and enabling the global public to better understand itself.

In the meantime, a concept of diversified cultural security should be fostered. A diversified cultural security system should cover ideological and core values, which are the cultural basis for the legitimacy of national sovereignty. It is also expected to include public cultural security, featuring an organic combination of traditions and modernity, and to implement cultural policies that can truly meet the needs of the people. Also, effective policies for the protection of cultural diversity in different regions and ethnic groups should be actively promoted to minimize the homogenizing impact that arises from rapid economic and social development on different cultures in the country, while revitalizing the increasingly weak cultures of different regions and ethnic minorities to the fullest extent. In addition, we also need to draw from the experience of the United States and other Western countries, that is, to diversify the participating vehicles and maintenance methods in connection with cultural security. Relying solely on acts of state can have many disadvantages; for example, it lacks operability and flexibility, and can easily lead to the misunderstanding that China is secretly seeking hegemony. Moreover, the forms of international communication tend to be increasingly diversified, which will inevitably require the diversification of participants. The development of information communication technology has facilitated the diversification of a nation's thinking framework, and the subjectivity of civil organizations and individual citizens has been unprecedentedly enhanced as well. In this context, China should have the ambition to think in greater depth.

4 Conclusion

The modernization experience of different countries has proved that disrupting traditions does not necessarily lead to modernity; on the contrary, it may cause the collapse of value systems and the loss of cultural identity, which is likely to damage the process of modernization itself. The practice in China since the 1950s has also repeatedly demonstrated that large-scale and effective social and cultural changes cannot be achieved if they are in fundamental conflict with traditions, that is, the common cultural orientations of members of the society. Whether to increase the competitiveness and influence of culture, or to resist the international pattern of West-centrism and hegemonism, or to address the multiple dilemmas and problems that modernity has caused in China, traditions need to be recovered and revitalized to form an effective path of resistance through collective efforts and to be integrated into a cultural value system that is aligned with China's modernization process.

The ongoing vigorous construction of soft power in China needs to have a future orientation and appropriate institutional arrangements; this requires a change in the attitude that regards soft power merely as a means to participate in the international political game, and instead should be a blueprint that is based on the long-term interests of the country and the people. China, a superpower with extremely complicated historical traditions and realities, has seen its cultural traditions being damaged repeatedly in the twists and turns of the last century. The remarkable economic development has been accompanied by an endless stream of social issues and a deepening erosion of culture. While enjoying the opportunities from increasingly frequent global exchanges, China is also facing the pressure to seek harmony between Chinese and foreign cultures, and to address the conflicts between different political and cultural values in China, as well as the contradiction between mainstream culture and subcultures. In this context, China's cultural undertaking is to prioritize its work on how to ensure national cultural security, to protect the spiritual homeland that is vital to the stability and survival of the Chinese nation, and to solicit support from historical traditions for further development.

Modernization should be a two-way journey, both from the West to China and from China to the world. The history of China in the last century has proved that every step forward in the cultural area is by no means easy. The future landscape of Chinese culture is hard to predict, as China is under pressure not only to seek harmony between Chinese and foreign cultures but also to address the conflicts between different political and cultural values within Chinese society, as well as the contradiction between mainstream culture and subcultures. As far as China's domestic situation and trends are concerned, it is still necessary to become mentally prepared for the process of going global: Chinese culture still has a long way to go before it can truly find its position in the global cultural system.

CHAPTER 6

Birth Trends and Economic Growth in China (1950–2014)

Zhou Tianyong

Since 2008, China has entered a downward stage of moderate growth. What are the reasons behind this sudden slowdown? An accurate answer requires an in-depth analysis of multiple factors including decelerating population growth, an aging population, constrained mobility and a reduction in labor supply.

Since the reform and opening up, China has not considered the inherent constraints of both the direct and opportunity costs of child-raising on birth and population growth, in the context of a market economy. The population growth is, in fact, an inverted U-shaped curve. In a market economy, the direct costs and opportunity costs of childbirth and rearing play a regulatory role; in other words, China will eventually reach the transformation phase of low growth, even without governmental intervention. This does not allow for the fact that technological advances may expand the capacity of resources for the survival of the increasing population nor for the possibility that we can overcome the challenges occurring in the early and middle phases of industrialization. Neither have we considered whether China can rely on its population to develop comparative advantages in its labor force, manufacturing and innovation, while importing sufficient food to meet people's needs, and ensuring basic self-sufficiency and food safety.

Z. Tianyong (✉)
The Institute for International Strategic Studies, The Central Party School of the Communist Party of China, Beijing, China

H. Men (ed.), *On China's Road*,
https://doi.org/10.1007/978-981-13-7880-5_6

The social practices outlined below have led to severe negative consequences for contemporary China as well as risking its future development. A hardline regulation of population and birth control has been enforced for 35 years with the aim of controlling the population at a moderate level of 600–700 million. And the household registration system has restricted population mobility. For example, farmers received little income from their land, yet neither could they succeed in the cities due to the excessively high cost of urban housing and the lack of equal access to public services such as education, medical care and social security. As a result, the process of urbanization has been interrupted. The implementation of this centralized planning and control of population, birth and mobility, and the government intervention that conflicts with the material production, distribution and consumer market economic systems and operations, will inevitably lead to distortion, losses and risks.

1 International Experience and the Lost 10–15 Years of China's Development

All economic activities such as production, distribution, exchange and consumption are based on human life and development. The size and growth rate of the population will undoubtedly affect the prosperity and growth of the national economy.

1.1 *International Data: Population Growth Transformation and Economic Slowdown*

Birth rates and population growth, even negative growth, are significantly correlated with GDP per capita and the economic growth rate. In general, *the lower the fertility rate, the higher the level of GDP per capita; and the slower the population growth, including negative growth, the slower the economic growth.* This chapter conducts a regression analysis based on 2013 World Bank cross-sectional data of 208 countries and regions. Let us first look at the relationship between the population increase rate and the economic growth rate in the scatter plot in Fig. 6.1.

Ignoring extreme outliers, in general, countries and regions with higher population increase rates boast higher economic growth rates; conversely, those with lower population increase rates or negative growth have lower economic growth rates. The mathematical relationship is

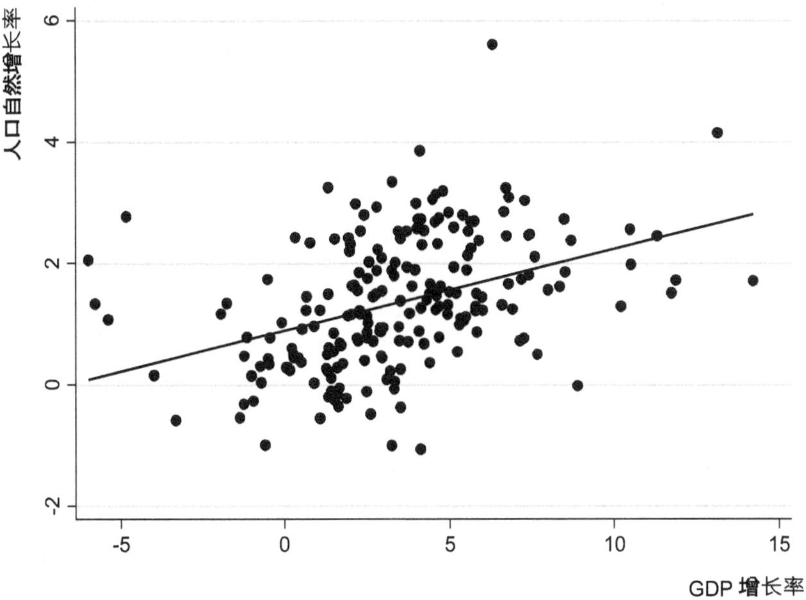

Fig. 6.1 Relationship between population increase and economic growth. Source: World Bank Database, http://data.worldbank.org.cn/indicator/all

$$\mathrm{RGDP} = 7.629\mathrm{RPOP} - 6.846$$

where RGDP is the growth rate of GDP and RPOP is the population growth rate, both in unit of %; P value = 0.000, adjusted R^2 = 0.16, and the p value of GDP growth rate variable = 0.000, which is significant.

The cross-sectional statistics of countries and regions at different levels of development can also reflect the dynamic changes in data as a country or region grows from a position of backwardness to one of economic advancement. China's GDP growth rate in 2013 was 7.67%. According to the regression model, the corresponding population increase rate should have been 18.9‰, but the actual figure was only 4.9‰. A possible explanation could be that factors other than population, such as demand and investment, greatly drove economic growth, or there were errors in the statistics of GDP growth. However, based on the general relationship between the population increase rate and the economic growth rate, in the absence of other driving factors, the Chinese economy faced enormous pressure to plunge into the medium- and low-speed growth ranges due to the fundamental effects of its ultra-low birth rate and low population growth rate.

Now, let's look at the relationship between fertility rate and the level of economic development in the scatter plot in Fig. 6.2.

It can be seen from Fig. 6.2 that the lower the GDP per capita, the higher the fertility rate, and the higher the GDP per capita, the lower the fertility rate. The total fertility rate dropped as the GDP per capita rose, but once the GDP per capita reached a certain level, the total fertility rate remained stable at a medium-to-low level. The critical value of GDP per capita was approximately USD 10,000, with a scatter plot for GDP per capita of less than USD 10,000 (Fig. 6.3).

To perform a regression analysis for countries and regions with GDP per capita of less than USD 10,000, the quantitative relationship between the fertility rate and the per capita GDP is

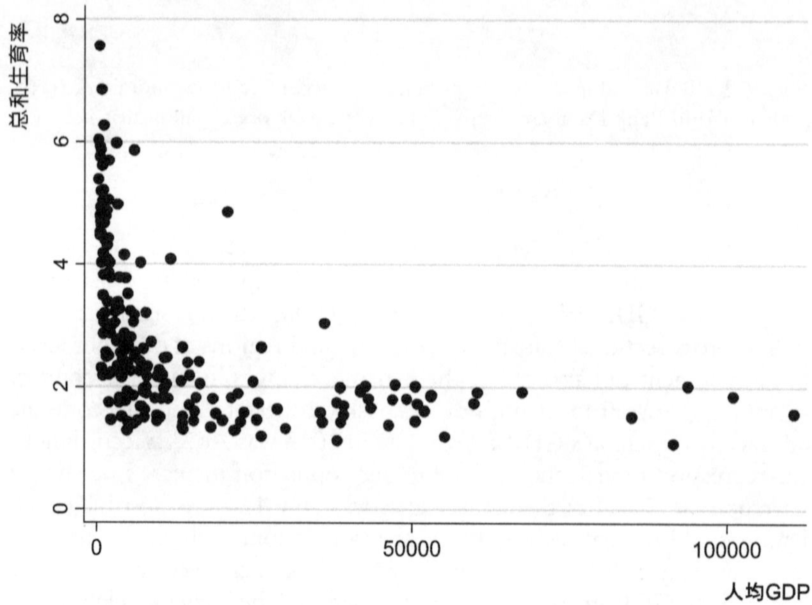

Fig. 6.2 Scattering of relationship between fertility rate and GDP per capita. Source: World Bank Database, http://data.worldbank.org.cn/indicator/all

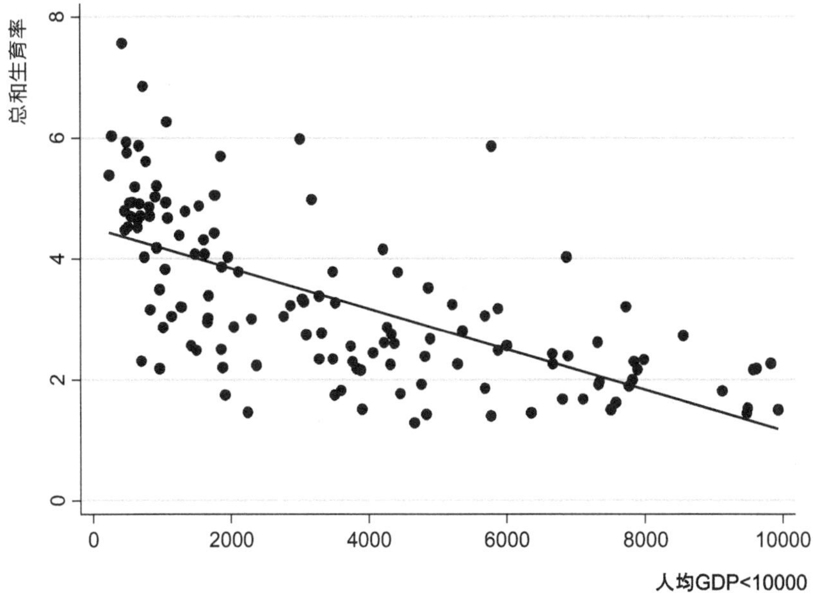

Fig. 6.3 Relationship between fertility rate and GDP per capita. Source: World Bank Database, http://data.worldbank.org.cn/indicator/all

$$\text{FERT} = 4.25 - 0.0003345 \times \text{PGDP}$$

where FERT is the total fertility rate, and PGDP is GDP per capita in USD; P value = 0.000, adjusted R^2 = 0.4269, and the p value of PGDP = 0.000, which is significant.

For every US dollar added to GDP per capita, the total fertility rate will fall by 0.0003345. While China's GDP per capita in 2013 was RMB 6807, the total fertility rate calculated by the regression equation should have been 2.24, but the actual figure was far lower at approximately 1.6 (World Bank data). *If calculated according to the GDP per capita of USD 5414 in 2011, which fell from the economic growth rate of 8%, the total fertility rate in that year should be 2.44, but the actual rate of China in 2011 was only around 1.2. As indicated by the statistics for developed countries with higher levels of GDP per capita, the relationship between the development level and childbirth is that the birth rate drops after the country becomes affluent, whereas in China the birth rate begins to reduce before it becomes rich.*

1.2 Loss of the Most Vital 10–15 Years for Transitioning Into a Developed Country

Many European and East Asian countries that now have low birth and low population growth, or even negative growth, do not promote birth control and only carry out guided family planning. Their population growth rates are basically smooth curves descending from high to low. Since the mid-1970s, China's fertility rate and population growth rate have started to shift from 'high birth, low mortality and high growth' to 'low birth, low mortality and low-to-medium growth'. Since the reform and opening up, however, its population's fertility has been subject to the centralized control of the government as well as to the direct and opportunity costs mechanisms of the market. Consequently, after a rebound in the early and mid-1980s, China's fertility rate and population growth rate entered low-level ranges ahead of schedule, earlier than many countries and regions in Europe (including Russia) and East Asia (including Japan, South Korea and Taiwan), forming a population dip caused by ultra-low fertility during this development stage. The family-planning-caused population dip refers to the section between the normal downward growth curve and the ultra-low descending curve.

The top downward-trending solid line indicates the population growth in South Korea, Taiwan and other countries and regions, while the lower downward-trending dotted curve refers to that of China. Beginning in the 1950s and 1960s, South Korea and Taiwan experienced 42–47 years of high-speed growth until the GDP growth rate fell from 8% in 1998 and 2003 respectively. In comparison, China experienced rapid economic growth for only 33 years, beginning in 1978 when the GDP per capita was USD 200. This puts China 10–15 years behind Taiwan and South Korea.

However, in terms of the median age of its population structure, China's status in 2011 was already equivalent to that of South Korea in 2002 and of Taiwan in 1997. Due to the dual regulation of fertility by family planning and the market, the middle and low-age section of the population structure of China was relatively small. As a result, in 2011, the over 65-year-old segment of its population was 1.7 to 2.7 percentage points higher than that of South Korea and Taiwan respectively in 1998 and 2003 when their GDP growth rate fell from 8%. In fact, with regard to the relationship of the per capita development level and the age structure of the population, mainland China was aging before getting rich, and declining before becoming a great power, while South Korea and Taiwan were aging after becoming wealthy, with economic growth sliding to the low-middle rate range after industrialization was completed (Table 6.1).

Table 6.1 Comparison with South Korea and Taiwan in data related to development stages

Country and region	*GDP growth rate*	*GDP per capita (USD)*	*Fertility rate*	*Median age*	*Aging (%) over 65 years old*	*Starting and ending year of high growth rate of 8%*
SK	10.0% (2000)	12,094 (2002)	1.17	36	7.0	1961–2002
Taiwan	8.4% (1997)	14,048 (1997)	1.70	35	8.0	1951–1997
China	9.3% (2011)	5414 (2011)	1.20	36	9.7	1979–2011

Note: The data is collected, calculated and arranged according to the websites of the Bureau of Statistics of China, South Korea and Taiwan of China

Birth control, especially the one-child policy, has cost China the most precious 10–15 years of high-speed growth in its development from a low- and middle-income country to a high-income one, which is the most crucial period in the transformation from an underdeveloped nation to a developed one. China's GDP per capita in 2011 was USD 5414. *If the national economy continued to grow at an annual rate of 8% until 2014, the GDP scale should have reached RMB 73.7441 trillion with the GDP per capita being USD 8696. Yet China's GDP in 2014 was actually RMB 63.6463 trillion with GDP per capita of USD 7500, RMB 10 trillion, which is nearly USD 1200 lower than expected.* The economic downturn in 2011, caused by the relative population shrinkage, has the potential to cause huge economic losses to China. This also begins to show the negative effect of population decline and aging on economic growth.

Supposing the population grows by 8‰ by 2020 and progresses smoothly to effectively push forward the urbanization process, *if GDP grows at a rate of 8% on average after 2011—if the exchange rate remains the same—by 2020, China will reach USD 13,155 in GDP per capita and will complete its industrialization and urbanization to attain a post-industrial phase and emerge as a new economically developed country. And if the rate of 8% can be maintained until 2025, its GDP per capita could reach over USD 19,000, as long as the exchange rate of 2014 remains unchanged.* Such a level of development is equivalent to that of the Czech Republic, Estonia, Greece and Portugal in 2014 and close to that of Taiwan in the same year. Due to *the population implosion and aging, as well as the interruption of the urbanization process to a certain extent, China has lost the most crucial and precious 10–15 years for achieving leapfrog development.*

2 The Mathematical Relationship and Practice of Demographic Changes Affecting Economic Growth

At present, there appears to be a deficiency in academic research, that is, scholars who observe economic operation and growth have neglected the effects of population increase, structure and mobility, while those who discuss population increase, structure and mobility have paid more attention to the population change itself or its relationship with the ecological environment of resources and changes in social structure, without probing into the possible profound impact of these changes on economic operation and growth.

With a closer look at the relationship between population increase and economic growth since China's reform and opening up, the rise and rapid decline of population growth begin to affect the upward and downward tendency of economic growth 20 years later. From 1978 to 1987, the population growth rate climbed from 11.80‰ to 16.61‰, and the economic growth rate rose all the way from 7.8% in 1998 to the peak 14.2% in 2007; and the economic growth rate dropped from the highest 14.2% in 2007 to 7.4% in 2014, while the population growth rate plummeted from 16.61‰ in 1987 to 9.2‰ in 1997.

So, what is the intrinsic ripple effect of population increase on economic growth? As the population base expands, consumption increases, which will affect the scale of GDP, and the population growth rate will also have a long-term continuous impact on the future GDP growth rate. However, a major defect of compulsory family planning is that it can only reduce the number of newborns to control the size of the population but it fails to adjust the proportion of different ages in a balanced manner. In short, the population size is controlled, but the age composition isn't. As a result, China's population structure has been changed. Except for the high-fertility years after 1962, the age distribution of the aged, the middle-aged, the young, teenagers, children and infants gradually changed from high-end-down to a high-end-up pentagonal structure.

The replacement rate of the population dropped from 2.0 in 1991 to 1.18 in 2010, meaning that if there is not a timely adjustment to the fertility policy, the trend of this dynamic change over a long period of time will be that the population in middle age and below will continue to decrease while the aged population will continue to increase. With an ever-shrinking population in the middle and lower parts of this pentagonal structure, what impact will this trend have on China's long-term national economic development and growth? The following is the mathematical description and implication analysis of the internal mechanism.

2.1 Mathematical Description

From the cited deduction, we can see the impact of the falling population growth rate and the rapid aging rate on national economic growth in the following four aspects (see the Appendix for the detailed proving process).

First, let's compare the steady state: since $\mathrm{dGDP}/d\beta = G_0/(1-\beta)^2 > 0$ is a monotonically increasing function, the smaller the marginal tendency, the lower the long-term steady-state output. Because $\beta_1 = \mathrm{NOPOP}^2 \times \beta_N + \mathrm{ROPOP}^2 \times \beta_R$ and $\beta = \mathrm{NOPOP} \times \beta_N + \mathrm{ROPOP} \times \beta_R$, $\beta - \beta_1 = \mathrm{NOPOP} \times \beta_N \times (1 - \mathrm{NOPOP}) + \mathrm{ROPOP} \times \beta_R \times (1 - \mathrm{ROPOP})$. When $\mathrm{NOPOP} + \mathrm{ROPOP} = 1$, $0 < \mathrm{NOPOP} < 1$ and $0 < \mathrm{RNOPOP} < 1$ are true, so $\beta > \beta_1$. Thus, $\mathrm{GDP}^* > \mathrm{GDP}_1^*$. Therefore, this has important implications, which leads to *Conclusion 1: An uneven population structure is unfavorable for the growth of long-term output of GNP.*

Secondly, we need to consider the impact of decreasing proportions of all age groups except the aged on the steady-state output: because $\mathrm{dGDP}_1^* / \mathrm{dNOPOP} = G_0 / (1-\beta_1)^2 \times d\beta_1 / \mathrm{dNOPOP}$ and $d\beta_1/\mathrm{dNOPOP} = 2 \times \mathrm{NOPOP} \times \beta_N + 2 \times \mathrm{ROPOP} \times \beta_R \times \mathrm{dROPOP}/\mathrm{dNOPOP}$, when $\mathrm{NOPOP} + \mathrm{ROPOP} = 1$, $\mathrm{dROPOP}/\mathrm{dNOPOP} = -1$ and then $d\beta_1/\mathrm{dNOPOP} = 2 \times (\mathrm{NOPOP} \times \beta_N - \mathrm{ROPOP} \times \beta_R)$. Despite β_N, the consumption intention of the middle-aged, the young, teenagers, children and infants is greater than that of the aged β_R, $\mathrm{NOPOP} \times \beta_N - \mathrm{ROPOP} \times \beta_R < 0$, which will be established when all age groups except the aged take a small enough proportion in the population structure, so $\mathrm{dGDP}_1^* / \mathrm{dNOPOP} < 0$, causing an even lower steady-state output after the reduction of such a proportion. This leads to *Conclusion 2: When the population structure is out of balance, if the proportion of infants, children, teenagers, the young and the middle-aged is reduced sufficiently to offset the addition in consumption by the aged, the long-term output of GNP will decline even more.*

Thirdly, the uneven demographic structure will also affect the changes in the consumption intention of the entire society. Because $dGDP_1^* / d\beta_N = G_0 / (1-\beta_1)^2 \times NOPOP^2 > 0$ and $dGDP_1^* / d\beta_N = G_0 / (1-\beta_1)^2 \times ROPOP^2 > 0$ shows that a greater intention to consume over all age groups helps increase the long-term steady-state output. With the increase in the aging population, and the comparative decrease in infants, children, teenagers, the young and the middle-aged, the demand for durable consumer goods and non-durable consumer goods will become saturated, causing the consumption intention to decline when the rigid demand is met. The demand for products required by the aged will be boosted for a short period of time as the aging population is growing, but it will decline afterwards with a lower marginal consumption intention as the aged pass away. Therefore, in the aging process, the total social output will go through a 'fall-rise-fall' fluctuation as the marginal demand of the young decreases while that of the aged increases and then decreases. Thus, *Conclusion 3: In an aging society, the marginal consumption intentions of the aged and all other age groups are not synchronized, so GNP may recover in the short term but will definitely decline in the long run.*

Finally, we consider the effect of acceleration. Because $dr_1/dv_1 = (1/2) \times \beta_1 \times (v_1\beta_1)^{-1/2} \times (NOPOP^2 \times \beta_N \times dv_N + ROPOP^2 \times \beta_R \times dv_R)$, when the proportion of all age groups except the aged significantly reduces, their investment intention (dv_N) will also fall. Although the investment intention of the aged (dv_R) rises temporarily, its growth degree will not be very high (and will also be lower than that of other age groups) and it will eventually shrink as the aged successively pass away. Therefore, the long-term investment intention of the entire society resulting from the decrease of infants, children, teenagers, the young and the middle-aged, that is, dv_1, will become smaller, resulting in a slower adjustment rate of the short-term GNP toward a long-term steady-state equilibrium. Even if macro policies are adopted to stimulate such a shift, it will still take a longer time to realize due to the weakened investment intention, reducing the efficiency of the stimulus policies. Thus, *Conclusion 4: With the aging of the demographic structure, the short-term investment intention of the aged will be stimulated, but the long-term investment intention of the entire society will decline because of the population decrease in all other age groups. The fluctuation in investment of the population once again indicates a 'fall-rise-*

fall' trend. The long-term GNP will decline with the reduction in total social investment, while macro stimulus policies will also need increased regulation due to the decline in investment intention, accompanied by the reduced effectiveness of monetary and fiscal policy.

2.2 *Impact of Demographic Changes on Actual Economic Operation and Growth*

The influences of birth, population growth and, especially, structural changes on the output are described above using their mathematical relationships. The following are further discussions on the data, plus practical observations about investment, consumption, exports and economic growth.

2.2.1 Demographic Changes and Relatively Shrinking Consumption

According to the data on consumption growth, the total of retail goods consumed by the whole of Chinese society from 2008 to 2014 increased by 21.6%, 15.5%, 18.3%, 17.1%, 14.3%, 13.1% and 12% respectively, and by 10.1% in May 2015, showing a downward trend.[1] In comparing the configuration and data, the downward curve of consumption growth is associated and aligned with that of the population growth of the previous period.

The pentagonal population structure that is turning to a high-end-up pattern affects the national economy. Initially, the population aged 0–14 progressively shrinks, resulting in the gradual weakening of consumption demands for infant milk powder, kindergartens (the current shortage of kindergartens in China is caused by the government's access regulations), toys, children's clothing, and so on; then, primary education demand shrinks and primary schools become over-supplied; and later, the needs for secondary and even university education will gradually decline.

Based on the data in Table 6.2, the number of general pupils *declined by 14.05 million in seven years, from 107.11 million in 2006 to 93.06 million in 2013; the number of junior high school students dropped by 11.74 million in six years, from 59.37 million in 2006 to 47.63 million in 2012; and similarly, the number of general senior high school students also began*

[1] See the Statistical Communiqué on Social and National Economic Economy as well as the statistical release for each year published on the website of the National Bureau of Statistics of the PRC.

Table 6.2 The decreasing trend in the number of primary schools and junior and senior high schools in China

	2006	*2007*	*2008*	*2009*	*2010*	*2011*	*2012*	*2013*	*2014*
General senior high schools	16,153	15,681	15,206	14,607	14,058	13,688	13,509	13,352	13,253
General junior high schools	60,550	59,109	57,701	56,167	54,823	54,063	53,167	52,764	–
General primary schools	341,639	320,061	300,854	280,184	257,410	241,249	228,585	213,529	201,377

Source: Database on the website of the National Bureau of Statistics of the PRC

to decline, from 24.76 million in 2008 to 24.00 million in 2014. Correspondingly, the number of schools also showed a downward trend. Of course, such reductions were partly due to school restructurings and mergers, but the primary reason behind them was the decline in the school-age population.

A fast-growing population will see greater income and higher living consumption due to an increase in the labor force, whereas a slow increase in population, especially with a decline in the youth sector, will lead to the slowdown of consumption growth and even to 'trading down' in certain sectors such as clothing, durable consumer goods, automobiles and housing. As the population in the below-middle-age bracket reduces, the need for children's clothing and fashion apparel will also decrease. When the household purchase of durable consumer goods reaches saturation, its production will also decline or even show negative growth. And undeniably, the decrease in the rigid demand for housing, indicated by the declining curve of the marriageable population after its peak in 2015, is an important factor in the current oversupply of real estate in China, along with the excessive development in the past caused by land finance-related policies.

2.2.2 Demographic Change and Investment Growth Slowdown

Lower population-related demand slows down the growth rate of investment in fixed assets. With respect to the investment in, and construction of, primary schools, secondary schools, vocational schools, universities, houses, factories, shops, banks, public service buildings, hospitals, nursing homes and so on, this will present a surplus-construction-surplus fluctuation coinciding with the structural change and aging of the population. While some buildings will need to be demolished or converted, except for nursing homes, hospitals and buildings related to tourism, which will show an increase in investment and construction, there will be insufficient social need to promote more investment in new facilities. From 2007 to 2014, the growth rate of total fixed asset investment of the entire society in China was 24.8%, 25.9%, 30.0%, 23.8%, 15.9%, 20.3%, 19.3% and 15.3% respectively, and, from January to May 2015, it continued to decline, with a nominal year-on-year growth of 11.4%.[2]

[2] See the Statistical Communiqué on Social and National Economic Economy as well as the statistical release for each year published on the website of the National Bureau of Statistics of the PRC.

The housing demand based on population is an important driving force for investment growth and also a source of growth for decorative and durable consumer goods and other forms of household consumption. However, urban and rural residential buildings in China are now in serious oversupply. From 1991 to the end of 2012, the cumulative number of urban residential units completed in China, with the original stock included, was about 220 million–250 million.[3] From 2013 to the first quarter of 2015, the total area of commercial apartments completed was 1.82 billion square meters, approximately 18.2 million units, and urban houses with limited property rights totaled about 70 million units covering 7 billion square meters. Assuming that new affordable housing offset demolished housing, there were about 308.2 million to 338.2 million residential units in cities and towns. At the end of March 2015, there were still 4.07713 billion square meters of commercial apartments under construction, which, once completed, would provide an additional 40.77 million units. At that time, the number of residential units would be 348.97 million to 37.897 million.[4]

For now, let's put aside any future construction of new houses. Since less than 1% of migrant workers purchased a house in the area where they worked,[5] and about 14% did so in cities and towns near their hometown, there were still 293.32 million to 333.2 million units over and above the 15 million they bought. *If the number of urban residents was counted as 150 million households, the average number of properties per household would be around 1.95 to 2.22.* According to the data, 21% of urban residents owned multiple units, 66% had one unit on average, and 13% owned or rented none;[6] if we subtract 15 million (houses purchased by migrant workers) and 10 million (the estimated vacant houses unsold yet) from the current housing stock of 293.32–333.2 million, this means 99 million urban households owned one unit, 1950 owned or rented none, while 3150 owned 5.37 to 6.63 units. This highlights the oversupply and uneven ownership of urban housing.

[3] Chen Yongjie, "The Average Apartment Owned per Household Is Over One in China," *Securities Daily*, April 12, 2013.

[4] From the database on the website of the National Bureau of Statistics of the PRC.

[5] National Bureau of Statistics of the PRC, "National Report on Migrant Worker Monitoring and Survey," website of the National Bureau of Statistics.

[6] Gan Li et al. with Survey and Research Center for China Household Finance in Southwestern University of Finance & Economics (SWUFE), "Survey of China Household Finance," published on May 20, 2014, on chfs.swufe.edu.cn.

As the population growth has slowed down, and particularly as the marriage rate has begun to drop, as well as the single-child group owning multiple units, and with houses left vacant after the death of the aged, the housing demand has declined correspondingly, causing the growth rate in residential investment from January to May between 2010 and 2015 to fall by 33.2%, 27.9%, 16.2%, 19.8%, 10.5% and 5.1% year-on-year respectively.

2.2.3 *The Rising Labor Cost and Export Downturn*

According to relevant data, the working-age population, aged 16–60 years, recorded a decrease of 3.45 million, 2.44 million and 3.71 million respectively from 2012 to 2014.[7] A slower growth rate of the labor force, or the decline in its absolute number, reduced the labor force that could create value for the economy in the same period, especially with respect to the supply of migrant workers, which led to difficulties in the recruitment of workers in the Pearl River Delta, the Yangtze River Delta and the southeast coast of China.

The working-age population growth downturn has increased the cost of labor and prematurely deprived China of the cost advantage of its manufacturing capacity in the international arena, weakening the pulling power of exports needed for growth (Table 6.3).

While the average wage of urban residents in 2014 was 3.25 times that of 2002, the wage of migrant workers increased 4.48 times faster in the same period. In addition to the relative reduction in demand from the US and Europe resulting from the US subprime mortgage debt and Europe's sovereign debt crisis, the key factor that dragged down China's export growth rate since 2008 was the decreasing supply

Table 6.3 Comparison of wage increase trends between migrant workers and urban employees

Year	*2002*	*2005*	*2010*	*2014*	*2014:2002*
Salary of migrant workers (RMB)	640	861	1690	2864	4.48
Salary of urban employees (RMB)	1031	1517	3045	3349	3.25

Source: Lu Feng, "The Trend of Wages for Migrant Workers in China: 1979–2010," published in *Social Sciences in China* in the 7th issue of 2012 and on the National Bureau of Statistics website and its *China Economic Report* in the 2nd issue of 2015

[7] Website of the National Bureau of Statistics of the PRC.

of its own migrant labor force, which resulted in higher labor costs than India and other countries and regions in South Asia, leading to the shifting of some of the labor-intensive industries to Southeast Asia and Africa, and the declining competitiveness of China's products. The data shows that the export growth rate of China from 2006 to 2014 was 23.86%, 20.57%, 7.30%, −13.72%, 30.46%, 15.15%, 4.97%, 6.0% and 6.10% respectively, and it increased by 0.8% from January to May in 2015.[8] The decline in exports in 2008 and 2009 was partly due to the impact of the US subprime mortgage crisis. As shown in Fig. 6.4, the deceleration in the growth rate of China's exports since 2007 generally reflected the causal relationship between the shrinking labor force and rising costs, which led to a decline in export competitiveness. The drop in the ratio of the gross value of imports and exports to GDP was actually due to the slower and negative growth of the working-age population.

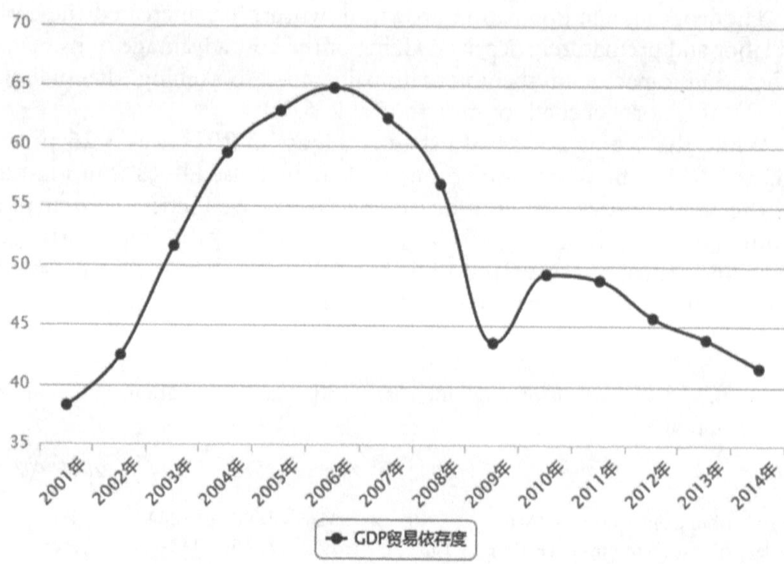

Fig. 6.4 Percentage of China's gross import and export value in GDP. Source: Data released annually by the General Administration of Customs of the PRC

[8]Website of General Administration of Customs of the PRC.

2.2.4 *The Weakened Impetus of Population Urbanization for Economic Growth*

The scholar Justin Yifu Lin emphasized that urbanization is still a driving force for the long-term high growth of the Chinese economy. He believed that by 2049, China's per capita GDP would reach the level of USD 40,000–50,000, with the urbanization rate up to 75%, and there would be more and more cities with a population of 20 million in the future. The Chinese economy would continue to grow at the rate of 8% for 15–20 years.[9] He also observed that by capitalizing on the late-mover advantage, South Korea, Taiwan, Singapore and other economies in East Asia managed to achieve a growth rate of 7.6% to 9.2% for two decades starting from a per capita income only 21% of that of the US. Given the fact that China's per capita GDP was about 15% of that of the US, it still had the potential for long-term high growth of the national economy.

The uniqueness of China's systems, structures and processes of development, however, determines the distortion of its urbanization course. Characterized by a huge population and an uneven regional development, China has experienced two totally different development periods since 1949, specifically, the planned economy with an economy model built on the People's Commune Movement, followed by the transition from the old system to a market economy. China differs greatly from many other countries, such as Germany, Japan, South Korea and Taiwan, particularly with regard to its population movement control policies, land systems and local fiscal systems. China's current economic operations and structures are closely and deeply connected with its historical systems and policies.

The urbanization of China is different from the general urban population flow of most nations in the world. In particular, the normal process is that rural people moving to towns and cities will seek jobs, residences, education, healthcare and pensions, as well as other public services, for the rest of their lives, as most of them will continue to work and live permanently as urban citizens. But in China, though its urbanization rate reached 54.77% in 2014, about 20% of this figure consisted of migrant workers and their families who lived and worked in cities and towns only for more than six months. In fact, the process is distorted by these rural Chinese who move to and gather in cities when they are young and return to their hometowns when they become old.

[9] Justin Yifu Lin, "Urbanization Is an Important Growth Point for China's Economic Development," *Nanfang Daily*, October 12, 2013.

Eighty-five percent of the migrant workers will eventually return to their homes in rural areas. This process impacts economic growth because it reduces the demand in areas such as housing, decorating, purchasing of furniture and electrical appliances, and the upgrading of lifestyle and living standards. Moreover, the aged workers who return to their hometowns have such a low marginal consumption rate that their consumption level is only 25% to 33% of their urban counterparts, resulting in a huge consumption collapse involving about 200–300 million people. Therefore, without radical changes, the concept that urbanization will strongly promote sustainable economic growth is not appropriate for describing China's actual urban and rural population and its economic process. The original plan was to sustain the rapid growth of the national economy by capitalizing on the opportunities created by the ongoing massive urbanization of the population and giving full play to the real estate industry in cities that were home to these newcomers, but it seems to have been severely disrupted.

In generalized studies of investment, consumption and export demand, as well as in the ascending and descending trends of national output multipliers and accelerators, there is an implicit assumption that the population variables are stable and negligible. Based on the above, however, the continuous economic downturn in recent years can be attributed to the reform of the allocation of national resources toward a market economy being adopted concurrently with the administrative plan for birth control, leading to a sharp decline in fertility and population growth under the double impact of both the market and the plan. Meanwhile, the control over population mobility and the slow reforms in land and other sectors have also disrupted the overall urbanization process. The economic consequence today is a corresponding decline in consumption, investment and exports, which has rendered an economic slump with a shrinking population and poor mobility.

3 Further Downward Pressure of Economic Growth

Our long-range development goal is to build a moderately prosperous society in all aspects and to reach the level of a moderately developed country by the middle of the twenty-first century. Therefore, the most critical questions are as follows: For how long will the national economy continue to decline and to what levels will the growth rate fall before it becomes stable? Will the national economy remain sluggish and fall into the trap set by the decreasing and aging population before the country becomes economically strong, thereby disrupting the great cause of the rejuvenation of the Chinese nation in the twenty-first century?

3.1 Impact of Demographic Changes on Future Short- and Medium-Term Economic Growth

The correlation between population change and economic fluctuation in the short and medium terms is mainly due to the impact of the decrease or increase of the population aged 0–14 on economic expansion or contraction, and on the consumption and education of that demographic. Therefore, we have analyzed the data relationships since 1973 and found that when the population grows or falls rapidly, it has a strong correlation with the economic growth rate 20 years later.

Based on the declining population trend of the 0–14 age bracket, the average population reduction per year from 2000 to 2010 was 8.81 million in the short, medium and long terms. The influences on education and consumption of each age group are reflected as follows: the decline in population during 2000–2003 and 2004–2010 occurred mainly in secondary school students and primary school students respectively; and since 2017, the enrollment of university students has begun to drop. Such a downward trend in the absolute number of students at all levels will reach a plateau by 2035. Economically, this means that the difficulties in kindergarten enrollment will be greatly relieved; in the short and medium terms, the education and consumption requirements of the students in primary and junior high schools will shrink sharply; the education and consumption of senior high school students will enter into recession; and the decline in education and consumption of college students will begin to appear during the '13th Five-Year Plan' period and will become increasingly severe in the following '14th Five-Year Plan' and '15th Five-Year Plan' periods, until it has stabilized by the time of the '16th Five-Year Plan'. If more and more Chinese children are sent to study abroad, the university education of China and the consumption of this age group will quickly fall into depression.

3.2 Historical Data on the Long-Term Effects of Demographic Changes on Economic Growth

There are three reasons demographic changes can affect the long-term economy:

1. When people turn 20 years old, the normal working age, they will join the existing labor force as new blood. The population growth rate of 20 years earlier will determine the number of laboring units invested in the national economy 20 years later, which in turn will influence the increment of national output.
2. Twenty years later, when the additional laborers find jobs, earn wages and other income, and develop into a group with consumption and savings capabilities, the national economy will have a greater consumption scale, more savings, better investment ability and enhanced export competitiveness, with a higher percentage of a young and middle-aged labor force.
3. People in their 20s begin to get married and have children, need to rent or buy an apartment, decorate their new houses, and purchase furniture, home appliances and other household supplies, including private cars, which boosts the demand for building materials, construction and installation, durable consumer goods, automobiles and other products. Below, we have run a regression for the correlation between the population growth rate from 1974 to 1994 and the economic growth rate 20 years later, from 1994 to 2014, and have obtained the following figures and correlation formulae (Fig. 6.5).

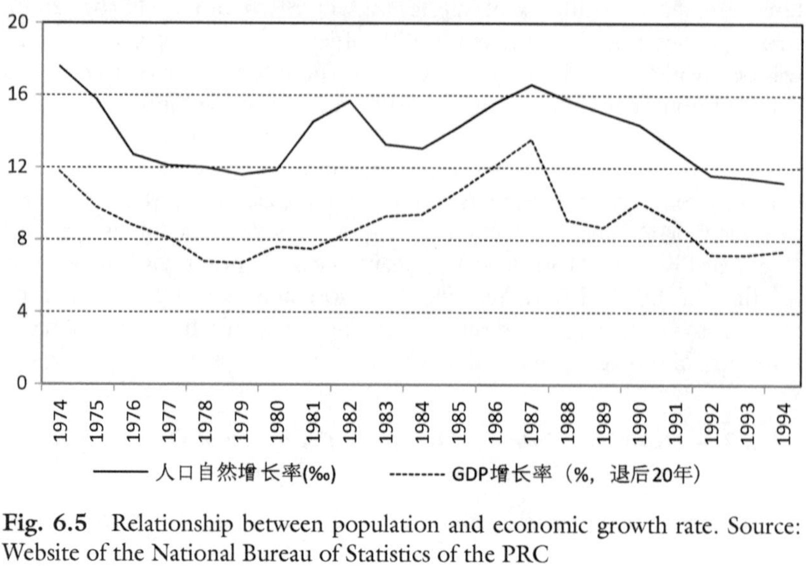

Fig. 6.5 Relationship between population and economic growth rate. Source: Website of the National Bureau of Statistics of the PRC

$$ry = -1.293 + 0.749 \times \text{pop}$$

R^2 = 0.6017, p value of pop = 0.000, which is significant; the population growth rate is from 1974 to 1994, and the nominal growth rate of GDP is from 1994 to 2014.

We will be looking separately at the impact of population increases and decreases on economic fluctuations 20 years later. For example, China was in a period of rapid population growth from 1979 to 1987. There were two main reasons. First, as the collective production system of the people's communes in rural areas was reformed into the contract responsibility system, the reproductive behavior in the natural economy rebounded. On the one hand, the rural production methods in this phase were changed from collective labor, work points-based calculation, public procurement, scarce sideline jobs and year-end work points-based distribution to a natural economy where every family accounted for itself; and, on the other hand, the large-scale population mobility that led to reduced fertility only began in 1988. As a result, the birth rate of the rural population was higher than that of the collective economy. Secondly, educated youth from the cities avoided getting married and having children during their stay in rural areas, even when they had reached marriageable age, because they were eager to go back to the cities. At the end of the 1970s, the campaign that called upon educated urban youth to go to the countryside was canceled. In addition, over 10 million of those young people in rural areas were allowed to return home, work and get married, so the delayed childbirth was concentrated in the following few years. It can be seen that the natural population growth rate rose from 11.61‰ in 1979 to 16.61‰ in 1987, while the GDP growth rate 20 years later climbed from 7.6% in 1999 to 11.7% in 2007. As shown in Fig. 6.6, they were both upward curves, for which a regression analysis was conducted to arrive at the following quantitative relationship:

$$ry = -4.049 + 0.962 \times \text{pop}$$

R^2 = 0.5336, p value of pop = 0.025, which is significant.

When the population growth declines, it also exerts downward pressure on economic growth 20 years later. From 1973 to 1978, the population growth rate dropped from a high point of 20.99‰ to 12‰, and 20 years

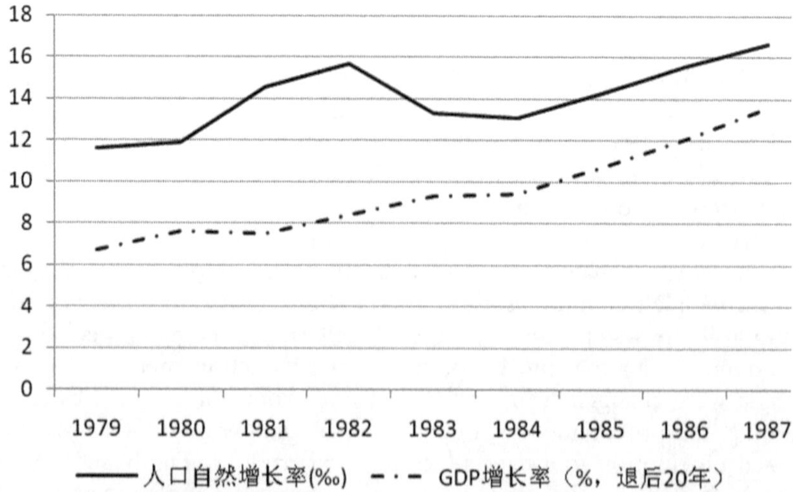

Fig. 6.6 Correlation between the population growth from 1979 to 1987 and the economic growth from 1999 to 2007. Source: Website of the National Bureau of Statistics of the PRC

later the GDP growth fell from 13.6% in 1993 to 7.3% in 1998. The population increase rate and economic growth rate at this stage all changed at the upper level. Then, from 1988 to 1994, the population growth rate dropped from 15.73‰ to 11.21‰, and the GDP growth rate dropped from 10.1% in 2008 to 7.4% in 2014. This time, the population change in the mid-to-low growth range also affected GDP and played a role in its entry into the state of mid-to-low growth.

To run a regression: in 1973–1978: $ry = 0.752 + 0.586 \times \text{pop}$; $R^2 = 0.911$; p value of pop = 0.003, significant; in 1988–1994: $ry = 1.908 + 0.491 \times \text{pop}$; $R^2 = 0.6509$, p value of pop = 0.028, significant.

According to the above regression analysis and the relationship between population growth and economic growth in both periods, as shown in Fig. 6.7, when the population growth either remained constant or changed at a particularly slow rate, the economic growth rate might be more affected by investment, exports, fiscal expenditure, changes in debt levels, currency fluctuations and other factors; and when the population rose or fell significantly, the economic growth rate would undoubtedly be subject to the fundamental and decisive influence of the demographic changes.

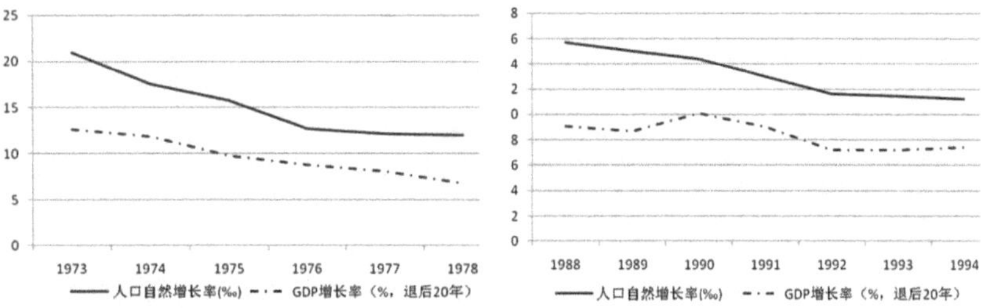

Fig. 6.7 Correlation between the declining population and the economic downturn in 1973–1978 and 1988–1994 in China. Source: Database on the website of the National Bureau of Statistics of the PRC

3.3 *The Pressure of Population Decline on China's Future Long-Term Economic Growth*

In 1994, the population fertility rate was 1.76 and the growth rate was 11.21‰; the growth rate dropped to 10.55‰ in 1995; and in 2014 the population fertility rate fell to 1.26 (estimated by the author) and the population growth rate to 4.79‰. There is a steep drop in the population growth rate from 1995 to 2014, during which the curves in 1997–2002 and in 2005–2010 were even steeper (Fig. 6.8).

Through regression, the relationship between the population increase rate and economic growth rate from 2015 to 2034 is: $ry = -1.035 + 0.738 \times \text{pop}$; $R^2 = 0.691$, p value of pop = 0.000, which is significant. This deduction is actually a forecast about the downward pressure of the declining trend in population growth of the previous 20 years on the economic growth after 2014, based on the premise that no other factors would affect future economic growth.

According to the regression analysis of the influence of changes in population growth in all periods on the changes in economic growth 20 years later (since the 1970s), the population growth rate was almost parallel to the economic growth rate 20 years later. The population growth rate's continuous decline and entry into the low growth range caused by the low population fertility rate from 1995 to 2014 will have a strong downward impact on the economic growth rate 20 years later. If not supported by other factors such as special reforms, technological development and innovation, strategies such as opening up and going out, and strong boosts from systems, policies and other measures, the economic growth rate will fall from about 7% to about 3% between 2016 and 2020, will drop from

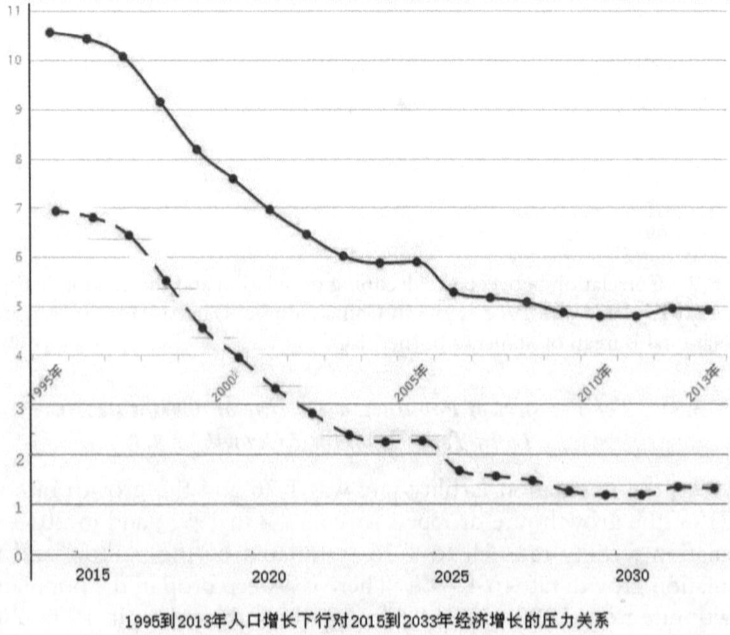

Fig. 6.8 Descending trend of population and economic growth. Note: On the vertical axis, the unit of economic growth rate is % in the dotted line; the population growth rate unit is ‰ in the solid line; population growth rate. Source: Database on the website of the National Bureau of Statistics of the PRC; the economic growth rate is derived from parallel correlations based on historical regression experience

about 3% to about 1% between 2021 and 2030, and will stay at 1.3% or so from 2030 to 2035. The national economy of China will remain sluggish for a long period of time, like Japan's. But the difference is that Japan became wealthy before growing old, but China is experiencing the opposite: it is growing old before getting rich, and is encountering increasingly greater obstacles to and difficulties in becoming rich.

If family planning were decisively and completely eliminated in 2016 to return the fertility rate gradually to about 2.1, the rise of the natural population growth rate might, after offsetting the rising mortality rate, return to about 8‰, and the resulting baby boom and the need for education, childcare, housekeeping and housing in the short term would stimulate consumption and investment, which would maintain the economic growth at about 6%. If people are willing and able to have children following the abolition of the family planning policy in 2016, the newly added population will reach working age by 2036, which means a cumulative increase in the labor supply, the addition of new adults who have the ability to consume, and an increase in the number of people who will get married, bear children and buy houses. Similar to the situation after 1999, there will be a wave of economic revitalization, which could prevent the Chinese nation from declining again in the 2040s after its global renaissance in the 2020s.

In countries and regions where people have reproductive freedom, for example, Japan, South Korea, Russia, Singapore and Taiwan, the fertility rate and the natural growth rate will still be lower than the birth replacement rate, because of factors such as the high direct and opportunity costs of childbearing and childcare, or infertility and other problems, or the growing number of people who prefer a late marriage or to remain single, meaning the natural growth rate will continue to decline despite various government incentives. The economic consequence is that consumption and investment will shrink even further, while the demand for education, housing, pensions and hospitals will be ebbing away. *By around 2035, the Chinese society will see a high degree of aging, with negative population growth, and the annual growth rate of GDP may be the same as that of Japan, which is around 0–2%. The result is the Chinese economy will get stuck in long-term sluggish development and fall into the population-dip trap of family planning.*

4 Prospective Difficulties in the National Economy Caused by Aging

The population structures of China, India and the US are as follows:

1. The population of infants, children, youth and the middle-aged in the lower part of China's population structure is decreasing, and the ratio of the workforce contributing to pensions to those able to collect pensions will change significantly. Moreover, when the pension system in China was set up, which was only in the mid-1990s, many of the aged did not contribute to pensions in their working years, so the pensions now contributed by the young people will be essential to provide support for the aged in the future.

2. The demographic structure of India is pyramidal. It has one thing in common with China in terms of pension withdrawal: it also needs pensions contributed by the young and middle-aged to support the retired population. At present, its pension system only covers about 12% of the labor force.[10] Unlike China, however, India's young population is larger than the aged, so there will be more and more young pension-contributors over time. Its pension pressure is actually much lighter.
3. The population structure of the US is basically bottle-shaped. As the aged collect pensions, this country is also faced with a pension gap due to inflation and other factors. And it has adopted measures, including the extension of the retirement age, to solve this problem.

Many scholars have conducted research on the pension gap created by the aging population in China. As estimated by Wei Jizhang, based on the basic urban pension system (excluding the rural pension), *in 2012 the implicit debt of the social pooling account was as high as RMB 83.6 trillion*, the implicit debt of the personal account was RMB 2.6 trillion, and the hidden debt under the unified pension system for urban employees' basic pension insurance was RMB 86.2 trillion, accounting for 166% of the GDP of the same year.[11]

Cao Yuanzheng and other scholars have projected that if the annual growth rate of GDP from 2010 was 6%, *the pension gap will expand to RMB 68.2 trillion by 2033, accounting for 38.7% of GDP of the same year.*[12]

Research by a team led by Ma Jun has forecast that, in contrast to 2011 when one retired man was supported by three laborers, 38 years later a retired man would be supported by only one laborer, with the pension gap expanding year by year. They also reported that, in addition to pension costs, one must consider that due to the aging of the population, the total cost of primary healthcare plus long-term care costs would rise to account for 10% of GDP 38 years later, one-third of which will need to be covered by the government. In their opinion, it is a *loose period* for the income and

[10] Li Yajun, "Review on the Development of Non Contributory Pensions in India," *South Asian Studies Quarterly*, Vol. 1, 2014.

[11] Wei Jizhang, "The Forecast and Measurement of Implicit Debts in the Current Pattern of Combination of Social Pooling with Individual Accounts," *China Pension Report 2014*, Beijing, China: Social Sciences Academic Press, 2014.

[12] Cao Yuanzheng et al., "Remodeling the Debt Capacity of China," *Caijing Magazine*, June 12, 2012.

expenses of China's urban pension from 2012 to 2021; it will enter into a *tightening period* from 2022 to 2035 when the retired pensioners increase rapidly and the growth of contributors is significantly slower, and then it will start to decline with the aging of the population alongside the slowdown of urbanization and the full realization of urban coverage. Afterwards, there will be a sharp *deterioration period* from 2035 to 2050 when the urban contributors decrease significantly while the retired group keeps expanding rapidly.[13]

Firstly, the increasing need for old-age care in the future will lead to higher taxes, which in turn will affect future investment, entrepreneurship and economic growth. When the proportion of the aged is too high while that of the middle-aged and young is too low, it is essential to increase the collection of money to support pensions. For example, the financial subsidies for pensions and the shortfall in pensions caused by inflation can only be balanced by more taxes levied by the government over companies and individuals. At present, China's actual macro tax burden has reached about 37% of GDP. With the heavier burden of old-age care, the tax burden will be increasingly greater. Given that the aging of the population starts earlier and lasts longer in China than in developed countries, the macro tax burden is likely to exceed 50% of GDP at its worst. Such a high tax burden will inevitably inhibit the supply and input of labor, technology, funds and other elements influencing the national economic output. In an aging society with sluggish economic growth, light taxes and tax cuts are generally required to stimulate economic growth, but the demands of such a high pension collection calls for high taxes. Therefore, economic policymaking is caught in a dilemma due to the conflict between needing low taxes to stimulate economic growth and high taxes to support pensions.

Secondly, when economic growth is affected by heavy fiscal burdens, tax revenue is reduced, which will lead to significant pension liabilities and an unstable financial system. In order to make up for the gap in the pension system, the national financial authorities will adopt a series of measures, including issuing long-term pension bonds at home and abroad to raise funds, with the guarantee of using the future fiscal revenue to repay the principal and pay interest; increasing the size of the fiscal deficit through bank overdraft in the event of a tight pension budget; and borrowing

[13] Ma Jun and Xiao Mingzhi, "Research on the Prediction and Reform of Pension Income and Expenditure of Urban Staff," *Chinese National Balance Sheet Study*, Beijing, China: Social Sciences Academic Press, 2012.

funds from personal deposit accounts in the case of insufficient government pensions. Pension debt is an integral part of the total national economic debt, which also includes state debt, corporate debt and household debt. China's future pensions will be characterized by the increasingly higher demand, the annual increase of the government's fiscal burden, the low yield from pension bonds, and possibly higher bad debt ratios caused by defaults of banks and other financial institutions, all of which could trigger a chain reaction among financial systems and eventually put the financial system and the national economy at high risk of collapse and severe recession.

Thirdly, in the future aging society, the huge urban-rural disparity in consumption will cause poverty of the aged in rural areas and consumption collapse. As reported above, for various reasons 85% of the migrant population did not settle in cities and towns as permanent residents. Many scholars focused on the future demand and shortfall of the urban pension on the assumption that approximately 80% of the population will move to cities over time, but they failed to observe the peculiar phenomenon of disrupted urbanization in China. In fact, a most likely scenario in the future is that 85% of the migrant workers in urban areas will return home in their old age and these people, plus the aged already in rural areas, may reach about 300–500 million. Due to China's limited financial capacity, they are unlikely to receive the same level of pension-related national treatment as their urban counterparts, which makes them a relatively poor community with little savings and spending power. These aged farmers will end up becoming the victims of China's family planning policies and its aging population.

Fourthly, in the long run, the increasingly heavy pension burden may weaken the global competitiveness of China's economy. The paid pension and related consumption linked to provision for the aged are actually important parts of GDP. Pension comes from products. The higher the percentage it takes from products and services, the lower is the international competitiveness of these products and services. By comparison, India's population ratio is patterned like a pyramid with a smaller pension burden, the US is bottle-shaped with all ages in balance, while only China has developed an inverted pentagonal structure when it is still economically underdeveloped. If national competitiveness is translated into economic implications, India will have an enormous demographic advantage in the long run, and a strong competitiveness due to the low pension cost of its products and services. Provided that any pension increase is synchronized with economic growth, and technological progress and the pension cost determined by the population structure are unchanged, the international competitiveness of India's products and services will remain stable. But when it comes to China, in the long-term future it will lose the global competitiveness of its national economy as the pension cost takes an increasingly high percentage of products and services, if there is no technological progress or industrial innovation. And even if there are technological advances, their benefits may be consumed by the tremendous pension cost. Of course, optimistically, technological progress and industrial innovation will make up for the pension deficit and withstand the economic downturn to protect the national economy from severe crises or risks.

Fifthly, with the coexistence of the labor shortage and structural unemployment, there will be a corresponding decline in working innovation and productivity. And the possible large-scale use of robots to replace human labor will make the lack of demand and overproduction even worse. On the one hand, the slowdown in the growth of the working-age population, especially the decrease of young laborers, has led to a labor shortage and a continued rise in labor costs; on the other hand, serious structural unemployment will also occur for two main reasons. First, the consumer demand for education and housing, and so on will decline with the population implosion, resulting in an overcapacity in relevant industries from which workers will become redundant, and consequently an unemployed population will be created. Secondly, retirement has gradually been postponed in order to close the pension gap. Extending the working age will inevitably reduce jobs for young people, leading to a higher unemployment rate just as Europe is now experiencing. Moreover, the aging workforce, with its outdated knowledge and stereotyped mindset, will impede innovation and vitality in technology and other fields. Older workers are slow to learn and react, and not energetic enough to work efficiently.

Some domestic researchers have suggested that China's future labor shortage can be compensated for by robots.[14] It is arguable that it is necessary to develop robots to make up for the lack of labor, and some industries also need robots to improve manufacturing accuracy and quality as well as production efficiency. However, there would also be some negative consequences to this:

[14] Zheng Jiabao, "China Will Become the No. 1 User of Industrial Robots in the World," www.qianzhan.com, April 3, 2015.

1. Developing robots, in effect, is a capital input. In the case of overproduction, the excessive use of robots to replace the labor force will lead to a higher unemployment rate.
2. The national wealth produced by robots, a kind of capital, is attributed to capital owners, which will not only reduce the opportunity for workers to create and distribute wealth, but also widen the income gap between capital owners and laborers.
3. When robots are more extensively applied to production and services, laborers will find it harder to gain income through participation in work. The products made by robots will not be consumed through lack of effective demand by laborers, leading to an overproduction in the national economy. More seriously, such underconsumption may even trigger a financial crisis.

5 Conclusion

In a market economy environment, population mobility and urbanization will adjust the momentum of excessive population growth on the macro level, while on the micro level, the education level of females, combined with the direct and opportunity costs of birth and child-raising, will affect household fertility decisions and regulate reproductive behaviors. From a global perspective, data analysis has shown that a number of countries that have never adopted national family planning policies have also undergone periodic changes in population growth, that is, from a population boom at the beginning of industrialization to moderate growth in the mid-term, and then to low or even negative growth when the industrialization era draws to an end. Based on the current world trend of demographic change, Thomas Robert Malthus' prediction that the human population would sustain its exponential growth will not become reality.

In order to rationalize its population to the moderate scale of 700 million advocated by some scholars, China began to promote family planning in the 1970s and enforced the one-child birth control policy in the 1980s. This revealed a marked institutional disassociation between wealth creation and human reproduction. So, when it started its transition to a market economy system in the late 1970s, the country changed its fertility policy from independent decision-making by each household to a centralized control of family planning by the government.

This government-imposed family planning had two major defects. *First, due to the combined impact of government regulation and the market, there was a steep population decline and significant population dip; and secondly, the population structure was severely unbalanced because the policy could only control the population scale but failed to adjust the demographic structure proportionally.*

In a market economy, the two forces—the internal and intrinsic force of the society combined with the external and mandatory force of the government—restrain the population growth, which has rapidly transformed from a population boom to a moderate increase and then to low growth, as shown in a very steep descending curve. So, these dual forces have become the fundamental factors that drive the economic growth rate.

From 1979 to the mid-1980s, the rural contract responsibility system helped the recovery of reproductive behaviors in the natural economy; in the meantime, a large number of educated youth returned to the cities, got married and had children. From 1999 to 2007, 20 years after the baby boom, a large number of new laborers were added to the economic sphere, which strongly promoted the growth of the national economy during this period through the development of processing industries and exports, especially after China's entry to the WTO in 2011. However, due to the adjustment of the dual forces of society and government, the population growth rate began to decline sharply in 1987, impacting on the post-2007 growth momentum of the national economy that has continued to decline until this day.

Based on mathematical modeling, we have sketched out the changes in the population and national economy as follows: China has experienced a rapid aging of its population as the growth rate fluctuates alongside the dynamic structural changes caused by family planning policies. Age-specific consumption, investment and export bring about waves of structural rises and falls, continuously creating downward pressure on economic growth in the long term. Also, changes in consumption and investment influenced by such structure-related population decline may play a part, as a multiplier and an accelerator, in affecting the prosperity or recession of the national economy.

One of the key questions is how population growth and changes will affect the future trend of national economic growth. Of course, the future economic growth rate is determined by multiple factors. The following prediction is based on the assumption that other factors remain constant: *During the period from 2015 to the mid-2030s, if China fails to adjust its population policy, and to develop technologies and industrial innovation on a par with the advanced countries, or to make new inroads in the world with its development, the economic growth rate in the future is likely to drop from 7% to 3% and down to nearly 1%–0%.*

Another major concern is the huge risk created by China's aging population. Although some developed countries that have not implemented institutionalized family planning have also entered an aging society due to the adjustment of internal mechanisms, China's enforcement of family planning has led to a series of consequences. First, it has lost the most precious 10–15 years for accelerating the pace of economic growth and timely industrialization by taking advantage of the demographic dividend. In contrast to the developed countries that have stepped into the post-industrial age, China is hit by aging and recession before it has grown to be wealthy and strong. Secondly, the number of the young and middle-aged that contribute to pensions is decreasing progressively, while the group of pensioners is growing increasingly large. As a result, the proportion of the pension cost inherent in production and services in the national economy stays at a high level, weakening its global competitiveness. Thirdly, such a huge pension gap may lead to heavy tax and financial burdens, a forced extension of the retirement age, and lack of innovation and low work-efficiency, which will not only impose downward pressures on further economic growth, but also bring a great risk of instability in the financial system and dramatic fluctuations in the national economy.

The following are some suggestions for strategies and policies proposed by the author.

Legislated birth control should be stopped as soon as possible in 2016, returning the right to make fertility decisions to families and abolishing the collection of social maintenance fees. This move has the following strategic significance for China and its people:

1. It will gradually bolster the consumption related to infants and children and recover the need for education and other relevant sectors. Also, it will ease the burden of social support, increase farmers' income and spending capacity, and encourage people to start businesses and buy houses, which will restore economic vitality and drive urbanization.
2. China's economy was at its lowest point in the 1930s. If the birth control policy is lifted in 2016, the new labor force will be able to gradually participate in economic activities from 2036, providing

impetus in terms of earning, consumption, marriage, childbirth, house purchasing and so on, as happened with the upward economic growth that started in 1999.

3. According to studies by Ma Jun et al., the pension gap will drop sharply after 2035. If the birth control policy is canceled ahead of schedule in 2016, the newly added population will reach working age in 2036 and expand the size of the pension-contributors, which will eventually cover deficits and ease fiscal pressure and debt, and avert financial crises.
4. Due to the high possibility of negative population growth in China, the total size of China's economy in the 2040s is likely to be overtaken again by the US, or even surpassed by India. However, if family planning is abandoned in 2016, and urban and rural households are willing and able to bear children, it is expected that, by the second half of the 2030s, China will secure its potential to be the largest economy in the world, thanks to the growth of a new workforce, recovered consumption, investment and exports, and the alleviation of the aging challenge.

Although China's economic and social development was gravely affected by the population dip caused by family planning, it still holds many development advantages. For example, the Chinese people are intelligent, diligent and thrifty, and have the tradition of saving money, and there is an enormous pool of manpower, including a sizeable talent base studying and working abroad. These are all favorable factors that can make up for and bridge the population dip.

Therefore, great efforts should be made to vigorously reform China's administrative system by taking the following steps: streamline administration and delegate power to the lower levels to build a service-oriented government; rationalize the number of people on the government payroll and reduce taxes; encourage innovation and entrepreneurship, inspiring the creativity and vitality of the private sector; give full play to our high achievers, attracting talented expatriates to return home; promote technological progress and strive for industrial innovation to build an innovation-oriented country that leads the world; enhance the international competitiveness of China's products and services; open up and go global at a higher level, creating cultural soft power, advanced technology, international industrial partnerships and dynamic systems with controllable risks that are recognized by our foreign counterparts; and explore markets for the development of the Chinese nation, so as to achieve an effective backflow of national income in the framework of win-win cooperation. Only by taking these measures will it be likely for China to avoid the trap caused by family planning and realize the dream of the great rejuvenation of the Chinese nation in the twenty-first century.

Appendix

Three Sectors Model of National Income Determination Excluding Population Structure

The American economists Alvin Hansen and Paul Samuelson combined the multiplier and accelerator theories for the first time to analyze how consumption and investment demand spontaneously caused cyclical fluctuations in the national economy. Based on the Hansen-Samuelson model, this paper assumes that in the three sectors model of national income determination, the total social consumption in the current period is determined by the marginal consumption intention and the GDP in the previous period, and the investment in the current period, as a kind of induced demand, is subject to the investment accelerator and previous consumption changes; then the following formula will be established[15]:

$$\mathrm{GDP}_t = C_t + I_t + G_t \tag{6.1}$$

$$C_t = \beta \times \mathrm{GDP}_{t-1} \tag{6.2}$$

$$I_t = v \times \left(C_{t-1} - C_{t-2}\right) \tag{6.3}$$

where t is time; GDP is gross domestic product, which also equals to national income in the absence of a net export sector; C is consumption; I is investment; and β and v are marginal consumption intention and investment accelerator respectively with $0 < \beta < 1$ and $v > 1$ being true.

To bring (6.2) and (6.3) into (6.1), there is:

[15] As the basis for the Hansen-Samuelson model, this assumption is also applied to wide-ranging domestic research such as Zhuang Liting: "Discussion about Investment Multiplier-Accelerator Model and the Cyclical Fluctuation of Chinese Economy," *Prices Monthly*, Vol. 4, 2010; and Huang Feixue, Zhao Xin, and Hou Tieshan, "Study on China's Economic Fluctuation Based on Four Sectors Multiplier-Accelerator Model," *Productivity Research*, Vol. 3, 2009.

$$\mathrm{GDP}_t = (\beta + \beta \times v)\mathrm{GDP}_{t-1} + v \times \mathrm{GDP}_{t-2} + G_t \tag{6.4}$$

Let $G_t = G_0$, when $\beta \times v < 1$, the general solution of the state Eq. (6.4) is

$$\mathrm{GDP}_t = r^t (A \sin \omega t + B \cos \omega t) + \frac{G_0}{1-\beta} \tag{6.5}$$

where $r = (\beta \times v)^{1/2}$. Obviously, when $t \to \infty$, GDP_t is convergent to $[G_0/(1-\beta)]$, which means the long-term steady-state equilibrium is:

$$\mathrm{GDP}^* = \frac{G_0}{1-\beta} \tag{6.6}$$

Three Sectors Model of National Income Determination Including Population Structure

The role of demographic structure was not considered in the classic Hansen-Samuelson model. In order to analyze how the consumption intention and investment intention of different age groups influence the multiplier-accelerator model and then play a role in the fluctuation of national income, we have classified the entire population into two types, the young and the aged. Suppose the total young population is NOP, the total aged population is ROP and the total population is N, the proportions of the young and the aged are

$$\mathrm{NOPOP} = \frac{\mathrm{NOP}}{N}, \quad \mathrm{ROPOP} = \frac{\mathrm{ROP}}{N}, \quad \mathrm{NOPOP} + \mathrm{ROPOP} \equiv 1 \tag{6.7}$$

Correspondingly, both the marginal consumption intention and investment accelerator of the whole society are weighted averages of the young and the aged

$$\beta = \mathrm{NOPOP} \times \beta_N + \mathrm{ROPOP} \times \beta_R \tag{6.8}$$

$$v = \mathrm{NOPOP} \times v_N + \mathrm{ROPOP} \times v_R \tag{6.9}$$

where β_N and β_R are the marginal consumption intentions for the young and the aged respectively, and $0 < \beta_N < 1$ and $0 < \beta_R < 1$ are established; and v_N and v_R are the investment accelerators for the young and the aged respectively, and $v_N > 1$ and $v_R > 1$ are established.

When total social consumption is constituted by the young and the aged, the total consumption is the weighted average of the two parts, that is, $C_t = \text{NOPOP} \times C_{\text{NOPOP}, t} + \text{ROPOP} \times C_{\text{ROPOP}, t}$, and the total investment is also the weighted average of the two parts, that is, $I_t = \text{NOPOP} \times I_{\text{NOPOP}, t} + \text{ROPOP} \times I_{\text{ROPOP}, t}$. Therefore, the national income of the three sectors is determined by the following equations:

$$\text{GDP}_t = C_t + I_t + G_t \tag{6.10}$$

$$C_t = \text{NOPOP} \times C_{\text{NOPOP},t} + \text{ROPOP} \times C_{\text{ROPOP},t} \tag{6.11}$$

$$I_t = \text{NOPOP} \times I_{\text{NOPOP},t} + \text{ROPOP} \times I_{\text{ROPOP},t} \tag{6.12}$$

For the young, total consumption should be equal to their marginal consumption intention multiplied by the previous total output:

$$C_{\text{NOPOP},t} = \beta_N \times \text{GDP}_{\text{NOPOP},t} \tag{6.13}$$

The total output of the young should also be equal to the proportion of the population multiplied by the total social output:

$$\text{GDP}_{\text{NOPOP},t} = \text{NOPOP} \times \text{GDP}_{t-1} \tag{6.14}$$

According to the relationship between total consumption and total output, the total consumption of the young is:

$$C_{\text{NOPOP},t} = \beta_N \times \text{NOPOP} \times \text{GDP}_{t-1} \tag{6.15}$$

Correspondingly, the total consumption of the aged should also be equal to their marginal consumption intention multiplied by the proportion of the population and then the total social output in the next period:

$$C_{\text{ROPOP},t} = \beta_R \times \text{ROPOP} \times \text{GDP}_{t-1} \tag{6.16}$$

Similarly, regarding investment, the total investment of the young is the accelerator multiplied by their previous consumption balance:

$$\begin{aligned} I_{\text{NOPOP},t} &= v_N \times \left(C_{\text{NOPOP},t-1} - C_{\text{NOPOP},t-2}\right) \\ &= v_N \times \left(\beta_N \times \text{NOPOP} \times \text{GDP}_{t-1} - \beta_N \times \text{NOPOP} \times \text{GDP}_{t-2}\right) \\ &= v_N \times \beta_N \times \text{NOPOP} \times \left(\text{GDP}_{t-1} - \text{GDP}_{t-2}\right) \end{aligned} \tag{6.17}$$

It is the same with the aged:

$$\begin{aligned} I_{\text{ROPOP},t} &= v_R \times \left(C_{\text{ROPOP},t-1} - C_{\text{ROPOP},t-2}\right) \\ &= v_R \times \left(\beta_R \times \text{ROPOP} \times \text{GDP}_{t-1} - \beta_R \times \text{ROPOP} \times \text{GDP}_{t-2}\right) \\ &= v_R \times \beta_R \times \text{ROPOP} \times \left(\text{GDP}_{t-1} - \text{GDP}_{t-2}\right) \end{aligned} \tag{6.18}$$

To bring (6.13)–(6.18) into (6.10), (6.11) and (6.12):

$$\text{GDP}_t = C_t + I_t + G_t \tag{6.19}$$

$$C_t = \left(\text{NOPOP}^2 \times \beta_N + \text{ROPOP}^2 \times \beta_R\right) \times \text{GDP}_{t-1} \tag{6.20}$$

$$I_t = \left(\text{NOPOP}^2 \times v_N \times \beta_N + \text{ROPOP}^2 \times v_R \times \beta_R\right) \times \left(\text{GDP}_{t-1} - \text{GDP}_{t-2}\right) \tag{6.21}$$

Let $\beta_1 = \text{NOPOP}^2 \times \beta_N + \text{ROPOP}^2 \times \beta_R$ and$v_1 = \text{NOPOP}^2 \times v_N \times \beta_N + \text{ROPOP}^2 \times v_R \times \beta_R$, then

$$\text{GDP}_t = \left(\beta_1 + \beta_1 \times v_1\right)\text{GDP}_{t-1} + v_1 \times \text{GDP}_{t-2} + G_t \tag{6.22}$$

When $G_t = G_0$ and $\beta_1 \times v_1 < 1$, the general solution of the above state Eq. (6.22) is:

$$\text{GDP}_t = r_1^t \left(A_1 \sin \omega_1 t + B_1 \cos \omega_1 t\right) + \frac{G_0}{1 - \beta_1} \tag{6.23}$$

where $r_1 = (\beta_1 \times v_1)^{1/2}$. Obviously, when $t \to \infty$, GDP_t is convergent to $(G_0/1 - \beta_1)$, which means the long-term steady-state equilibrium is:

$$\text{GDP}_1^* = \frac{G_0}{1 - \beta_1} \tag{6.24}$$

Comparison and Verification

First, let's compare the steady-state output. In the function GDP = $G_0/(1-\beta)$, since $(dGDP/d\beta) = [(G_0/(1-\beta)^2) > 0]$, which is a monotonically increasing function, the smaller the marginal intention, the lower the long-term steady-state output.

Also because $\beta_1 = NOPOP^2 \times \beta_N + ROPOP^2 \times \beta_R$ and $\beta = NOPOP \times \beta_N + ROPOP \times \beta_R$, $\beta - \beta_1 = NOPOP \times \beta_N \times (1 - NOPOP) + ROPOP \times \beta_R \times (1 - ROPOP)$ is established. According to the equation $NOPOP + ROPOP \equiv 1$ in (6.7), $0 < NOPOP < 1$ and $0 < ROPOP < 1$ are true, so that $\beta - \beta_1 > 0$ holds, which means $\beta > \beta_1$. Then according to the monotonically increasing nature of the function GDP = $G_0/(1-\beta)$, $GDP^* > GDP_1^*$ is established, which verifies Conclusion 1: *An uneven population structure is unfavorable for the growth of long-term output of GNP.*

Then, let's look into the impact of the reduction in the proportion of the young on steady-state output. Because $\left(dGDP_1^* / dNOPOP\right) = \left(G_0 / (1-\beta_1)^2\right) \times \left(d\beta_1 / dNOPOP\right)$ and $(d\beta_1/dNOPOP) = 2 \times NOPOP \times \beta_N + 2 \times ROPOP \times \beta_R \times (dROPOP/dNOPOP)$, when $NOPOP + ROPOP \equiv 1$, $(dROPOP/dNOPOP) = -1$, so $(d\beta_1/dNOPOP) = 2 \times (NOPOP \times \beta_N - ROPOP \times \beta_R)$.

Despite the fact that the consumption intention of the young β_N may be greater than that of the aged β_R, $NOPOP \times \beta_N - ROPOP \times \beta_R < 0$ will be established when the young takes a small enough proportion in the population structure, so $\left(dGDP_1^* / dNOPOP\right) < 0$, causing even lower steady-state output after the reduction of the proportion of the young. Therefore, Conclusion 2 is reached: *When the population structure is out of balance, if the proportion of the young is reduced sufficiently to offset the addition in consumption by the aged, the long-term output of GNP will decline even more.*

An unbalanced demographic structure will also affect the changes in the consumption intention of the entire society. According to the definitions of Eq. (6.24) and β_1, $\left(dGDP_1^* / d\beta_N\right) = \left[\left(G_0 \times NOPOP^2 / (1-\beta_1)^2\right)\right] > 0$ and $\left(dGDP_1^* / d\beta_R\right) = \left[G_0 \times ROPOP^2 / (1-\beta_1)^2\right] > 0$ are established. Then it can be concluded that it is the young and the aged who can contribute to the growth of a long-term steady-state output by increasing consumption intentions.

With the aging of the population, as the young people decrease, the demand for durable consumer goods and non-durable consumer goods will become saturated, and then the consumption intention will decline when the rigid demand is met. In other words, the decline in β_N leads to the reduction of GDP_1^*. Meanwhile, the demand for products required by the aged will be boosted in a short period of time as the aging population is growing, so that GDP_1^* will grow as β_R becomes greater, but it will decline afterwards with a lower marginal consumption intention when the aged pass away, which means the decline in β_R leads to a further reduction of GDP_1^* . Therefore, in the aging process, the total social output will go through a 'fall-rise-fall' fluctuation as the marginal demand of the young decreases while the that of the aged increases and then decreases. Hence, Conclusion 3 can be reached: *In an aged society, the marginal consumption intentions of the young and the aged are not synchronized, so GNP may recover in the short term but will definitely decline in the long run.*

Finally, let's look into the effect of accelerator. Because $(dr_1/dv_1) = [\beta_1(v_1\beta_1)^{-1/2}(NOPOP^2\beta_N dv_N + ROPOP^2\beta_R dv_R)]/2$, when the proportion of the young significantly reduces, their investment intention dv_N will fall too. Although the investment intention of the aged dv_R may rise temporarily, its degree of growth will not be very high (and will also be lower than that of the young) and will even shrink in the long run as the aged successively pass away. Therefore, the long-term investment intention of the entire society after the decrease of the young, that is, dv_1, will become smaller, resulting in a slower adjustment rate of short-term GNP toward long-term steady-state equilibrium. Even if macro policies are adopted to encourage such a shift, it will still take a longer time to realize due to the weakened investment intention, reducing the efficiency of the stimulus policies. So, Conclusion 4 is reached: With the aging of the demographic structure, the short-term investment intention of the aged will be stimulated, but the long-term investment intention of the entire society will decline because of the population decrease of the young. The fluctuation in investment of the population once again indicates a 'fall-rise-fall' trend. The long-term GNP will decline with the reduction in total social investment, while macro stimulus policies will also need longer time to regulate due to the decline in investment intention, accompanied by the reduced effectiveness of monetary and fiscal policy.

PART IV

International Dimensions of China's Road

CHAPTER 7

China's Road to Peaceful Development: Cultural Foundation, Strategic Orientation, and Double Significance

Xiao Xi

A peaceful path to development is the strategic choice of the Chinese government and people based on the tide of development in the current era in conjunction with personal interests. History has shown that the correctness of China's judgment of global political trends, including a comprehensive understanding of the developmental orientations of major political trends worldwide, and rational decision making in light of their interrelations and influence at all stages, is crucial to the success or failure of this endeavor. By reflecting on the experiences and lessons drawn from the country's reform over the past 30 years, Chinese leaders have proposed two ideas, "peace" and "development." In the context of the joint influence and agitation of various complex political trends, "peace" and "development" have gradually emerged as the main pursuits of a majority of countries and their peoples, and is the major direction of global political development.[1] Experience has shown that as its lasting development strat-

[1] Niu Jun, *Longitude of Foreign Relations of the People's Republic of China*, collected in *Foreign Affairs Review*, Issue 3, 2010, pp. 59–73.

X. Xi (✉)
The School of International and Public Affairs, Jilin University, Changchun, China

H. Men (ed.), *On China's Road*,
https://doi.org/10.1007/978-981-13-7880-5_7

egy, the path to peaceful development is adaptive to China's circumstances and characteristics, and has made outstanding contributions to peace and development here and across the world.

1 Proposal and Establishment of China's Path to Peaceful Development

The proposal and establishment of China's path to peaceful development involves a scientific representation of the road to Socialism with Chinese characteristics, and clearly embodies the unified internal and external guidelines of the Communist Party of China (CPC) and the country.[2] The peaceful transformation of the international system at present is parallel to China's path to peaceful development, and presents a rare strategic opportunity. Participation in the transformation of the international system and the acceleration of innovations in its internal system are two necessary conditions for China's path to peaceful development.[3] This involves the adjustment and intensification of state strategy according to changes in the national and international situation. It is a resounding response and a solemn oath to the world, and embodies the direction and path of the future development of China. The delineation of this path has involved the construction of a theoretical framework, as well as the determination and proposal of a detailed conception of it to yield outstanding achievements.

Since the very beginning, the idea of peaceful development was the strategic judgment of the Chinese government according to the "Theme of the Times" proposed by Deng Xiaoping in the 1970s and 1980s. In 1977, Xiaoping claimed that "we may endeavor to put off the war outburst"; in 1982, he stated that "the war factors are increasing, and factors that restrict the war are also increasing." In March 1985, while meeting with a Japanese delegation, Xiaoping pointed out that "there are two real serious and global strategic issues in the world: one is the issue of peace,

[2] Zheng Bijian, *Thinking Course—Origin, Foundation, Connotation and Prospect of China's Path to Peaceful Development*, Beijing: The Central Party School Publishing House, 2006, pp. 1–2.

[3] Huang Renwei, *Transformation of International System and China's Peaceful Development Road*, collected in *Research on Theories of Mao Zedong and Deng Xiaoping*, Issue 5, 2006, pp. 5–13.

and the other is the issue of economic development."[4] The proposal of peace and development motivates China to join the international community and comprehensively participate in the international order. At the beginning of the twenty-first century, as its economic development gathered pace, on the one hand, China provided a formidable impetus for global economic development; on the other hand, it also caused doubts in the international community regarding the intention, speed, and scale of Chinese development. A series of negative theses, such as the "China Threat Theory" and the "China Collapse Theory," were formulated one after another. Some Western countries and allies claimed that China could implement a global hegemony through violent means, such as invasion and expansion. This significantly informed China's international image and status. However, China's fundamental interests, the character of the state, its political system, and basic state policy dictate that it will not follow a path of invasion and expansionism. Chinese historical and cultural traditions, its development status, and current trends in global development have guided the direction of Chinese development: China will develop in peace.

In November 2003, in the speech *China's Peaceful Rise New Road and the Future of Asia* at the Boao Forum for Asia, Zheng Bijian first proposed the theme of "China's peaceful rise." He claimed that "proved by the historical, repeated striving for hegemony of the great powers since modern times, the rise of a great power always leads to a radical change in the international pattern and world order, and [can lead to] even world war. One of the important reasons is that they follow a development road relying on invasion, war, and external expansion. However, such roads must end in failure ... [W]e can only choose to rise in peace: strive for developing ourselves in a peaceful international environment and maintain world peace with our development."[5] Starting with this thesis, Chinese academics and politicians carried out systematic research on the significant theme of China's peaceful rise and established firm theoretical foundations for its path to peaceful development in politics, economy, culture, and society.

In April 2004, Hu Jintao made a significant address called *China's Development Is an Opportunity for Asia* at the opening ceremony of the

[4] *Selected Works of Deng Xiaoping*, Vol. 3, Beijing: People's Publishing House, 1993, p. 105.

[5] Zheng Bijian, *China's Peaceful Rise New Road and New Role of Asia*, collected in *Study Times*, November 24, 2003, Edition 1.

Boao Forum for Asia, and formally proposed that China's development should adhere to "the path to peaceful development." He said, "China cannot develop without Asia and Asia cannot realize prosperity without China. China will adhere to peaceful development, uphold the banner of peace, development, and cooperation, and co-create a new pattern of Asian rejuvenation with other countries of Asia, and work hard to make greater contributions to the lofty cause: human peace and development."[6] In March 2005, Wen Jiabao emphasized the significance of the "path to peaceful development" to Chinese development in a government work report, and pointed out that "China will unswervingly adhere to the path to peaceful development, adhere to an independent foreign policy of peace, carry out mutual-benefit- and win-win-based opening strategies, and make unremitting endeavors with other countries worldwide to facilitate human civilization, promote the benefits of the peoples of these countries, and build a harmonious world with enduring peace and co-prosperity."[7] This signifies that the Chinese government understands "peaceful rise" as "peaceful development," and considers China's path to peaceful development as an important strategy for national development in the future.

In December 2005, the State Council Information Office published a white paper on China's path to peaceful development, and provided the first comprehensive explanation of this path. Through a discussion of five aspects—"peaceful development is the necessary path for the modernization of Chinese construction," "facilitate the peaceful development of the world with our own development," "depend on own power to reform, create, and realize development," "realize mutual benefits, win-win scenarios, and co-development with other countries," and "build enduring and peaceful co-prosperity in a harmonious world"—the Chinese government and people are determined to walk along a path to peaceful development.[8] It was pointed out at a central foreign affairs' working conference convened in August 2006 that only if we uphold the banner of peace,

[6] Hu Jintao, *China's Development is an Opportunity for Asia*, http://www.gmw.cn/01gmrb/2004-04/25/content_17425.htm, May 3, 2015.

[7] Wen Jiabao, *Government Work Report for 2005—On the Third Session of the 10th National Congress of the Communist Party of China on March 5, 2005*, http://www.gov.cn/test/2006-02/16/content_201218.htm, May 3, 2015.

[8] State Council Information Office of the PRC, *White Paper China's Peaceful Development Road*, http://news.xinhuanet.com/politics/2005-12/22/content_3954937.htm, May 3, 2015.

development, and cooperation, insist on a path to peaceful development, maintain world peace to develop ourselves, and promote world peace with our own development, and peaceful coexistence and cooperation with other countries, can we create better international conditions for China's development and realize lasting development.[9] Subsequently, the sixth session of the 16th National Congress of the CPC, held in October 2006, passed several historically significant decisions concerning the construction of a Socialist, harmonious society, and further explained and discussed China's path to peaceful development. It has become a significant strategic document for China's direction of development.[10]

In October 2007, the report of the 17th National Congress of the CPC promised that China would unswervingly follow the path to peaceful development. China is a peace-loving nation, a firm power to safeguard world peace.[11] In September 2011, the State Council Information Office published a white paper entitled *China's Peaceful Development*. It further defined the creation and general objectives of and foreign guidelines and policy for China's path to peaceful development. It pointed out that peaceful development was a historically inevitable choice, and discussed the global significance of China's peaceful development.[12] In November 2012, a report by the 18th National Congress of the CPC emphasized that China would unswervingly adhere to the path to peaceful development, and to carrying out independent and peaceful diplomatic policies. The document affirmed China's opposition to the hegemony and power politics of all forms, and vowed that it would never seek hegemony and expansion.[13] In

[9] *Adhere to Peaceful Development Road and Advance the Construction of Harmonious World*, http://news.xinhuanet.com/politics/2006-08/23/content_4999339.htm, May 13, 2015.

[10] *Historical Decisions for Several Significant Problems of the CPC on Constructing Socialist Harmonious Society*, http://cpc.people.com.cn/GB/64093/64094/4932424.html, May 3, 2015.

[11] *Report of Hu Jintao, General Secretary, on the Seventeenth National Congress of the CPC*, http://news.xinhuanet.com/newscenter/2007-10/24/content_6938568.htm, May 13, 2015.

[12] State Council Information Office of the PRC, *White Paper China's Peaceful Development Road*, http://news.xinhuanet.com/politics/2011-09/06/c_121982103.htm, May 3, 2015.

[13] Hu Jintao, *March Forward Unswervingly along the Road of Building|Socialism with Chinese Characteristics and Strive for Building a Moderately Well-off Society in All Aspects—Report on the 18th National Congress of the CPC* (November 8, 2012), Beijing: People's Publishing House, p. 48.

March 2013, Xi Jinping visited Russia for the first time since having taken office as President of China. He addressed the Moscow State Institute of International Relations, and proposed that "since modern times, Chinese has suffered foreign invasions and internal chaos caused by wars for a hundred years, and deeply knows the preciousness of peace. The Chinese government needs to urgently carry out national construction and unceasingly improve people's lives. China will unswervingly adhere to a path to peaceful development, be devoted to facilitating open development, cooperative development, and win-win development, and will meanwhile call for a path to peaceful development together with other countries."[14] In June 2014, in a speech to the 60th anniversary conference of the Five Principles of Peaceful Coexistence, Xi Jinping pointed out that the Chinese uphold the principle of "don't do to others what you don't want others to do to you." The Chinese disagree with the idea that "a country must become strong through seeking hegemony," and does not have this gene. China would unswervingly adhere to a path to peaceful development. This would be conducive to China, Asia, and the world. No power is able to change the Chinese belief of insisting on peaceful development.[15] In October 2017, a report by the 19th National Congress of the CPC emphasized China's path to peaceful development and advancing the construction of the Community of Human Destiny. It affirmed that China would uphold the banner of peace, development, cooperation, and win-win results, obey the diplomatic tenet of safeguarding world peace and facilitating common development, unswervingly develop friendly cooperation with countries on the basis of the Five Principles of Peaceful Coexistence, and drive the construction of mutual respect, fairness, justice, and cooperative and win-win-type international relations.[16]

[14] *Xi Jinping's Speech in Moscow State Institute of International Relations*, http://news.xinhuanet.com/world/2013-03/24/c_124495576.htm, May 3, 2015.

[15] Xi Jinping, *Carry Forward the Five Principles of Peaceful Coexistence and Build Cooperative and Win-Win Great World—Speech on the 60th Anniversary of the Five Principles of Peaceful Coexistence*, http://news.xinhuanet.com/world/2014-06/28/c_1111364206.htm, May 3, 2015.

[16] Xi Jinping, *Secure a Decisive Victory in Building a Moderately Prosperous Society in All Respects and Strive for the Great Success of Socialism with Chinese Characteristics for a New Era—Report on the 19th National Congress of CPC* (October 18, 2017), Beijing: People's Publishing House, 2017, pp. 57–58.

2 Cultural Foundation of China's Path to Peaceful Development

China's path to peaceful development has been proposed on the basis of five millennia of history and culture. Chinese tradition is long-standing, extensive, and profound. "Harmony" is a principle that runs through Chinese culture, and signifies the Chinese humanistic spirit. Harmony is a generally accepted and common principle. No matter the changes to the universe, humans, nature, society, human relations, politics, economy, systems, moral principles, values, mental structures, and aesthetic emotion, the spirit of harmony or "concordance" runs through all.[17] Harmony could be found usually in oracle bone scripts of the legendary Shang Dynasty. It implies fusing two or more elements and factors.[18] Harmony has rich and profound connotations. Confucianism, Taoism, Mohism, Guanism, and Legalism in the Pre-Qin Period all strove for harmony. Confucianism and Mohism emphasized the harmony of benevolence, Taoism emphasized unificationist harmony, Guanism emphasized energy-based harmony, and Legalism emphasized principal and subordinate harmony.[19] In traditional Chinese culture, the lasting co-existence of "Confucianism, Buddhism, and Taoism" is based on their interlinked core value, namely "harmony." The core of Confucianism is "benevolence" and "harmony," which mainly explain the manner of interaction among people. Buddhism calls for transmigration and resolution, and emphasizes "harmony" instead of obtaining solutions via conflicts. Taoism encourages allowing nature to take its course and doing nothing, which is the manner of a harmonious interaction between human and nature. The reason for the long-standing of the Chinese nation is that "harmony" is precious and "gathering" accepts diversity.[20] *"Harmony is most precious," "harmony but no sameness," and "nature and man unite as one" are three important layers of the connotation of the Chinese cultural concept of "harmony."*

First, "harmony is most precious." Confucianism agrees that "courtesy costs nothing but harmony"[21] (*The Analects of Confucius—Xue Er*). The promotion and application of courtesy should be oriented toward

[17] Zhang Liwen, *Harmony I*, Beijing: China Renmin University Press, 2006, p. 276.

[18] Zhang Liwen, *Harmony I*, pp. 375–376.

[19] Zhang Liwen, *Harmony I*, pp. 276–280.

[20] Huang Renwei, *How to Know China Better Through "China Studies,"* collected in *Social Outlook*, Issue 12, 2010, p. 6.

[21] *The Analects of Confucius*, Changchun: Jilin People's Publishing House, *Xue Er*, p. 18.

harmony. Confucius called for harmonious administration. "Broad in fierceness, fierceness in economy, and politics in peace" ("Zhao Gong Zuo Chuan Notes in the Spring and Autumn Annals"). "Rule of virtue and rule by law should supplement each other, and then the country will be harmonious"[22] (Notation to Spring and Autumn Annals: The 20th Year of Zhaogong). When thinking of the wars for supremacy at the time among princes for successive years, Menci pointed out that "the time isn't as important as the terrain, but the terrain isn't as important as unity with the people"[23] (Menci Gongsun Chou II). Of the three main factors influencing the results of war, namely "time," "terrain," and "unity with people," the latter is prioritized and considered as the most important factor. Xuncius claimed that all things on Earth may exist if in harmony[24] (Xuncius Discussion of Heaven). It aims to promote the idea that harmony leads to existence, and emphasizes that it is the basis for all things to unceasingly grow and upgrade. Nothing can generate new life or new things without "harmony." Dong Zhongshu claimed that "harmony is the universe in balance, the neutralization of Yin and Yang. It is beneficial for the generation of things. The ones who are inclined to harmony let Nature take its course."[25] He considered "harmony" the most general principle in the universe. The Chinese love peace, adhere to the Five Principles of Peaceful Coexistence, and are deeply influenced by the idea that "peace is precious."

Second, "harmony but no sameness." Harmony advocates harmony and peace but does not mean obliterating difference and conflicts. On the contrary, it seeks cooperation, peace, and harmony with the precondition of admitting difference and conflict. There was a well-known "harmony and consistence debate" in Chinese history. Guoyu, in Discourses of Zheng, recorded Shibo's discourse about harmony and consistence in the last years of the West Zhou Dynasty.[26] Shibo claimed that it should be called

[22] Chen Shuguo, *Notation to the Spring and Autumn Annals*, Vol. 2, Changsha: Yuelu Press, 2006, The 20th Year of Zhaogong, p. 1022.

[23] *Menci*, Changchun: Jilin People's Publishing House, 1999, Gongsun Chou II, p. 64.

[24] *Xuncius*, Shanghai: Shanghai Chinese Classics Publishing House, 1989, Tianlun, p. 96.

[25] *Chunqiu Fanlu—Yinyang Meaning*, Shanghai: Shanghai Chinese Classics Publishing House, 1989, *Let the Nature Take Its Course*, p. 92.

[26] "Harmony is the integration of different elements and the precondition is difference and diversity. Only in this way can harmony exist for a long time and integrated things develop. If abandoning harmony but pursuing pure consistence, this is not far from ending. Therefore, all things consist of many elements. Different seasonings are harmonized to a good tasting;

"harmony" as it reconciles different things, and should be called "consistence" to simply collect the same things together. That is to say, only when different elements are combined organically to form a diversified and unified state can a harmonious effect be achieved. If only the same things are stacked together, the result is only an increase in quantity but no qualitative change. Thus, it is impossible to produce new things, and they will not develop further. The Spring and Autumn Annals also recorded conversations on the difference between "harmony" and "consistence," between Yanyiing and Duke Jing of Qi.[27] Yanying compared "harmony" to making soup and playing music. He claimed that only if the materials are allocated well can the cook make delicious, fresh soup. While playing music, only when the notes are well deployed can the player play good music. He also linked this to the monarch–subject relationship, and enriched the connotation of "harmony" through the ideas of "combining economics" and "complementation."

Confucius inherited this idea of valuing harmony and removing sameness, and said, "Gentlemen are harmonious but not the same, while vile characters are the same but not harmonious"[28] (*The Analects of Confucius—Zilu*).

arms and two are practiced to a good body; six rhythms are allocated to a good melody; seven sense organs are harmonized to a good thinking; eight parts of the body are harmonized to a good completeness; nine internal organs are harmonized to a pure morality; ten kinds of grades are harmonized to teach the officials a lesson...Then the king has broad land, earns income to support people, teaches and uses them by loyalty and makes theme harmonious and happy as families. In this way, it reaches the top of the harmony." See Zhang Liwen, *Harmony (Volume I)*, Beijing: China Renmin University Press, 2006.

[27] Duke Jing asked: "Are harmony and consistence different?" Yanying answered: "Yes, they are different. Harmony is like boiling soup. The cooker boils fish and meat with water, fire, vinegar, soy sauce, salt and plum and cooks with fire. The cooker allocates the seasonings to receive a good taste; adds seasonings if the taste is not enough; reduces seasonings if the taste is excessive. The gentleman eats for calming down. It is the same for the relationship between the king and the officials. The king considers it is right but there is an improper part. The officials point out the improper part to make it much perfect; the king considers it improper but there is a right part. The officials point out the right part and abandon the improper part. Therefore, the political affairs are in order without breaching courtesy and the people are not in a mind to fight. The music is like the taste and consists of various aspects in allocation. The gentleman listens to it, with his heart at peace. If the mind calms down, the morality may be harmonized...Who can eat if using water to taste water? Who can bear listening to the music played with only one rhythm? The law that pursuit for mere consistence is not proper is like this." See Zhang Liwen, *Harmony (Volume I)*, Beijing: China Renmin University Press, 2006.

[28] *The Analects of Confucius*, Changchun: Jilin People's Publishing House, 1999, Zilu, p. 115.

Taking the difference between "harmony" and "consistence" as the standard of division of "gentlemen" and "vile characters" reflects the orientation in the value of preferring harmony to consistency. The idea of "harmony but no sameness" becomes an important source of theory and practice in Chinese diplomacy. China adheres to an independent foreign policy of peace, and meanwhile respects the benefits of other countries, calls for consistence and tolerating differences, and seeks mutual benefits and win-win scenarios.

Third, "nature and man unite as one." This claim calls for coordination, concord, and harmony between humans and nature, and emphasizes that humans should know nature, cognize it, and master its laws and implement a complete integration between themselves and nature. It has reflected the harmonious spirit of traditional Chinese culture. At the same time, "nature and man unite as one" also conveys the idea that the Chinese nation pursues harmony in human relations as well as international relations. The idea has evolved over time, and was proposed as early as the Pre-Qin Period. However, it was first proposed by Zhang Zai, a well-known philosopher of the Beisong Dynasty, as a definite theme.[29] In the Spring and Autumn Period, Zichan, senior official of Zheng Country, says, "Courtesy is the law of nature and people's behavior regulator. Specifications, regulations, and behavioral rules are the most fundamental standards for people"[30] (*Notation to the Spring and Autumn Annals—The 25th Year of Zhaogong*). He thought that "courtesy" was the inevitable law of nature, and humans must behave according to it. It linked natural rules to human properties, and reflected on the idea that nature and humans can communicate with each other and operate according to unified rules. In the Warring States period, Menci claimed, "A person who thinks sufficiently knows the human property. If knowing the human property, the person must know the nature"[31] (Menci—Sufficient Thinking). Menci linked human properties to nature, and claimed that the two may communicate with each other. In the Han Dynasty, the idea of nature and man uniting was formulated as Dong Zhongshu's nature–human induction theory. Dong Zhongshu's theory of yin and yang, and the five elements, was introduced into Confucianism. He proposed that

[29] Edited by Fang Keli in chief, *A Brief Introduction to Chinese Culture*, Beijing: Beijing Normal University Publishing, 1994, pp. 377–380.

[30] Chen Shuguo, *Notation to the Spring and Autumn Annals*, Vol. 2, Changsha: Yuelu Press, 2006, The 20th Year of Zhaogong, p. 1058.

[31] *Menci*, Changchun: Jilin People's Publishing House, 1999, Jinxin I, p. 207.

the "human is subordinate to nature." He compared humans to seasons in nature, and claimed that nature has yin and yang, as do humans. He advocated that "the nature and human are unified"[32] (Chunqiu Fanlu—yin and yang). In the times of the Two Song Dynasties, the idea of integrating nature and humans became the leading social–cultural tide. In the history of Chinese culture, Zhang Zai first definitively proposed the theme of "harmony between nature and human." He claimed that the Confucians "were reasonable to believe and then realize that nature and man unite as one. Enough study may lead to superiority. Do not underestimate life even if having beliefs" (Zhengmeng Qiancheng). Zhang Zai thought that the world's origin was the universal *pneuma*, and humans and all things consisted of pneuma. Pneuma is the basis of nature and man united as one. Zhang Zai considered nature and man united as one to be the highest realm that humans pursue. In his opinion, the highest realm of life was the coordination of humans and nature.[33] The "harmony between nature and human" embodies the unification of human and nature, the coordination and consistence of moral reasonability and natural reasonability. At present, it focuses on the idea of contained harmony—the unification of and harmony between human and nature, human and human, human and society, and even countries.

In the opinion of Yu Yingshi, the theoretical analysis of the traditional Chinese society must focus on two basic elements: an individual with the capacity for value awareness, and a "family" of natural relations. "Clan," "state," and "nature" are all expansions of the family. The Chinese think that all levels of a community are the same as "family," and are built on the basis of natural relations. As they are "families," they should get along with one another harmoniously. According to the Chinese social outlook, the central value to maintain natural relationships is "harmony," "equality," and "peace." It is the general way, while conflicts and contradictions represent a changing way.[34] In a manner of speaking, as the humanistic spirit and value ideality of Chinese traditional culture, "harmony" has generated an important influence on the establishment of China's path to peaceful development.

[32] Chunqiu Fanlu, *Yin and Yang Meaning*, Shanghai: Shanghai Guji Publishing House, 1989, *Yin and Yang Meaning*, p. 71.

[33] Edited by Fang Keli in chief, *A Brief Introduction to Chinese Culture*, Beijing: Beijing Normal University Publishing, 1994, p. 379.

[34] Yu Yingshi, *Modern Explanation to Chinese Traditional Thoughts*, Nanjing: Jiangsu People's Publishing House, 2003, p. 20.

Peaceful development is the fruits of the Chinese idea of harmony, and helps Chinese traditional culture progress further. Confucianism claims that "peace is precious," and adheres to the behavior rule—"what you do not wish on yourself, do not do unto others"—in dealing with interpersonal affairs[35] (The Analects of Confucius—Yanyuan). It demands that humans "develop the self before helping others to develop"[36] (*The Analects of Confucius*). China's path to peaceful development does not involve invading other countries, conquering the world, or seeking hegemony, and agrees that a country may have lasting development only if it develops itself and helps others develop. This is the embodiment of "harmony" in traditional Chinese culture.

3 Strategic Orientation of China's Road to Peaceful Development

China's peaceful development is rooted in Chinese history and culture, sources of Chinese development practices, is established in Chinese conditions, and follows the cooperative trend of the world and China's state policy. Dai Bingguo spoke thus about the strategic orientation of China's path to peaceful development: "Firstly, China's peaceful development has its own root and source, namely long-standing historical and cultural origin; secondly, China's path to peaceful development is not figured out by a minority from papers, but is explored and established gradually in practice in over 60 years after the foundation of the new China, especially after the reform and opening up; thirdly, China's path to peaceful development is not a stopgap, or to conceal its true features or intentions, but is a lasting strategic choice that roots in its own basic conditions, and is sincere, conscious, and voluntary; fourthly, China's path to peaceful development is not to lie to foreigners, but is a reasonable selection that is made according to calm analysis and scientific judgment on the current situation of the world to follow global trends, and will be implemented; fifthly, China's declaration for walking the path to peaceful development is not malarkey, but has firm politics, policy, and a strategic foundation. It is consistent both in words and behaviors; sixthly, instead of reaching the end, the

[35] *The Analects of Confucius*, Changchun: Jilin People's Publishing House, 1999, Yanyuan, p. 100.

[36] *The Analects of Confucius*, Changchun: Jilin People's Publishing House, 1999, Yongye, p. 58.

exploration and practice of China's path to peaceful development will be an endless, unceasingly explored, and improving course; seventhly, China's path to peaceful development is not only China's own business but needs the understanding, support and cooperation of the international society."[37] The discourse incisively concludes the strategic orientation of the path to peaceful development. The orientation of China's path to peaceful development deepens due to the selection of a developmental road to a transcendence of the past and an exploration of the future.

First, China will adhere to the Five Principles of Peaceful Coexistence and carry out a policy of independent diplomacy. This requires that it uphold the great banner of peace, development, cooperation, and win-win results; obey the diplomatic target of safeguarding world peace and promoting common development; carry out friendly cooperation with countries on the unswerving basis of the Five Principles of Peaceful Coexistence; deal well with other countries in the world; and strive for a healthy international environment for its own development. By positively developing global partnerships and creating a network that features conversation but does not confront, and accompanies but does not align, China has built partnerships of different forms with about 100 countries and international organizations that involve all the great powers, and neighboring developing countries[38]; enlarges the benefits of areas of the intersection of interest with other countries; drives coordination and cooperation with great powers; constructs a relationship framework for the great powers that enjoy a general stability and balanced development; deepens the relationship with surrounding countries according to the diplomatic guidelines of friendliness to neighboring countries; adheres to the correct ideas of morality and profit; and strengthens unification and cooperation with developing countries.[39]

Second, China will adhere to reform and opening up, and seek mutual benefits and win-win results through cooperation. It was proposed in the report of the 17th National Congress of the CPC that "China will pur-

[37] Dai Bingguo, *China Walks Peaceful Development Road Unswervingly*, collected in *International Problem Study*, Issue 6, 2011, pp. 1–4.

[38] Party Committee of the Ministry of Foreign Affairs, *Five Years of Up-and-Coming Major-Country Diplomacy with Chinese Characteristics*, http://theory.people.com.cn/n1/2017/0930/c40531-29569994.html, December 1, 2017.

[39] Xi Jinping, *Secure a Decisive Victory in Building a Moderately Prosperous Society in All Respects and Strive for the Great Success of Socialism with Chinese Characteristics for a New Era—Report on the 19th National Congress of CPC* (October 18, 2017), Beijing: People's Publishing House, 2017, pp. 59–60.

sue the mutual-beneficial and win-win strategy of opening up unswervingly."[40] The report of the 18th National Congress of the CPC emphasized this as follows: "China will unswervingly carry out opening strategy based on mutual benefit and win-win-based opening strategy and facilitate powerful, sustainable, and balanced growth of the world economy through deepening cooperation. China is committed to narrowing down the gap between the North and the South, as well as supporting developing countries in strengthening their capacity for independent development."[41] The report of the 19th National Congress of the CPC pointed out that China insisted on the basic state policy of opening itself to the outside world, and was committed to opening the door to construction, actively facilitating international cooperation in The Belt and Road Initiative, and working hard to realize policy Unicom communication, facility linking, transaction unblocking, capital circulation, connection among people, creating new platforms for international cooperation, and adding impetus to common development and enhancing assistance to developing countries, especially the most underdeveloped countries. China supports a multilateral trading system, and has pushed forward the construction of a free trade zone and driven the establishment of an opening world economy.[42] Opening itself to the outside is an essential characteristic of China's path to peaceful development, and will help the all-round development of a moderately well-off society, reach domestic harmony, advance world harmony, and promote its international influence.[43] In today's era of political multipolarity and economic globalization, reform and opening itself to the world are among the basic policies that China should insist on continually, while cooperation with other countries to seek

[40] *Hu Jintao's Report at the 17th National Congress of the CPC*, http://news.xinhuanet.com/newscenter/2007-10/24/content_6938568.htm, May 3, 2015.

[41] Hu Jintao, *March Forward Unswervingly along Road of Socialism with Chinese Characteristics and Strive for Building a Moderately Well-off Society in All Aspects—Report on the 18th National Congress of the CPC* (November 8, 2012), Beijing: People's Publishing House, p. 48.

[42] Xi Jinping, *Secure a Decisive Victory in Building a Moderately Prosperous Society in All Respects and Strive for the Great Success of Socialism with Chinese Characteristics for a New Era—Report on the 19th National Congress of CPC* (October 18, 2017), Beijing: People's Publishing House, 2017, p. 60.

[43] Men Honghua, *Opening and National Strategy System*, Beijing: People's Publishing House, 2008, p. 9.

mutually beneficial outcomes is to the fundamental benefit of China on the condition that this improves its relationship with the relevant countries and enhances mutual dependence.

Third, China will realize its development peacefully and facilitate the development of other countries through its own. The significance of China's peaceful development involves promoting its own power while benefiting peace and development in the Asia-Pacific Region and the world. "The fundamental character of China's path to peaceful development is to independently build Socialism with Chinese characteristics in the course of becoming connected with economic globalization, but not getting rid of and realizing mutual benefits and win-win with international society."[44] The 19th National Congress of the CPC presented the plan for the introduction of Chinese diplomacy to these times, mainly involving the promotion of new types of international relations and the construction of a Community of Human Destiny. This novel type of international relations aims to abandon the law of the jungle that oppresses the weak and bullies the small in favor of mutual respect, justice, fairness, and cooperation among countries. The Community of Human Destiny aims at responding to various global challenges and providing a Chinese solution to significant problems by building an enduring, peaceful, prosperous, tolerant, clean, and beautiful world.[45] China's path to peaceful development will unify domestic development with openness to the outside, link Chinese development to world development, and combine Chinese benefits with those of the people of the world.[46]

4 Dual Significances of China's Path to Peaceful Development

Since it was proposed, China's path to peaceful development has yielded significant dividends in its application from theory to practice. Through its application to the domains of politics, economy, military, culture, and diplomacy, China's path to peaceful development has realized historical

[44] Zheng Bijian, *Thinking Course—Origin, Foundation, Connotation and Prospect*, Beijing: Central Party School Publishing House, 2006, p. 291.

[45] *Wang Yi Talked about the Achievements and Significance of the 19th National Congress of CPC*, http://www.fmprc.gov.cn/web/wjbzhd/t1507077.shtml, December 1, 2017.

[46] Xu Shan, *Peaceful Development: China's Confidence and Commitment—An Analysis of the Theory of China's Path to Peaceful Development Since the 16th National Congress of the CPC*, collected in *Documents of the CPC*, Issue 5, 2011, pp. 100–106.

transcendence and contributed to its own development as well as world peace and prosperity. In other words, Chinese power has been clearly enhanced through its insistence on reform, openness, and peaceful development. Approximately 1.3 billion Chinese are forging ahead along the road to rejuvenating the great dream of the Chinese nation. The country effectively responded to the international financial crisis and positively joined in international efforts to mitigate it. China has played an important role in facilitating the economic rejuvenation of the world and responding to global challenges, and has become an important member of the new global economic governance mechanism. It unswervingly walks the path to peaceful development, adheres to the correct idea of the balance between moral and profit, advances the establishment of a new type of international relations involving cooperation and mutual benefit as core, propagates the program of "One Belt and One Road," and drives the Community of Human Destiny.

China's path to peaceful development has profound theoretical significance. It has Chinese characteristics, being based on extensive historical and cultural traditions, and is the inheritance and development of the civilization of the country. China's path abandons the old path of Western capitalist countries and traditional Socialist powers, and offers a new strategy for national development according to the principles of Marxism and its national development since foundation. This provides directional instruction for internal administration and diplomacy. *Its theoretical significance can be detailed as follows.*

First, China's adherence to the path to peaceful development is an inheritance and development of traditional Chinese culture. "Harmony" embodies the essential value and essence of all things. It permeates the entire development course of traditional culture, and has been promoted by various ideological and cultural schools of Chinese culture. "Harmony orientation," "harmony but not sameness," and "harmony between nature and human" are the three important levels of its connotation: "Harmony orientation" is the cultural idea whereby the Chinese love peace, and adhere to the Five Principles of Peaceful Coexistence and the path to peaceful development. "Harmony but not sameness" is a significant source of the theory and practice of Chinese diplomacy. China adheres to an independent foreign policy of peace, respects the interests of other countries, and calls for a coexistence of harmony but not sameness, and mutual benefit and win-win scenarios. "Harmony between nature and human" uses the Chinese idea of pursuing harmony in human relations and international relations, and embodies the unification of humans and nature, and the coordinative consistence of moral reason and natural reason. It emphasizes the idea of harmony in modern times: unification and harmony between humans and nature, humans and other humans, humans and society, and even countries. The path to peaceful development is clarified through a comprehensive study of traditional Chinese culture, and inherits such ideas of Confucian culture as "harmony orientation," "friendly relations with all countries," and "harmony helps the world reach great prosperity." The relevant guideline for diplomacy is that of being kind to neighboring countries and considering them partners, and promoting harmony, prosperity, and security to implement the traditional idea of "neighborliness." The path to peaceful development calls for democracy in international relations and diversity of modes of development, respecting the diversity of cultures, political systems, and modes of development of countries, and seeking common points while reserving differences to realize common development goals. It is the application of "harmony but not sameness" in modern times. Cultural diversity to human society is akin to biological diversity to nature, and is a kind of objective reality. Only through respecting cultural diversity can human civilization be developed. The coexistence and development of different civilizations is the final aim of "harmony." It includes peace between countries, harmony between people, and harmony between humans and nature;[47] China never seeks hegemony and power politics no matter its level of development. It embodies "adopting benevolent government and abandoning hegemony." "Our party lays emphasis both on strengthening hard powers, such as economy, military and science, and technology, and promoting soft powers such as culture, national spirit, and national cohesion. It is modern application and development of the ideas of moderation and neutralization."[48] The inheritance and development of the traditional culture not only embody the Chinese characteristics of the path to peaceful development, but also show features attuned to the tide of the times.

[47] Qin Yaqing, *Harmonious World: China's New Diplomacy Idea*, collected in *Qianxian*, Issue 12, 2006, pp. 30–32.

[48] Wang Yi, *Study and Analysis on the Traditional Cultural Source of China's Peaceful Development Strategy—In the View of State Relation Idea of the Confucianism*, collected in the *Journal of Guizhou Normal University*, Issue 2, 2006, pp. 12–17.

Second, China's path to peaceful development is a new development of Marxism that deepens its sinicization. Marxism is the most fundamental guiding idea of the administration of the CPC. The sinicization of Marxism is the harmony between basic Marxist theory and Chinese conditions. Deng Xiaoping called for combining Marxist theory with peaceful development, the theme at the time, and building a Socialist path to peaceful development with Chinese characteristics. It was the first strategic integration of peace and development along China's path to peaceful development, and has profoundly reflected the themes of peace and development. It also integrated the direction of Chinese development and its objective, and has provided detailed instructions concerning internal administration and diplomacy. The path to peaceful development is a significant constituent of Socialism with Chinese characteristics. To adhere to the path to peaceful development is to build Socialism with Chinese characteristics, which reflects the innovation and changing with the times of the CPC. This path is the strategic development of the CPC in administrative theory as well as the sinicization of Marxism in China.

Third, China's path to peaceful development is the enrichment and development of the Chinese theories of diplomacy and international relations, and imbues them with features more germane to the times, and with more obvious Chinese characteristics. Since the foundation of new China, as the international environment in which China is involved changes and international reform deepens, the Chinese theories of diplomacy and international relations have experienced development from nothing to something and from something to prosperity, which reflects changes in characteristics of the times, international patterns, and state strategy in every period. Once the country adopted reform and openness, the international trend was inclined toward peace and stability, and China has gained significantly from it. The theme of peace and development proposed by Deng Xiaoping became the new face of Chinese diplomacy and international relations, while the proposal and application of concepts such as a peaceful rise and safety enriched them.

Fourth, China's path to peaceful development provides theoretical support to cancel the influence of negative public opinion in the international community, such as the "China threat theory" and the "China collapse theory." Since its foundation, China has always adhered to the Five Principles of Peaceful Coexistence and an independent foreign policy of peace. However, in recent years, as Chinese power has grown, negative public opinion, in the form of the "China threat theory" and the "China collapse theory," has seriously influenced the image of the Chinese state and its international status, and impeded the development of sound relations between China and other countries. China's path to peaceful development is a sufficiently clear answer to doubts about Chinese development in the international community and a powerful counterattack against vicious slander by some countries and people. China's path clearly defines its direction of development, and declares its basic principle of relations with the world, namely "Chinese development is peaceful. No matter at what level, China will never seek hegemony and will not get involved in power politics." If China is to become more prosperous, rich, and strong, peaceful development is necessary. Only by removing doubts among the international community about Chinese development can the country enjoy further development and advance world peace.

China's path to peaceful development has profound practical significance, on both the state and international levels. It can be described as follows.

First, the path to peaceful development defines the strategic path for Chinese development, and provides directional instruction for internal administration and diplomacy. The path to peaceful development demands that China integrate internal reform and openness, its own peaceful development and that of the world, the fundamental interests of China and the Chinese, and those of the countries and people of the world. It requires that the state adhere to independence and self-reliance, rely on its own power, advance its development via international cooperation in a peaceful and stable international environment, and facilitate the peace, prosperity, and development of the world together with other countries. As a rising power, flaws in China's internal political and economic systems, and problems relating to population and resource pressures, pose formidable challenges to the administration of the CPC. China occupies a place of considerably greater importance in international affairs than in the past, and its diplomatic status is viewed much more positively than before. However, there remain ideological differences that are difficult to surpass. China has a series of urgent problems in both its internal administration and diplomacy. The path to peaceful development guides China to seek development in peace, promote peace, and advance the common development of China and other countries of the world.

Second, China's peaceful development is conducive to promoting Chinese soft power, and advancing the coexistence of soft and hard power as well as the comprehensive development of the state. "Whether China realizes its rise depends on not only its hard power, but also its soft power, and its real rise should be complemented by soft power and hard power."[49] Since its reform and openness, rapid economic development, advances in scientific and technological pursuits, and a strengthened military have formed the foundations of China's hard power. However, due to such factors as culture, tradition, ideology, and mode of development, Chinese soft power is not in direct proportion to its hard power. The path to peaceful development encourages China to develop itself and devote to the co-development of other countries, and engage in efforts for world peace. It needs the understanding, support, and cooperation of other countries. Only by strengthening both soft and hard power at the same time can China establish a good image, obtain a status corresponding to its strength, realize national development in all aspects, and become a real world power.

Third, China's path to peaceful development is conducive to the promotion of the comprehensive power of the state and the realization of the great rejuvenation of the Chinese nation. It was pointed out in the decision of the sixth plenary session of the 16th Central Committee that "the foundation of new China starts the great rejuvenation of Chinese civilization on a Socialist basis. Since China entered into a new period of historical development signified by the third plenary session of the 11th Central Committee of the CPC, a new, powerful entelechy and vitality was endowed to the rejuvenation."[50] The main means of realizing the great rejuvenation of the Chinese nation is to promote the state's power. The path to peaceful development involves implementing development using reform and innovation in a peaceful and stable international environment while advancing world peace and prosperity via its own development. Adhering to the path to peaceful development is conducive to realizing the objective of enriching the nation and strengthening the country.

Fourth, China's adherence to the path to peaceful development is conducive to the sound development of international relations, and promotes a more just and rational international political and economic order. The path to peaceful development demands that China adhere to reform and openness, and has provided rich resources and a broad market for the development of international commerce. China joins in international cooperation and resource complementation among countries, which allows global

[49] Men Honghua, *Introduction to Chinese International Strategy*, Beijing: Tsinghua University Press, 2009, p. 63.

[50] *The 6th Plenary Session Bulletin of the 16th Central Committee of the CPC*, http://www.southcn.com/nflr/llzhuanti/lzqh/toutiao/200610240193.htm, May 3, 2015.

resources to be allocated more rationally. It is an important path to safeguarding world peace and advancing common development to build a fair and rational political and economic international order. China supports and improves international transactions and financial systems, encourages the freedom and convenience of investment, and deals well with conflicts in the economic domain via negotiations and coordination. China will not harm others to benefit itself or benefit itself at the expense of its neighbors. The path to peaceful development is conducive to working with developing countries, establishing communication and cooperation with them, considering the fundamental benefits of all countries in a peaceful manner, making adjustments to global resource allocation, and formulating effective international rules to build a fair and rational international political and economic order.

Fifth, China's path to peaceful development is conducive to a world with lasting peace, universal security, common prosperity, openness, tolerance, and beauty. China's peaceful development may stabilize the world and safeguard global peace because it is a responsible power in the international community, and a positive participant and builder in the construction and evolution of the international order. The path to peaceful development demands that China adhere to an independent foreign policy of peace, development, cooperation, and win-win outcomes, and to friendliness, sincerity, mutual benefit, and the idea of tolerance and partnership with surrounding countries; deepen relationships with neighboring countries; persist in the correct balance between morality and profit; and realize common development and prosperity. Based on the spirit of democracy, harmony, justice, and tolerance, adhering to a path to peaceful development is conducive to working hard with other countries to facilitate peace and common prosperity in the world.

CHAPTER 8

China's Peaceful Development and Transformation of International Order (1985–2015)

Honghua Men

The creation and gradual improvement of China's peaceful development road depends not only on the implementation of domestic strategies but also, to a great extent, on successful international engagements. Thus, this represents the joining of domestic and international arrangements. At the international level, China's road shares a natural relation with the reform of the international order. It can be said that the achievement of a stable international order symbolizes a great power's true success.[1] The construction of an international order is a strategic and diplomatic topic that every rising great power should address. As China ascends, the world is looking to see how China will address and participate in reshaping the international order (RIO). It will also become an important template for those countries waiting to see the effect of China's rise.

The rise and fall of countries, globalization, and regional integration are the three impetuses behind the world's current evolution. A nation's rise and fall have occurred since ancient times and represents

[1] Barry Buzan, *Sino-Japanese and Sino-US Relations in China's Peaceful Rise*, collected in *World Economics and Politics*, Issue 7, 2006, pp. 15–18.

H. Men (✉)
Institute for China & World Studies, Tongji University, Shanghai, China

H. Men (ed.), *On China's Road*,
https://doi.org/10.1007/978-981-13-7880-5_8

the fundamental motivation to form and create a world presence. Globalization and regional integration are complementary, and push forward the rise and fall of great powers as well as influence the characteristics of such ascents and declines. Globalization can lead to a new period of development and decline for a country, as well as acting to advance the process of regional cooperation. Globalization is changing the operating rules of the world system and further emphasizes the "democratic deficit" of the existing international order. It not only brings forth new opportunities for countries but also (and inevitably) generates destructive power. Nations want to join in the globalization process but are fearful of being too removed to do so. Furthermore, they have noticed that in the era in which globalization and regional integration can coexist without conflict, the prosperity of nations can only be safeguarded by the overall prosperity of their region. Therefore, regional cooperation has been transformed toward integration, and countries are now paying more attention to the concept of regional integration. Regarding nations' desire for some sort of order, the construction of both regional and international order has revealed important values. With the manifestation of a country's subjectivity, the enhancement of regional integration, and the deepening of global governance, emerge various forms of coexistence that are accentuated by national reform and regional cooperation, as is the generation of complex construction logistics.

China's peaceful development is considered an important force that influences the international order. China's future strategy orientation is receiving significant attention from the international community and affects the strategic adjustment of the core nations around the world. In 2005, China's *White Paper on Peaceful Development* proposed a strategy for a new international order, that is, an "advanced international order developed in a much fairer and more rational direction." For more than 30 years, China has been quiet on this topic, meaning that China now has a new policy orientation after its integration into the international community, one aimed at a harmonious world. However, since 2010, the international community has become much more sensitive toward China's strategic direction. Following the creation of China's new big strategy framework, new international systems such as the development banks of Brazil, Russia, India, China, and South Africa (BRICS) and the Asian Infrastructure Investment Bank (AIIB) have been designed and built.

Similarly, the "One Belt and One Road" initiative was proposed and implemented. Thus, whether or not China is trying to change the existing international order and aims to become the builder of a new (or the challenger of the existing) international order, it will be a leading power that is watched closely by the international community.

In consideration of three main variables—state power, international goals, and strategic design—this article explores relations between China and the international order. Furthermore, it analyzes how China established and enriched the path of peaceful development since Deng Xiaoping first proposed the theme of peaceful development in 1982, and examines how China proposed its own ideas and strategies in respect of the construction of an international order.

1 Analysis Framework of the Rise of the Great Power and Interactions with the International Order

The order of the international community refers to the formal or informal arrangements between nations. These arrangements provide a determinable and stable international environment for these nations and enable them to pursue group goals based on the application of rules such as the peaceful settlement of disputes.[2] Hedley Bull pointed out that the order refers to a pattern that leads to a specific result and one targeted at realizing a social arrangement with a specific goal or value.[3] The international order also refers to the pattern or layout of international behaviors, and it seeks the basic, major, or universal goals of the state and society, including the maintenance of the existence of the international system, state, society, and the independence or sovereignty of the state, and lastly peace.[4] According to current understanding, the international order includes the following aspects: first, the international order is the pattern established by the principal actors based on their respective powers in a certain period of time. In other words, the international order is built on the basis of a power comparison among actors, especially core countries. Thus, the

[2] Muthiah Alagappa, ed., *Asian Security Order: Instrumental and Normative Features*, New York: Stanford University Press, 2003, p. 39.

[3] Hedley Bull, *The Anarchical Society: A Study of Order in World Politics*, New York: Columbia University Press, 1980, p. 1.

[4] Hedley Bull, *The Anarchical Society: A Study of Order in World Politics*, pp. 16–20.

international order is the result of a power distribution. Second, the international order refers to international rules of behavior and safeguard mechanisms that the actors of the international community determine via mutually affecting means and benefits to realize a certain goal in a certain time period. That is to say, the international order is the result of the distribution of benefits between the countries, especially the great powers. Third, whether the international order is stable in a certain period always depends upon whether main great powers can reach and maintain a tacit understanding (or reach an appropriate compromise) of a core idea. In other words, the formation of a shared idea in the international system will be the key variable that decides whether an international order can be built and whether stability can be maintained. Fourth, the international order means that the actors (e.g., sovereign states, state groups, and international organizations) in the international community deal with relations according to certain principles, regulations, goals, and means, and they build or maintain mechanisms under which international politics and economics operate. That is, the international system is the decisive variable in constructing and maintaining the international order. In summary, in the opinion of the author, *the international order is based on the concept of sharing and is the result of the distribution of power and benefits among the main actors, especially the great powers, in the international community. A key example of this is the foundation and operation of the global international system.*

In consideration of the above knowledge, the international order can be described as an international public good. It is mainly provided by the main actors and expresses and leads to cooperation and conflict between the great powers. The dispute over the international order is, in essence, a dispute over power and benefits, and is again reflected as strategic competition, and competition in the international system. In view of the fact that the balance among the strengths of the great powers is based on history and law, the distribution of benefits is based on power, a guiding strategy, and an international system that reflects three kinds of distribution frames and processes that must be present for any change to occur. The international order is a dynamic idea, with evolution being an essential characteristic. However, there is some degree of stability and even some delay in the power and benefit structure, the concepts, and in the international system. The transformation of new and old orders occurs over a long time period. The progress and speed of the international political and economic order depends upon changes to the power balance. However, the latter will not impact on the existing structure and system. The international order sits at the top of these structures and systems. Therefore, any lag is also considered a basic feature of the international order.

Powerful countries have a huge influence on the international order. Bull once said that a great power could influence the international order because countries such as these hold unequal amounts of power within the international system. The inequality of state power leads to the simplification of international relations. Great powers may adopt policies that maintain or harm the international order according to the analysis. Bull found that the international order maintained by the great powers obtained broad support from the international community. However, the great powers are continually faced with the issue of how to let weaker countries recognize their special role in the international system. The world is a place where different powers compete and no great power can build an order that perfectly meets its own interests. Therefore, the great powers must not seek to formalize and determine their own special status, and they must avoid engaging in behavior that clearly acts to destroy the order. These nations must also satisfy (or partially satisfy) the requirements of fair reform and coordinate and maintain the balance of regional power with second-tier powers.[5]

The great powers are the protagonists in constructing and remodeling the international order. The general laws are as follows: the soft and hard powers of the great powers improve, followed by demands for benefits; a new international goal is formed and a principal or secondary strategic design is implemented during a change in the international order; and the great powers become the actual champions of the reform of the international order and implement their strategic actions at both global and regional levels. Since the twentieth century, the international order has changed frequently and the struggle for order has never ceased. It is in this way that competition between the great powers is generated. During the construction of the international order, state power is a fundamental condition, and the reform strategy always plays the leading role. As globalization and regional integration develops and deepens, concepts such as global governance and regional community are proposed and gradually accepted. However, the concept of hegemonic guidance still exists today and traditional and innovative thinking engage in a fierce competition. The restructuring of the order is carried out at both global and regional levels.

[5] Hedley Bull, *The Anarchical Society: A Study of Order in World Politics*, pp. 199–222.

2 Historical Evolution of the International Order

An investigation into the development progress of the international order reveals that it is built upon the coexistence of multiple regions' order. These orders all share one common feature: the dominance of a single country. An "international" balance of power was first established in Europe, emerging with the rise and fall of great powers and early globalization (e.g., characterized by exploration to other countries). The great European powers gained further control after the industrial revolution, and their dominance soon expanded worldwide. As a result, regional orders turned toward establishing a global economic order, finally forming a global order after the two world wars. Of course, to certain extent, the global order has not completely over taken efforts (or attempts) to establish regional orders; this can be seen in the United States' attempts to establish a hegemonic order in Latin America and the hegemonic order under the Soviet Union in Eastern Europe during the Second World War (SWW). After the SWW, especially since the 1960s, changes to the international order displayed certain dominant features: as European self-reliance and national liberation movements in Asia, Africa, and Latin America gained momentum, the rejuvenation of regional orders became a tidal wave, and a new form of regional community order stepped on to the historical stage. Since the 1990s, the RIO and the rejuvenation of the construction of regional orders have become the main features of the construction of the international order.

Looking back, no country has yet possessed the power or influence to dominate the world or worldwide interests; similarly, no international system has managed to lead at a global scale. Regarding the coexistence of various regional orders, the East Asia order with China as the core largely reflects traditional Chinese political concepts and wisdom. The appearance of a real global system depends on great geographical discoveries. Since the fifteenth and sixteenth centuries, great European powers have expanded beyond the continent and created a stable global navigation system and corresponding global trade system. By the mid-nineteenth century, when China experienced a colonial invasion, a global international system had been established. This period was followed by the industrial revolution, transportation revolution, and communication revolution. The tight connections inside the system finally created a global international economic order. The signing of the *Peace of Westphalia* in

1648 recognized the principle of sovereign equality among nations and established a novel political foundation for the later creation of an international political order. It is worth noting that two essential conditions must be present to achieve an international order: the formation and stabilization of a balanced European order.

The end of the nineteenth century and the beginning of the twentieth represented the acceptance of an international division of labor and the appearance of a world market and world currency system. That period also marked the emergence of the colonial system and an international political and economic system. Within this system, the great European powers were transformed into modern nations and possessed the necessary power and will to protect themselves from threats of invasion and to engage in colonial expansion. The British Empire became the overlord and the United States emerged as the world's first great economic power. Japan also successfully rose as a great Asian power under the Meiji Restoration. The most prominent phenomenon in the second half of the nineteenth century was internal and external expansion of the great powers and the dissolution of the traditional order of East Asia: the United States abandoned its isolationism policy and not only searched for a dominant position in the American order (this started with "Monologism") but also started interfering with the reconstruction of the order in East Asia (e.g., its occupation of the Philippines and its proposed "open-door" policy).[6] The balance of power in Europe changed rapidly due to the rise and fall of continental countries. Germany realized its ascent via unification and challenged the Westphalian system. The result of the wars among these big powers was the appearance of the first international order. This relied upon the establishment of an international alliance and was signified by the determination of the Versailles–Washington System. In a manner of speaking, the creation of global orders between countries represented the demand for a new order in the twentieth century. On the one hand, it was the practical achievement of idealism and signified the enduring efforts for world peace; on the other hand, it was the continuation of the global expansion of the European international order and the continuation of the interstate order established by capitalist countries with a global scope. The order has always been flavored by hegemony and power politics.

[6] Men Honghua, *Hegemony's Wing: Strategic Research on American International System*, Peking University Press, 2005, Chapter IV.

Considering the spoils of the natural divisions and the internal inequality of the Versailles–Washington Order, the instability of the international order was inevitable. Germany's re-emergence marked the rise of fascism within the country, and it was similarly embraced by Japan and Italy during the 1920s–1930s. Thus, the power and will to attack the order emerged and a new world war was inevitable. The main influence during that time was the United States, as it had the power to be a global overlord but it refused to bear the subsequent responsibilities. Instead, the United States attempted to seek worldwide interests. The rise of a socialist Soviet Union provided the best excuse for the big powers to maneuver themselves among various political groupings and to get ready for war. Therefore, the SWW was the decisive battle between the people of the world and fascism, and it represented an attempt by capitalists to use fascism as an excuse to eliminate socialism. The result of the war was that fascism died out, but the socialist Soviet Union became stronger. Thus, a significant challenge emerged: how best to build a post-war international order.

The efforts made by the great powers to establish an international order before and after the SWW represented an appeal for the second new order of the twentieth century. The great powers followed the power and interest principles and created an international order following the Yalta Conference; the ensuing order possessed a strong geopolitical color in terms of the division of power. This international order represented significant progress, achieving success around the world in the fight against fascism and socialism. Politically, the new order lead to the founding of UN-determined institutional principles, such as sovereign equality and national self-determination. In terms of economic developments, the International Monetary Fund, World Bank, and General Agreement on Tariff and Trade (GATT) were established, representing the desire to facilitate global economic development. The international order at that time was a global extension of the Westphalia Order. The principle of sovereign equality became a worldwide guiding principle. The inclusion of the principle of sovereign equality in the *Charter of the United Nations* was a significant milestone regarding the international order. However, the order failed to remove the negative influences of hegemony and power politics. A clear illustration of this is the struggle between the Soviet Union and the United States in their fight for hegemony, and the world then got caught in the Cold War for decades. Important foundation conditions were necessary for the two countries to seek hegemony: the United States had consolidated the order in the Americas and the Soviet Union determined the hegemonic order of Eastern Europe. However, the socialist Soviet Union soon dropped into the imperialism mire. Furthermore, its dominance in the security order of East Asia ensured the United States' geopolitical superiority in the hegemonic competition.

In a sense, the Yalta order (established after the SWW) came with an inevitable historical burden, bringing inequalities established as early as one century before. This order is therefore called the old international political and economic order. The old international economic order refers to an unequal international order characterized by the exploitation and plundering of developing and undeveloped countries by developed countries. It also included an international productive order based on an irrational international division of labor, an international trade order featuring unequal exchanges, and an international financial order based on monopolies. The old international political order refers to an international political order characterized by hegemony and power politics.

Meanwhile, the international political and economic order is changing. Fundamentally, such revolution comes from economic and technological development. The development of different societies in different areas worldwide occurs at different speeds and depends not only upon the type of change affecting technology, production, and trade, but also the capacity of increasing production and wealth, and acceptance of these new forms. While certain areas enjoy progress, other areas experience relative or (sometimes) absolute delay.[7] The information revolution is a decisive power for the world's transformation, and it has rapidly changed comparisons of international competence and further enlarged the huge gap between countries. It has also changed the status of wars and national security. The information revolution has had an inconvenient influence on the international order of the future. However, continual economic growth and the world market economy have relaxed international relations. In modern times, a country largely gains greater interests through economic efficiency, cooperation, and the international division of labor, as opposed through war, imperialism, and exclusive economic means. However, the prospect of economic dependence and mutual benefit does not eliminate competition and distrust between countries. Trade is not always a means to maintain peace. In addition, the wealth of some countries

[7] Paul Kennedy, *The Rise and Fall of the Great Powers*, Beijing: China Economic Publishing House, 1989, p. 538.

and the poverty of the majority have created a huge global gap, and this gap has become a new pathway to discord.[8] Of course, this process is occurring in an era whereby global issues are becoming even more dominant, and both the international order and international mechanism have entered an era of change.

First, the power pattern constituting the foundation of the international order has undergone a number of remarkable changes. After the SWW, the position of the great powers underwent dramatic changes. The Soviet Empire, which was once powerful and prosperous, suddenly collapsed; a group of developing great powers (e.g., China) rose to the fore, impacting the existing global patterns of power and interests. There were also changes in Western Europe: after a painful experience, Western European countries united and became self-reliant, thus they became rapid-development pioneers in the region. After establishing the European Union (EU) and expanding eastwards, they once again became the core power advancing the international revolution. Japan too experienced change: first, it enjoyed prosperity and then decline; it then became trapped in the "lost decades" at the beginning of the 1990s, and a deviation to the political right disturbed the pattern in East Asia. Since the 1960s and 1970s, Third World countries have enjoyed development that has enabled them to become important political powers,[9] and they have demanded the reform of the world political and economic order. The most prominent influence in the change of the pattern of power was the reconstruction of regional orders. The construction of a community order in Western Europe took the lead in regional cooperation and facilitated such reconstruction in other regions.

Second, with changes to the power structure, various countries proposed corresponding interest demands, and international interests also underwent a huge transformation. This was reflected not only in the interest conflicts between the North and the South but also within Northern countries.

Third, as globalization and interactions deepened, international cooperation became a leading international notion. New concepts such as global governance enjoyed popular support, accompanied by a more subtle change to the concept of international order. Economic globalization,

[8] Robert Gil-pin, *War and Change in World Politics*, Beijing: People's Publishing House of China, 1994, pp. 216–218.

[9] Refer to *The History of International Relations*, chief-edited by Wang Yingzu, Vol. 9, Beijing: World Affairs Press, 1996, pp. 41–75.

however, is a double-edged sword in the construction of the global order. Interdependence leads to fiercer international competition, while interdependence itself becomes a tool to sanction other parties. However, it may encourage countries to adopt attitudes that are more rational and to choose dialogue rather than war when dealing with conflicts.

Fourth, a silent reformation of the international mechanism also occurred. Since modern times, especially after the First World War, the international community continuously sought cooperation and wished to build a supranational world order. Such impulsions led to the generation of a series of international laws and international political rules, and have created a series of institutionalized organizations and institutions. As the power becomes dispersed, the influence of the concept of international governance is enlarged, and more countries join to make and improve the international mechanisms. Thus, the fair nature of the international mechanism has been further exemplified. The acceleration of the world's transformation impacts the existing international order framework and hastens the RIO based on common interests. The transformation of the international order is increasingly based on multipolarization, the gathering and systemization of common interests, and the sharing of common responsibilities (the great powers should assume the important responsibilities and other countries should share the responsibilities).

Because of the abovementioned changes, the dispute over the international order has become very fierce. Before the Cold War ended, the call to establish a new international order mainly came from Third World countries; they sought to overturn the negative status within the old international economic order and to create a beneficial international environment for the development of a national economy. Shortly after the end of the Cold War, the power of the developed countries grew and they proposed the establishment of a new order. The United States promoted the construction of a new world order that matched its national strategy, and urgently sought to create a world order that would place itself in a leading position. At the same time, EU countries sought to restore Europe's traditional status, and Japan proposed a new international order with Japan, the United States, and Europe as the three poles of power. In essence, the new world order advocated by the developed countries is the continuation and consolidation of the old order, whereby they mean to make use of their advantageous status to maintain their own interests to the largest extent. Thus, they aimed to include all countries in the international political and economic system that they led by maintaining existing international rules or making international rules that benefited themselves. Upon entering the twenty-first century, the focus of the creation of national orders returned to the regional level. After the beginning of the global financial crisis in the second half of 2008, many countries were forced to further recognize the value of regional cooperation. While facilitating global economic governance (e.g., the activities of the Group of 20 countries [G20]), countries were devoted to consolidate their regional status, explore new ways to reconstruct the global order via advancing regional cooperation, and accumulate power to facilitate a global revolution.[10]

3 Historical Background to Relations Between China and the International Order

Before the nineteenth century, China continued to develop in a relatively isolated geopolitical environment in East Asia and was relatively insulated from the rest of the world. In the mid-nineteenth century, the big European powers included China in the international order they led, and this started the tumultuous interactive process between China and the international order. Examples of China's participation in the international order can be seen in two key ways: the transition from "China's World" to the "World's China," and the transition from an "outsider" to a "member." These two features are interactively combined and supplement each other, resulting in several changes in China's role in the international order.

Throughout history, China has always been a leading great power. For more than 1000 years, Chinese science and technology has led the world. Furthermore, China's gross national product (GNP) ranked the first in the world at the beginning of the nineteenth century. China had its own systematic long-standing civilization and constituted its own systematic imperialist system in East Asia. The Confucian social and political order designed by China followed a pattern of unification whereby "all the land in the world belonged to the lord and all the people living on the land were subordinate to the lord." This unification structure constituted a so-called international order with China at the core and offered a concentric hierarchical world system[11]; this can be considered the origin of the East Asian order. This order placed China as a unique ruler that could specify

[10] Men Honghua, Establishment Logistics of Regional Order, collected in *World Economy and Politics*, Issue 7, 2014, pp. 5–22.

[11] Fei Zhengqing edited in chief, *The Cambridge History of China*, Vol. 2, Beijing: China Social Sciences Publishing House, 1985, p. 37.

reality, and the grace of the Chinese Empire was used to humanize all people worldwide. A tributary order followed Chinese rules for political relations, namely the continuity and application of decentralization in diplomatic relations. This emphasized that "China may maintain peace as long as neighboring countries develop in sequence," "convince others by morality," and "are kind to people and all come to pay allegiance and appease the dukes and the world shows respect." China sought to distinguish the Han People and minorities through culture instead of race.[12] The economic system and international order with China at the core aimed to obtain the external security necessary for internal stability and prosperity, as well as deal with surrounding relations according to the principle of giving more and receiving less. Thus, it was a flexible style of hegemonic order. The regional order established in ancient China was based on the tributary system. Although there may have been some aspects of inequality, the use of inherited culture and trade was used to maintain the peaceful and mutually beneficial order (Fig. 8.1).

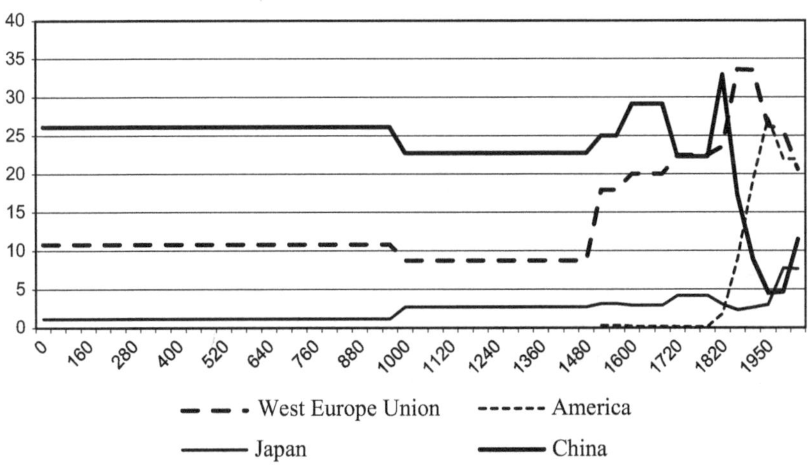

Fig. 8.1 Ratio of Chinese GDP to the world (Year One: 1988). Data Source: Angus Maddison, *The World Economy: A Millennial Perspective*, OECD: Paris, 2001

[12] Feng Youlan, *A Short History of Chinese Philosophy*, Peking University Press, 1985, p. 221.

Traditional Chinese society stood still and refused to make progress; it lacked an innovative spirit and the awareness to expand. By comparison, upon leaving the Middle Ages, Europe enjoyed rapid development and accelerated the pace of its expansion to the outside world. In the seventeenth century, European powers sunk their colonial claws into the southeast coastal region of China. In the nineteenth century, after failing to establish a much broader and more direct link with the Qing Dynasty via diplomatic means, Western powers resorted to warfare. They launched a series of wars against China, broke the Chinese pattern of unification with gunboats, and by force, brought China into the international order. As a nation, China transformed from one characterized by a pattern of unification to a national country with modern significance. Since its inclusion into the international order by force, China has long been insulted by the major powers and its land has been recklessly divided up, with no recognition of its sovereignty. After entering the twentieth century, China's main status regarding external diplomacy has changed from that as an imperial court to one seeking equal status.

As the international order expanded from regions to the world, the prominent feature was the creation of the League of Nations. Just prior to this, China's desire to actively join the international order grew. In 1916, China participated in the First World War and, for the first time since modern times, achieved numerous victories. However, at the 1919 Paris Peace Conference, held to determine the future international order, China (a victorious country) had no right to join in the discussions regarding the post-war international order. Thus, it was unable to safeguard its own interests. An important step for China in its attempts to join the international community was membership to the League of Nations. Nevertheless, Japan launched a large-scale war of aggression against China in 1931 and China appealed to the dispute settlement mechanism of the League of Nations. China lodged a complaint to the League of Nations and demanded sanctions against the invasion in accordance with the provisions of the treaty of the League. Although the League of Nations dispatched a delegation and released an investigative report, the report took the side of Japan and refused to declare Japan an invader, representing the first serious failure of the League of Nations in its short history. Until the end of the SWW, China was caught up in a new multipolar world.[13]

[13] Henry Kissinger, *Diplomacy*, Haikou: Hainan Publishing House, 1998, p. 9.

During the SWW, China took action to conqueror the Japanese in Far East battlegrounds, and made significant contributions to defeat fascism. As a great power, China participated in the process to found the UN and became one of the five permanent members (with voting rights) of the UN Security Council. Its great power status was affirmed under the mechanism of the UN. Thus, for the first time, China became a positive participant within the international order. However, after the Communist Party of China (CPC) founded New China in 1949, core Western countries such as the United States refused to acknowledge the People's Republic of China (PRC). Instead, it continued to recognize the Chiang Kai-shek clique that had settled in Taiwan and supported it to gain seats on international organizations, such as the UN, and Mainland China was expelled from existing global international systems. After careful consideration, Chinese leaders introduced a "one-sided" diplomacy policy. China's chosen strategy and the start of the Korean War had a substantial influence on the international order. The 1960s and 1970s marked significant polarization and alliances in international power. The Sino-Soviet Alliance dissolved and the socialist camp was dismantled, and capitalism further developed with the United States, Europe, and Japan at the core. Developing countries, as independent political powers, stepped on to the world stage. China proposed two intermediate zone theories and demanded to "fight through two lines" and even "make attacks in all directions." Thus, it further challenged the hegemony and the international system. At the start of the 1970s, with the Soviet Union's hegemony posing a major threat to China, China again adjusted its international strategy and proposed "three-world" theory. It also achieved breakthrough diplomatic relations with Western countries such as the United States. In October 1970, China regained its seat in the United Nations as a permanent member; this earned China broader international acceptance. However, China's doubts about the UN and other international organizations had not been completely dispelled.[14]

In consideration of China's experience of participating in the post-war international order and then its exclusion from decision making, the Chinese government proposed to create new international relations and a new international order. At the end of 1953, when meeting a delegation from the Indian government, Zhou Enlai proposed five principles: mutual

[14] Zhao Quansheng, *Explanation of Chinese Diplomacy Policy: Research Method Combining Microscopic and Macroscopic Research*, Taibei: Yuedan Publishing House, 1999, p. 105.

respect for sovereignty and territorial integrity, non-aggression, non-interference with internal affairs, equality and mutual benefits, and peaceful coexistence. Since their proposal, the so-called Five Principles of Peaceful Coexistence have now been widely accepted around the world. The principles have not only been affirmed in bilateral agreements signed by China and other countries (e.g., treaties, declarations, and statements), but have also been repeatedly quoted or reiterated at many significant international conferences and in numerous international documents. The wide acceptance of these five principles is one of China's great contributions to the basic principle of international relations as well as the first important attempt of the PRC to improve the international order.

China has always supported the appeals of Third World countries to create a new international economic order. In 1974, at the sixth special session of the UN General Assembly, China put forward a proposal to establish a new international political and economic order: first, build political and economic relations among countries on the basis of the Five Principles of Peaceful Coexistence; second, international economic affairs should be co-managed by the countries of the world; third, world trade should be conducted on the basis of equality, mutual benefits, and the mutual exchange of necessary goods; fourth, exclude political and military elements from the economic aid given to developing countries and respect the sovereignty of the country receiving the aid; and lastly, the international community should provide more technological aid to developing countries.[15]

In 1978, China first implemented its opening-up policy and sought to quicken its integration into the international community. China began to adhere to existing international rules and joined existing international systems instead of starting all over again via other means. China also adopted a constructive attitude to its regional system and embodied the desire to continually facilitate a connection with the international community. Thus, China's involvement with the international order was increasingly developed and enriched.

In summary, since the foundation of the PRC, China has had a positive influence on the international order. China was once excluded from any decision making regarding the international order. However, its role in the process has changed from onlooker to participant and its attitude has changed from a negative one to a positive one. During this time, China's understanding of the international order has gradually grown.

[15] Edited by Pei Jianzhang and Wang Taiping in chief, *Diplomacy History of the PRC*, Vol. 3, Beijing: World Affairs Press, 1999, p. 480.

4 China's Strategies to Integrate into the World (1985–2005)

In 1978, the Third Plenary Session of the 11th National Congress of the CPC symbolized a significant change in Chinese history. In 1982, the 12th National Congress of the CPC further defined the blueprint of its quest for socialist modernization. In 1982, a general theme of peace and development provided the strategic idea for China to integrate with the international community and join the international order. On this basis, China followed a road of peaceful development whereby it changed itself and influenced the world. During the process whereby China gradually began to participate in global affairs, China still recognized the importance of its own power and localization, and gradually considered cooperation with East Asia (with China at the core) to facilitate participation in international affairs. Thus, strategies to create an international order have gradually led to the situation whereby the world and regional orders are parallel.

The Third Plenary Session of the 11th National Congress of the CPC symbolized the moment that China abandoned its strategy based on class struggles and instead focused on economic construction. In December 1979, Deng Xiaoping first proposed the idea of establishing a "moderately well-off society" by the end of the twentieth century. In 1982, the 12th National Congress of the CPC introduced an objective under a moderately well-off society to quadruple the annual industrial and agricultural output value of the country at the end of the century. The congress also emphasized the need to create an excellent economic system, which would act as the core of three construction tasks in the 1980s: anti-hegemony and peacekeeping, motherland unification, and modernization construction. Between 1980 and 1985, the gross value of China's industrial and agricultural output increased by 11.0%, exceeding the strategic expectations of the Twelfth National Congress of the CPC. On this basis, Deng Xiaoping looked at China's unique conditions and changed and redesigned the long-term development goal of Chinese modernization. He then developed the "three-step" strategic concept for the primary stage of socialism.[16] On April 30, 1987, Deng Xiaoping, introduced his "three-step" modernization development strategy: the first step was to double GDP from 1981 to 1991 (the 1980 value being the base value from which

[16] Section III of the Party History Research Center of the CPC Central Committee, *China's Reform and Opening-up History*, Shenyang: Liaoning People's Publishing House, 2002, p. 73.

to reach USD 500); the second step was to again double GDP by the end of the twentieth century (per capita income reached USD 1000); and the third step was to spend 30–50 years to quadruple GDP (it would reach USD 4000 per capita).[17] In 1987, the 13th National Congress of the CPC further stated that China has entered the primary stage of socialism and its fundamental task was to emancipate and develop productivity. The adjustment of the national general strategy was the starting point of China's reform of its international strategy: the focus changed from military security, national independence, and self-reliance to economic construction, wealth and the prosperity of the people, and opening-up. Thus, China hoped to create a positive international environment for its socialist modernization. The change in emphasis from safeguarding national security to development became the fundamental element in China's international strategy. Meanwhile, changes in the international situation and China's international environment also provided historic opportunities to adjust China's international strategy. China's international environment improved when the Soviet Union began to follow more aggressive policies and the United States became more conservative. This led to China and the United States creating new diplomatic relations on January 1, 1979. Because of the adjustments to US policy, China and the Soviet Union both sought to improve their relations. After 12 rounds of political negotiations spanning seven years (1982–1989), both parties gradually re-established links in various field. Meanwhile, as China's reform and opening-up was implemented and developed, China's huge economic and market potential attracted foreign investors and this helped to extend and improve relations between China and other countries. Therefore, China's foreign relations developed to a new high. China opened and accelerated its integration into the international community. The reform of the relation between China and the international order was imminent. From that point onwards, China was an important power in facilitating the reform of the international order and its influence only became stronger.

In the 1980s, China made a fundamental adjustment to its international strategy. This adjustment was based on the following change in strategy: China's focus moved from "the class struggle" to "economic construction," and the overall objective for that era turned from war and revolution to peace and development. The objective of that period was

[17] *Selective Works of Deng Xiaoping*, Vol. 2, Beijing: People's Publishing House, 1994, p. 226.

first based on domestic needs but then gradually spread to the international community. In 1977, Deng Xiaoping said that, "we may strive to delay the start of the war," and he said again in 1982 that, "the reasons for war are increasing and the reasons not to go to war are also increasing." On March 4, 1985, while meeting a Japanese delegation, Deng Xiaoping pointed out "the current significant problems in the world are global strategic problems: the first is the peace problem and the other is the economic problem or development problem."[18] On December 21, 1988, when meeting the Prime Minister of India, Rajiv Gandhi, Deng Xiaoping stated that, "there are mainly two issues at present in the world. The first is the peace issue and the other is the development issue ... we should recognize the development issue affects all of mankind. It is necessary to observe and solve the issues taking this in to consideration. Only in this way can we understand that the development issue is the responsibility of the developing countries as well as the responsibility of the developed countries."[19] The quest for peace and development represents a turning point in recognizing the interactive relations between China and the world. On this basis, the administrative strategy of the CPC realized the transformation from the "philosophy of struggle" to the "philosophy of construction," as well as changes to its political focus, shifting from the "class struggle" to "economic construction." Similarly, there was a shift from "doctrinarism" to "practice is the sole criterion for testing the truth." This was accompanied by the reform of the economic strategy, shifting from a planned economy to a socialist market economy. The introduction of the theme of peace and development influenced China's national strategy and established the foundation for the general coordination of both domestic and international strategies.

The strategic adjustment was marked by the convening of the 12th National Congress of the CPC in September 1982. China began to abandon its "one-line" strategic layout, and further emphasized the need for an independent peaceful diplomatic policy. It also shifted its focus from the Soviet Union and looked instead to developing all-round diplomatic relations with other countries around the world. Meanwhile, Deng Xiaoping developed the "three-world" theory and highlighted the West–East problem and the North–South problem: "At present, the biggest problems in

[18] *Selective Works of Deng Xiaoping*, Vol. 3, Beijing: People's Publishing House, 1993, p. 105.

[19] *Selective Works of Deng Xiaoping*, Vol. 3, pp. 281–282.

the world are global strategic problems. One is the peace problem and the other is the economic problem or development problem. The peace problem is a West–East relation problem and the development problem is the North–South relation problem. In summary, it is West, East, North and South. The North–South problem is central."[20] On this basis, Deng Xiaoping actively called for North–South conservations and South–South cooperation. He also proposed his "One Country, Two Systems" policy as an answer to the problem of Taiwan's unification and a "suspend disputes and develop together" policy to resolve the disputes concerning the South China Sea. As the international situation developed and Chinese power increased, Deng Xiaoping began to focus on building a new international political and economic order. He was the first world leader who raised the issue of a "new international order" both before and after the Cold War. In 1988, Deng Xiaoping proposed to "take the Five Principles of Peaceful Coexistence as the guidelines for guiding international relations" when constructing a new international order.[21]

As China's general strategy was adjusted, reform and opening-up became the key elements of its international strategy. Opening-up is a process that not only introduces funding and technology but also enables the learning of advanced ideas and systems. Similarly, it represents an important path that supports China to integrate with the international community and change relations between China and the international order. During this process, China accelerated its integration into the international system. Because of the restraints caused by historical factors and actual conditions, China's strategy in this period especially viewed participation in the international economic system as essential and reflected its focus on economic interests and objectives. China began to emphasize its connection with international trends and made efforts to create a role as a positive participant and follow international norms. During this period, China's perception of the international community changed, and it began to follow the rules of the international community and joined key global international systems. Thus, China did not take the revolutionary path to reform the international community but joined the international community as a necessary precondition and an important pathway to achieve modernization. China's potential and its huge market earned significant attention from the international community,

[20] *Selective Works of Deng Xiaoping*, Vol. 3, p. 105.

[21] *Selective Works of Deng Xiaoping*, Vol. 3, pp. 282–283.

and it became a key power in reshaping international order. Thus, it was for this reason that relations between China and the international community improved.

In the late 1980s and beginning of the 1990s, the international situation again experienced considerable changes. For example, 1989 marked a series of revolutions, followed soon by the end of the Cold War. On this important historic occasion, China sailed against the current and further developed its opening-up policy. Looking to the transformation to capital-intensive manufacturing and high-tech labor-intensive manufacturing in developed countries, China further developed its export economy. Meanwhile, in considering international disputes after the Cold War, China innovatively proposed to introduce a socialist market economy and then liberated China–world relations from the ideology vortex, showing high-level political wisdom and strategic courage. In 1992, the 14th National Congress of the CPC outlined a strategy to build a socialist market economy and China entered a period of high-speed development. In particular, the aim to double China's GDP by 2000 was realized five years early and the average living standard moved away from the poverty level toward "fairly well-off." Thus, China's economic development was improving in all respects. From 1990 to 2000, China's GDP growth rate reached 10.4%, ranking first among the great powers. Because of China's development and global changes, the United States soon came to view China as its No. 1 potential strategic opponent.[22]

Before and after the Cold War, socialism suffered serious worldwide setbacks and China experienced a number of political disturbances. Furthermore, various economic challenges had negative impacts on China's reform and development. Furthermore, now that the Soviet Union was no longer a threat, the United States no longer required its alliance with China. Thus, China became a key opponent in the minds of US strategists. Since June 1989, the United States has taken the lead in imposing "sanctions" against China, and Sino-US relations deteriorated. Both parties have engaged in fierce competitions on a number of issues including human rights, "most favored nation" trade status, and weapon proliferation. In the second half of 1989, regarding the huge changes in

[22] As early as the beginning of the 1990s, US strategic experts engaged in fierce discussions about whether China posed a threat against the interests and safety of the United States and East Asia. For a relevant analysis, please see: Thomas J. Christensen, "Posing Problems without Catching Up: China's Rise and Challenges for U.S. Security Policy," *International Security*, Vol. 25, Issue 4, Spring 2001, pp. 5–40.

domestic and overseas situations, Deng Xiaoping proposed a series of strategic guidelines: "observe calmly, stabilize the camp, respond sedately, hide capacities and bide time, be honest, never stand out, and do something." Furthermore, he insisted on never being a mistreated bird and aimed to avoid letting the overall situation get out of control because of confrontations with other great powers. He insisted on doing something and saying something about the significant issues around interests that concerned Chinese sovereignty and security. Deng Xiaoping also stated the need to calmly evaluate the development of the situation, make the most of opportunities, and to do something on the basis of hiding China's capacities and biding time. These strategic guidelines focused on hiding capacities and biding time, doing something, the refusal to act as a mistreated bird, and to avoid fighting against the West. Thus, China withstood the pressure from Western sanctions and, in the end, voices of the international anti-China chorus had little effect. Meanwhile, Chinese leaders introduced a series of new and innovative ideas regarding China's international strategy. These specifically concerned the construction of a new international political and economic order, the construction, and creation of a strategic partnership, the advancement of regional cooperation, and fostering initiative.

As early as the 1980s, Deng Xiaoping examined the significant and profound changes in the international situation and proposed to build a fair and rational new political and economic order. On December 24, 1990, Deng Xiaoping commented to comrades in the central government that "it is impossible to do nothing on international issues. We should do something. What to do? I propose to actively facilitate the construction of a new international political and economic order."[23] Key leaders such as Jiang Zemin included the subject of establishing a new international political and economic order in subsequent speeches and political reports. China felt it necessary to facilitate the construction of a new international political and economic order to emphasize the inequality within the current international economic order (whereby the power lay with Western countries), to obtain the right to speak about the international order, and to strive for the sympathy and support of international public opinion. China then further mastered its strategy initiative, and managed to engage in the unification and cooperation of international powers, and this helped to direct the development of the international environment to benefit

[23] *Selective Works of Deng Xiaoping*, Vol. 3, p. 363.

Chinese development. Of course, after the Cold War ended, the reconstruction of the international order became the main objective of many countries. For instance, the United States continued to advocate an international order with itself as leader and was devoted to the pursuit of unipolar hegemony. In contrast, Japan proposed an international order that included the United States, Japan, and Europe as the core countries. Many developing countries also presented opinions about the reform of the international order. China joined in the discussion and continued to promote its Five Principles of Peaceful Coexistence. For instance, in 2002, Jiang Zemin included numerous Chinese propositions in the report presented at the 16th National Congress of the CPC: all countries should be mutually respectful and coordinate with other countries instead of imposing their will on others; the countries should mutually promote economic and common development instead of causing extreme disparity between the rich and poor; countries should learn from each other and aim for co-prosperity instead of expelling the culture of other races; countries should trust each other for security, act to safeguard each other, establish a new security concept of mutual trust, mutual benefits, equality, and coordination, and solve disputes via dialogue and cooperation instead of resorting to weapons or military force.[24] On May 28, 2003, Hu Jintao made a speech at the Moscow State Institute of International Relations and presented five recommendations to ensure the creation of a fair and rational new international political and economic order: to encourage the democratic practice of international relations; to maintain and respect the diversity of the world; to establish a new security concept of mutual trust, mutual benefits, equality, and coordination; advance balanced global economic development; and to respect the important role played by the UN and the UN Security Council. Meanwhile, China associated the new order with multipolarization, and considered multipolarization as the foundation to facilitate the construction of a new international order. Furthermore, it reached agreement on the strategic intention to facilitate multipolarization and the construction of a new international order via a joint declaration. China then obtained the important right to speak on the construction of the international order. During this period, China's state power enjoyed significant growth, and cooperation between China and the international community grew stronger. Similarly, common interests grew and the compatibility of national interests strengthened, which provided important

[24] *Document Collection of the 16th National Congress of the CPC*, Beijing: Renmin Publishing House, 2002, p. 46.

support for positive interactions between China and the international order, as well as the necessary conditions for the use of initiative.

Because of the pressure of Western sanctions after the Cold War and the promotion of environmental reform, the improvement of relations among the great powers and surrounding relations became a priority for China, and this became an important strategic measure with which to promote the construction of development partnerships. In 1993, China and Brazil first proposed a strategic partnership, and in 1994, China and Russia reached consensus regarding forming a partnership (it was the first partnership determined in public by China via a joint declaration). In 1996, the initiative to create Chinese partnerships expanded to neighboring countries and China created partnerships with Pakistan and Nepal, and the partnership with Russia was later upgraded to a strategic coordinative partnership. In 1997, China and France established a comprehensive partnership, and China and the United States decided to create a constructive strategic partnership. In 1998, China and Britain established a comprehensive partnership. China and various European countries have established long-term stable and constructive partnerships and China has also established a partnership with South Korea. In 2000, China began a partnership with South Africa. In the 1990s, the proposal and implementation of Chinese partnership improved the Chinese environment and became an important path for China to facilitate the sound reform of the international order. Upon entering the twenty-first century, China's partnership strategy can be viewed as a huge success.[25] China currently has partnerships with nearly 100 countries and national organizations, and has created a worldwide partnership network. This partnership strategy represented a new means of exploration that enabled China to build new international relations and facilitate the construction of a new international order.

When the Cold War ended, the "China threat theory" was propagated in the international community and especially among those countries neighboring China; it was, of course, purposefully instigated by certain countries. However, the shock of China's rise indeed impacted on neighboring countries and concerns about China's future direction grew. China then had to determine how it could pacify neighboring countries and promote the concept of sharing and stability; this became a key priority. China also recognized

[25] Men Honghua and Liu Xiaoyang, *Strategic Evaluation and Outlook of Chinese Partnership*, collected in *World Economics and Politics*, Issue 2, 2015, pp. 65–95.

its location as a great advantage, and ignored the impulse to join in the power competition among the international community. China sought to establish relations in East Asia, built on diplomacy, and began to effectively unify the construction of global and regional orders. Thus, China realized the value of its concepts and strategies for a new international order.

With the rise of China's national strength, its influence on affairs in East Asia increased. In the mid-1990s, China left behind its indifferent and passive attitude toward regional cooperation and instead engaged in a new pattern of behavior: China engaged in positive cooperation with neighboring countries in terms of the economy, security, and military, and became a key proponent of the construction of a regional order in East Asia. Regarding the economy, China pushed forward the creation of the China–ASEAN Free Trade Area (CAFTA) and stated that the "10+3 mechanism" can be developed into a major channel for cooperation in East Asia. China also worked hard to construct cooperative regional economic, trade, investment, and security frameworks. In terms of security, China proposed mutual trust, mutual benefits, equality, and coordination, and turned these new security concepts into practice with the construction of the Shanghai Cooperation Organization; this then extended to the creation of CAFTA. These achievements provided a positive base from which China could cooperate with other Asian countries.[26] China also strengthened cooperation with ASEAN countries in the non-traditional field of security. Regarding the military, China has actively broadened its cooperation with other central great powers and has embodied an unprecedented positive attitude toward anti-terrorism, the prevention of the spread of weapons, and united military exercises. The mechanism for cooperation in East Asia (and facilitated by China) represents the country's new diplomatic policy whereby it aims to create and cultivate a regional order that is equal, cooperative, mutually beneficial, and provides mutual aid. This is created on the basis of common interests in the region, which are affiliated to China's interests, and aims to put an end to long-standing misunderstanding and complaints. Thus, China seeks to explore and gradually determine new guidelines for relations between countries and international relations.

Since 1997, China has taken the maxim, "responsible power," as the benchmark for its international status and has further focused to establish its own international image. China is turning from a great regional power

[26] Men Honghua, *Reconstruction of Chinese Strategic Culture: A Survey on the Agenda*, collected in *Teaching and Research*, Issue 1, 2006, pp. 57–63.

with global influence to a world power, and now plays an increasingly important role in global peace, security, and development. This demands that China should establish a responsible, constructive, and appropriate image of a great power and provide more global and regional public goods. During Asia's financial crisis in 1997–1999, China established the image of a responsible great power and won the respect of other Asian countries.

Since then, China's strategy has turned from one of introversion to extroversion. China has worked hard to become integrated into the international community, and it has expanded its strategic interests to become an active global participant. The end of the Cold War motivated China to end its diplomatic isolation. Thus, for China, an important element of the strategy is how it can gain the acceptance of the international community. Only in this way can China ensure the appropriate international environment to achieve its basic objective of national development. As China accelerates its integration into the international community, its strategy has more room in which to operate, but its vulnerability to external impacts increases. Furthermore, as China's power grows, so too does international pressure resulting from the "China threat theory." China's accelerated integration with Europe and the United States has also produced considerable international pressure. This pressure encouraged China toward integration with East Asia. China possesses sound judgment regarding the international environment and clearly understands its own state power. Thus, there is a degree of flexibility within its national objectives and international goals.

China's strategy announcement of "responsible power" reflects the country's significant shift in self-identification. It represents the meeting of China's traditional identification as an independent great power, with sovereignty at the core, and a new perception as a responsible great power. The latter has a very direct affiliation with China's integration into the international system, meaning that China's state behavior is changing because of such involvement. Thus, integration into the international system requires that China breaks long-term barriers and earns goodwill. In respect of the international community or significant global issues, China's integration process is constantly improving and is becoming increasingly cooperative. In addition, China not only promotes participation in the international system but shows growing positivity. Thus, China is a positive participant and therefore its capacity for agenda creation has been enhanced. China decided to pursue a strategy of integration into the international community and expanded its state strategic benefits via participating, creating, and guiding the international system. China has also actively participated in the improvement of the international system and in the creation of the international system in new fields. Thus, China is increasingly leaving its mark on the international system, and its capacity to shape the international system has also been enhanced.[27]

As China's international status improves, its views on the international order are considered more reasonable. China recognizes that the current international order is dominated by the West and that it is indeed unfair and irrational in many respects. However, China's position in the present international order has gradually improved. In addition, based on China's objective evaluations of the advantages and disadvantages of the current international order, and under the present UN-dominant global institutional system, China occupies a clearly favorable political position; there are also more economic advantages than disadvantages. Thus, the current international order is a double-edged sword for China: as China joins the international community, both its power and benefits have grown; however, because the current international order is based on fixed power and benefit patterns, this limits the expansion of China's power and benefits. China must therefore participate in the construction and reform of the international political and economic order to remedy the unfair and irrational aspects of the current order. This should be done in a gradual, peaceful, and democratic approach, that is, in the manner of a responsible great power. China is also now aware of the arduous nature of constructing a new international order. It has actively facilitated the construction of the East Asian order in a pragmatic manner and has new ideas for the construction of the international order.

5 China's Strategic Path to Forming a New World Order (2005–)

Upon entering the twenty-first century, China's development accelerated and its level of GDP exceeded the original objective, which of itself seemed impossibly high. In 2010, China surpassed Japan to become the second largest economic power. Chinese foreign trade also enjoyed rapid

[27] Men Honghua, *Pressure, Cognition and International Image—Historical Explanation on Chinese Participation in International System Strategy*, collected in *World Economics and Politics*, Issue 4, 2005, pp. 17–22.

growth and, in 2014, China became the largest foreign trade country in the world. As China's Go Out policy develops, especially regarding the proposal and implementation of the BRICS Development Bank, the Asian Infrastructure Investment Bank, and the "One Belt and One Road" strategy, so too has its foreign investment. China is also paying more attention to the construction of cultural soft power, which will further consolidate a foundation for China's peaceful ascent. Thus, China continues to deepen its integration into the international community in all aspects, as well as further its reform. In doing so, China engages in self-improvement. In face of the global financial crisis, China began to actively participate in a process to reshape the world order, seeking to gradually form a strategic framework to achieve integration and reform. Thus, a key element of China's great strategy is the reform of the international order.

The strategic framework for China's peaceful development has been gradually established and enriched in the twenty-first century. After decades of exploration and subsequent results, in December 2005, China published a white article titled *China's Path to Peaceful Development*. This article was the first to propose the idea of "advancing the international order to develop in a fairer and more rational direction." This is a new formulation that shows that China is willing to engage in the reform of the current international political and economic order as a responsible great power. Thus, China believes that the reform of the international order should occur in a gradual, peaceful, and democratic way. The report presented at the 18th National Congress of the CPC proposed to "promote the international order and international system to develop in a fair and rational direction." This also suggests that China, as a responsible great power, is willing to engage in the gradual, peaceful, and democratic reform of the international order. Thus, Chinese leaders have outlined a new harmonious society and expounded a traditional idea as a solution to international issues. They have presented the idea of a harmonious world, a harmonious Asia, and a harmonious region, and emphasize that the existence of a harmonious society and world are dependent upon each other. The proposal of a harmonious world represents a utopian ideal for the international order. Harmony is also a commitment, not only for domestic populations but also for the whole world. The commitment equates to a responsibility and becomes a kind of restraint on the "responsible power" self-strategy of China's government. This means that Chinese leaders are clearly aware of the influence that China's development has on the international community, and regard the harmonious world as a strategic intermediate point with which to combine domestic harmony and external cooperation.

If the idea of a "harmonious world" is expressed in terms of a strategy, the corresponding realistic strategic path is the pursuit of common interests, mutual benefits, and win-win outcomes. The term "common interest" was first included in the political report of the 15th National Congress of the CPC in September 1997 and proposed to "seek the convergence point of common interests" with developed countries. The political report of the 16th National Congress of the CPC expressed the goal to "expand common interests with developed countries." Similarly, leaders such as Hu Jintao and Wen Jiabao advised that it is essential to "maintain the common interests of developing countries." The report presented at the 17th National Congress of the CPC clearly outlined a strategy for common interests: "share development opportunities, respond to various challenges, and push forward processes for the peace and development of humankind." The report presented at the 18th National Congress of the CPC further pointed out that China should be "advocating a sense of community of human destiny, giving consideration to the pursuit of one's own interests and rational care for other countries; facilitating the common development of countries while seeking one's own development, as well as building an equal and balanced new global development partnership. Help each other, bear rights and liabilities together, and enhance the common interests of humankind." China's leaders are also aware that China's engagement in international affairs represents the rapid expansion of the relevant agenda and that it is both possible and necessary to consolidate and expand common interests with other countries. China has become an affiliated party to both global and regional benefits, and must strengthen and expand shared interests. This follows China's international strategy and complies with China's long-term strategic interests.[28] In October 2005, the Fifth Plenary Session of the 16th Central Committee of the CPC proposed to implement a strategy comprising mutual benefits and win-win outcomes. Thus, the Central Committee emphasized that only mutual benefits and win-win outcomes can safeguard the continuing success of China's basic national policy of opening-up to the outside. This strategy will also safeguard the further development of China's overseas

[28] Men Honghua, *Openness and State Strategy System*, Beijing: Renmin Publishing House, 2008, pp. 199–202.

benefits. Furthermore, it will not only realize the strategic objective of China's development but also help to establish a respectable image in terms of China's peaceful development. Mutual benefits and win-win results have been identified as the necessary foundation for relations with the outside world, in which China's international competence is enhanced and reflects the fact that China is paying significant attention to the interests of other countries while achieving its own development. Mutual benefits and win-win outcomes are the key elements of China's opening strategy in a new historical period. They reflect China's pursuit of its goals as a responsible great power. The report presented at the 18th National Congress of the CPC emphasized that China would unswervingly pursue a strategy of mutual benefits and win-win outcomes, as well as facilitate the powerful, sustainable, and balanced economic growth of the world through further cooperation. China is focused on narrowing the gap between the North and the South, and aims to support developing countries to strengthen their capacity for independent development. China will reinforce the coordination of macroscopic political policies with main economic entities, and properly solve economic and trading conflicts via negotiation. China also insists on balancing its rights and obligations, and will actively engage in global economic governance. Similarly, it aims to continue to push forward the liberalization and facilitation of its trade and investments, and opposes various forms of protectionism.

Since the 18th National Congress of the CPC, the new central leaders have worked hard to facilitate the creation of a modernized system of Chinese national governance and capacity. Furthermore, they wish to lead China to further integration within the international community and strive to have a greater international influence. To achieve these aims would symbolize that China has entered a new era whereby China's reform and opening-up is further developed. Entering the second decade of the twenty-first century, Chinese state power has been further advanced. For example, China's economic power and comprehensive power now rank second in the world and its industrial added value and foreign trade turnover rank first in the world. The report presented at the 18th National Congress of the CPC included the aim to establish a moderately well-off society in all aspects by 2020. Xi Jinping proposed "China's Dream" and the "Two Centenary Objectives." Following the above strategies, China's decision makers have actively pursued the further reform of the system, and seek to construct a national system of governance and to promote the state's governance capacity. The leaders have also participated in international affairs and this has helped China to achieve the status of a constructive participant and a dominant power in terms of global economic governance and the construction of the world order. Thus, China's role as a great power is prominent. China's leaders have also introduced a new series of diplomatic ideas and these have enriched China's diplomatic system. China's rise in the world has been very clear to China's leaders, and they have been mindful to "promote the world by virtue and admire the world," while insisting on mutual benefits and win-win results. They have also emphasized cooperation based on the common interests of countries, and have offered to bear a greater share of the international responsibilities. Furthermore, China is building and developing a common-interest community, a responsible community, and a community of common destiny with other countries. China is now calling for "communities of common destiny," and has introduced a number of new projects including establishing new great power relations, co-constructing a "Silk Road Economic Belt" and "Maritime Silk Road," and moving forward with a new "benevolent outlook." China also advocates for developing countries to give greater attention to both morals and profits, but with a preference for morals, and links a country's development to its neighbors and developing countries. It is also crucial that mutual trust and cooperation among countries is improved.

China seeks to expand its national strategic benefits and now focuses on entering a new era of diplomacy characterized by "common benefits," "mutual benefits and win-win outcomes," and "Chinese responsibilities."[29] In the face of international vicissitudes, Chinese diplomacy has become built on initiative. China's leaders have a strong desire to seek cooperation and achieve win-win outcomes for the world. They also express the need to actively engage in the international order and global governance. Thus, they have suggested a series of important projects and have entered many important agreements; these will directly influence regional benefits and further initiate the evolution of the world pattern, and also strengthen China's right to speak about international affairs, especially regional affairs. China proposes and has actively implemented "new relations between great powers" with the United States and advocates the sound development of Sino-US relations in bilateral and multilateral settings. China is aware of the

[29] Men Honghua, *Open a New Era of China's Comprehensive Deepening Reform and Opening—And China's Great Strategic Direction in Following Ten Years*, collected in *Study & Exploration*, Issue 8, 2015, pp. 41–45.

global shake up stemming from its rise in the world, but seeks a peaceful development road, and welcomes other countries to develop alongside it. China wishes to develop friendly cooperative relations with other countries around the world and for all to share in any development bonuses. Thus, China recognizes the importance of developing relations with neighboring countries and as such diplomacy is the showing of good will and friendship to neighbors. Such behavior will bring harmony, security, and prosperity to neighbors, and it emphasizes the concepts of friendliness, sincerity, benefits, and tolerance.[30] To further expand the concept of diplomacy, China has created a master blueprint and proposed various projects such an upgraded version of the Sino-ASEAN Free Trade Zone, the Asian Infrastructure Investment Bank, and a twenty-first-century "Silk Road Economic Belt" and "Maritime Silk Road." China has also made calls for countries to create mutual benefits and a win-win "community of shared interests" and a "community of common destiny" with common development and prosperity. Thus, China seeks to energetically promote cooperative relations with neighboring countries. Because China is a great regional power and is marching toward becoming a great world power, East Asia is growing in importance as the regional core of China's big strategy. China seeks to upgrade its East Asian strategy and to actively facilitate the systematization of cooperation in the region. This includes cooperation among East Asian countries to build a Sino-ASEAN community of common destiny and to establish a Sino-ASEAN Maritime Cooperation Fund. Similarly, China plans to develop maritime cooperation and work with other East Asian countries to build a "Maritime Silk Road" for the twenty-first century. Proposals have also been made to create an upgraded version of the Sino-ASEAN Free Trade Zone, to guide the foundation of the Asian Infrastructure Investment Bank, and to support East Asian countries to establish a Bangladesh–China–India–Myanmar economic corridor. By offering guidance for regional arrangements and facilitating other East Asian countries to adjust to its ascent, China's development has led the way for all-region cooperation, allays the concerns of East Asia, brings together common interests, and deepens regional awareness. It also strives to play a powerful building and guidance role in the construction of a new order in East Asia and even in the Asia–Pacific region.[31]

[30] Xi Jinping, *Xi Jinping Discusses Governance and Administration*, Beijing: Foreign Language Press, 2014, p. 297.

[31] Men Honghua, *Discussion on the Prospect of Order Construction in East Asia*, collected in *Teaching and Research*, Issue 2, 2015, pp. 56–62.

In summary, China's ascent both impacts and changes the patterns of international power and interests. It follows then that China's various initiatives, the Five Principles of Peaceful Coexistence, the new concept of security, and overall concept of national security, democracy in international relations, civilization diversity, harmonious world, and the world dream, have become important factors influencing the reform of the international order. As China's integration into the international community deepens, it will not only become a valued participant in the global international system but also actively engage in helping to establish a regional system. China has become an important force in reshaping the distribution of international power. China is still rising, and as such, with its constructive, cooperative, and appropriate status, it continues to challenge the international order to develop in a fair and rational direction. Regarding the international political order, China asks that others respect the world's diversity, and pushes forward democratic practices in international relations, while also encouraging multilateralism and general national security. China proposes the use of dialogue to resolve international disputes, and regarding the international economic order, China recommends common prosperity and common development, and steps to narrow the gap between the North and South. China believes it is important to facilitate balanced and sustainable global economic and social development. In terms of detailed mobilization, China calls for comprehensive security at a global level as well as strengthening cooperative security regulation and system protection. Furthermore, at the regional level, China wishes to accelerate the capacity for regional development, while also seeking to establish a new regional order and to provide a reference for the foundation of a new international order and the creation of a new regional foundation.

The recent collapse of the international financial order presented China with an opportunity. China now seeks to help re-establish a new order, while playing a greater role and bearing more responsibilities within the international community. China also hopes to advance the RIO at both regional and global levels. At the global level, China insists on safeguarding the authority of the UN and facilitating the UN to play a positive role. China also hopes to expand its international influence by establishing a worldwide partnership network and by promoting China's role in the international community via the implementation of the "One Belt and One Road" strategy, the implementation of a financial cooperation mechanism for countries, and the strengthening of the "Go Out" strategy.

Similarly, China's leaders are working hard to turn its economic influence into a political influence. At the regional level, China proposes the concept of a friendly, sincere, beneficial, and prosperous regional order, and hopes to develop greater regional cooperation and also allay the concerns of East Asia. Furthermore, China will ensure common benefits, deepen regional awareness, and play a powerful role in building and guiding the construction of a new East Asian order, or even a new Asian order. China has begun the RIO process, starting from a point with advanced technology, greater transparency, and certain advantages. For instance, the reform of the international financial order has been aided by guidance from investment banks and by mobilizing the Asian infrastructure. In other words, China aims to achieve a fairer and more rational international order in two ways: by first establishing an East Asian order and then a financial order. Thus, China's framework for peaceful development, its integration with the international community, and its own reform, have all led to the gradual creation of a new international order. China's construction of an international order is based on the growth of its state power and via the concepts of benefits (especially common benefit), ideas, and the construction of an international system.

6 Participating in the RIO at a Steady Pace

China's rise has largely occurred at the same time as the transformation of the international order. China has gradually become an important power in the RIO process. At present, the transformation of the international order provides numerous international conditions necessary for China's comprehensive rise. Countries from around the world drive the quest to develop the international order in a fair and rational direction; this also ensures essential international conditions for China's continued growth. In view of China's history, this is the first time that China has played a positive and comprehensive role in implementing change at a global level. The RIO is a systematic project, and the process needs to be carefully considered including the relevant concepts, power, and benefits. Only then should moves be made to gradually advance from bilateral implementation to multilateral implementation and from regional implementation to global implementation. This is explained below in detail:

First, China's positive participation in the RIO has enhanced its power and expanded its benefits. Furthermore, a country's role in the new order relies on its own comprehensive power. Thus, the international order is based on a distribution of power. It is only because China emerged as a powerful country that it has been able to reshape the international order. The strengthening of state power comes not only from the development and cultivation of its domestic market but also from seeking strategic resources under globalization. Equally important is the strengthening of a country's hard power and soft power. Thus, a greater soft power sits at the core of enhancing state power. Furthermore, the international order comes from the distribution of benefits. Thus, developing countries must achieve greater benefits before any effective improvements and advancements occur within the international order.

Second, various cultural beliefs have had a positive effect on the construction of the international order. Chinese traditional culture is longstanding and profound. Many beliefs have philosophical meaning; for example, "be harmonious and friendly to neighboring countries," and "all living creatures grow together without harming each other, and run parallel without interfering with one another." Thus, such principles denote China's valuable inheritance and aid its development. With such a heritage, China should provide further guiding principles to the international order.

Third, it is important to recognize the effect of the international system on the construction of the international order. During any period of transformation, international conflicts always occur over international norms that have a strong impact on the development of the international order. China should aim to improve the basic rules of the globalized international system. It should also actively call for and guide the revision and improvement of the international system and the construction of a new international system. On the other hand, China should improve its agenda-setting capacity and fully participate in the readjustment of global rules. China also needs to advance the RIO with the construction of a new system and effectively maintain and facilitate China's national strategic benefits. It is also important to emphasize the effect of the UN and to actively push forward the reform of the UN to assure its authoritative status as the basis of the international system.

Fourth, there needs to be a greater emphasis on the establishment of an order in East Asia, which will act as the base point. China should fully recognize the regional effect of its ascent, work to reduce any negative impacts stemming from its rise, and promote regional stability and common development. The CPC needs to improve "discussions about China" by the East Asian community, advance the design for a regional system, and strive to develop a transparent process for the construction of an East Asian community based on common benefits. Efforts must also be made to develop an East Asian community of shared benefits via systematic cooperation. A community must be established, one that is based on responsibilities whereby countries bear responsibilities together and important responsibilities are assigned to the great powers. An East Asian community of a common destiny should also be promoted. It is also essential that China cultivates and consolidates an equal, cooperative, East Asian order that is mutually beneficial, based on shared benefits, and an order where members assist each other. As the party affiliated to the key benefits of East Asia, China looks forward to entering an era, whereby it makes greater contributions to peaceful regional development, assumes regional responsibilities, and develops skills to its utmost potential. This process should follow the principle of gradual progress. Meanwhile, current regional affairs are numerous and complex and the countries all have different benefit requirements. A systemized foundation for regional cooperation can only be achieved following a gradual and orderly process to build a responsible community that bears responsibilities together and distributes important responsibilities to the great powers. Thus, awareness regarding a regional community of common destiny will be gradually strengthened. Therefore, China needs to deepen its understanding of regional public goods, work with other countries to achieve peaceful regional development, and objectively evaluate the fundamental benefit demands of other countries in the region. China must not only provide timely help but also realize shared prosperity to deepen awareness regarding an East Asian community of common destiny and to create an East Asian order.

Lastly, countries must actively bear the responsibility that comes with being a great power and establish a responsible, well-constructed, and appropriate image for inclusion in the international order. In an era characterized by the transformation of the international community, the need for basic moral principles remains; in fact, their value continues to grow. The moral image of a great power can be created in the following three ways: strengthen cooperation and coordination between countries, safeguard international morality, and preserve the basic principles of international law. Such actions are also necessary for China to expand state benefits to the world. China is marching forward, transitioning from a great regional power with global influence toward a great global power with a greater effect on global peace, security, and development. This, however, requires that China further improve its image as a responsible great power in the international community, provide more global and regional public goods, and become a responsible contributor in the creation of a new international order.

CHAPTER 9

China's Road and Its Illuminations Toward Developing Countries

Li Bin

In the past 40 years since China's adoption of its reform and opening-up policy, Chinese society has witnessed profound and dramatic changes on both the material and spiritual level and, in contrast to when the People's Republic of China was founded, it has exerted an unprecedented global impact on the world. However, it must be acknowledged that China has still followed a dependent development path in the past 40 years, though featuring the least dependency and the greatest autonomy among all the developing countries that have taken a similar approach. China's development experience not only is significant for the enhancement and development of the underdevelopment theory but also serves as a role model for those developing countries that wish to free themselves from dependency in their own development. The theoretical significance of China's development for the underdevelopment theory is that it acknowledges the possibility that the capitalist world economy can provide developing countries with certain opportunities for development, and emphasizes the necessity for developing countries to transform their inappropriate systems and formulate suitable development strategies in order to seize opportunities for development. What developing countries can learn from China's develop-

L. Bin (✉)
School of Political Science & International Relations, Tongji University, Shanghai, China

H. Men (ed.), *On China's Road*,
https://doi.org/10.1007/978-981-13-7880-5_9

ment is that export-oriented development is the only way for them to realize modernization. However, they should also be reminded to embrace an organic and progressive opening-up rather than pursuing an irrational and uncontrolled integration into the world economy. The government, as an extremely important player in this process, should be strong enough to provide a stable political environment and a sustainable nationalist development strategy because these are essential to attracting foreign capital and to reforming the domestic economy.

1 Evolution of the Underdevelopment Theory

The underdevelopment theory was formulated by foreign left-wing scholars to explore the causes of underdevelopment and development strategies, with its theoretical origin largely linked to Marxism. However, from Karl Marx to today's left-wing development theorists, the understanding of development issues has changed. With respect to the causes of underdevelopment, Marx believed that it was caused by the traditional social mode of production or the social structure of developing countries, while the post-war Marxists disagree with this view and claim that the primary cause of underdevelopment lies in the world political and economic order formed by the capitalist mode of production. In terms of the road to development, Marx deemed that underdeveloped countries can also become developed countries as long as they import the capitalist mode of production, as in the typical cases of the United States and Australia. However, the post-war underdevelopment theorists have a different perspective. According to the structuralism theory, the underdevelopment of developing countries is attributed to the international economic structure devised by developed countries, a structure that has resulted in unequal exchanges between the core economies and the peripheral countries, which leads to the further backwardness of these peripheral underdeveloped countries. The dependency theorists argue that the capitalist mode of production dictates that advanced capitalism is bound to squeeze economic surplus from developing countries, subjugating the latter in the global economic order that is dominated by the developed countries. This is similar to the capitalist domestic production process in which the workers remain poor under the exploitation of capitalists. However, after the 1970s, some of these scholars began to re-examine the causes of underdevelopment in developing countries. They believe that such underdevelopment has resulted from the capitalist world economy as well as from some intrinsic characteristics of underdeveloped countries, rather than from the capitalist world economy alone.

Marx's analysis of the reasons for the backwardness of underdeveloped nations was based on their traditional social patterns. In *The Future Results of British Rule in India*, Marx states that 'Britain must fulfill its dual mission in India: one is a mission of destruction, which is to destroy the old Asian-style society; and the other is a mission of construction, which is to lay the material foundation for a Western-style society in Asia'.[1] Marx believed that Britain's development of capitalism in India would neither truly liberate the Indian people nor improve their social conditions, yet it could develop their productivity.[2] Here, Marx put forward the important hypothesis that the infiltration of capitalism in underdeveloped nations would disrupt their original modes of production and social systems and initiate the construction of a capitalist civilization that would ultimately transform them into developed countries. (In this article, Marx postulated that the future of India under British rule would be identical to that of the developed Britain). Marx thought that such development would not bring fortune and liberation to the ordinary British people nor to the local Indian people, because the productivity was not owned by the people, even if the infiltration of capitalism had created the material basis for a new civilization. However, Marx actually blamed India's backwardness on its traditional mode of production. In the preface to *Das Kapital*, Marx made this point of view more explicit. When referring to the relatively underdeveloped Germany at that time, Marx said that countries like Germany, which lagged behind Britain, 'suffer from both the development and the underdevelopment of capitalist production. In addition to modern disasters, we are also oppressed by many legacy disasters which arise from the old-fashioned modes of production and the outdated yet still existing social and political relations accompanying them'.[3] Therefore, Marx attributed the underdevelopment largely to the insufficiency of capitalist development and the constraints of pre-capitalist modes of production, including the deficiencies in the relations of production.

Most of the post-war radical development theorists address the causes of underdevelopment from the perspective of the capitalist world economic structure and try to demystify these causes based on the distribution

[1] *Marx/Engels Collected Works*, Vol. 1, Beijing: People's Publishing House, 1995, p. 768.
[2] Ibid., p. 771.
[3] *Marx/Engels Collected Works*, Vol. 2, Beijing: People's Publishing House, 1995, p. 100.

of such a production structure. The underdevelopment theory is divided into the structuralism theory and the more radical dependency theory.

According to the structuralists, trade does not play an effective role in propelling the economic development of developing countries. Due to the historical international division of labor in developed countries, there has been a fixed exchange pattern for industrial capital goods and primary products, under which peripheral developing countries provide agricultural products, mineral products, and primary processed products to central developed countries. Because of the low flexibility in the demand for these products, underdeveloped countries have long been subject to unfair trade arrangements and have been unable to benefit and develop from international trade. Structuralists point out that the key to economic development and productivity improvement is technological progress. However, the international exchange resulting from the historically formed division of labor between the central and peripheral countries, though having facilitated technological progress in the developing countries, has prevented them from improving their international trade conditions and caused the dilemma of 'immiserating growth', with growth in production but not in profits. As a result, they are unable to gain the momentum for technological development that the liberal trade theorists suggest. This explains why the structuralists believe that the underlying reason for the backwardness of underdeveloped countries lies in the international division of labor and the resultant trade patterns.

According to the dependency theory, underdevelopment results from the Western powers' desire to attach developing countries to developed capitalism and their refusal to fully develop the capitalist mode of production in these countries. Paul Baran, the father of the dependency theory, believes that 'the economic development of underdeveloped countries is very detrimental to the interests of developed capitalist countries', because underdeveloped countries 'provide substantial profits and investment solutions' to developed countries, serving as a necessary hinterland for the developed capitalist countries of the West; therefore, the United States and other Western powers strongly oppose the industrialization of developing countries.[4] In Baran's opinion, the Western capitalist world requires underdeveloped countries to maintain their traditional modes of

[4] Paul Baran, *The Political Economy of Growth*, Cai Zhongxing and Yang Yuguang, trans., Beijing: The Commercial Press, 2000, p. 96.

production, because the non-capitalist modes of production in developing countries can cause an accumulation of their dependency on the capitalist modes of production in the world market, thereby directly providing economic surpluses for the capitalist world market. Trade and investment are the economic means by which developed countries extract a large amount of the economic surplus from developing countries. Such a global production and division of labor structure has prevented underdeveloped countries from fully developing the capitalist mode of production. They have no choice but to succumb to the capitalist economy and are proscribed from growing into developed countries that are comparable to the existing developed countries. This thinking has its origins in the 'law of unbalanced and comprehensive development'. Specifically, the economic development of underdeveloped countries is in an unbalanced state, with a combination of both the capitalist mode of production and the pre-capitalist mode of production. The non-capitalist one provides accumulation for the capitalist one, and the capitalist one provides accumulation for the world economy. This is how the developing countries remain underdeveloped. In such cases, 'dependent' is the best expression to describe the status of developing countries in the world's capitalist production process.

It is precisely for such economic reasons that the dependency theory assumes that international capital must control the politics of developing countries, manipulating their political structure to the benefit of the global capitalist economy so as to extract economic surpluses from them. This political structure has transitioned from the past colonial rule to the military autocracy system, and then to today's neoliberalism. At the same time, international capital, through its political agencies, also suppresses and isolates any developing countries that attempt to free themselves from the capitalist world economic system. In addition, in order to facilitate such an economic dependency, international capital also spreads a kind of 'Coca-Cola' culture in developing countries, mesmerizing the general public into ideologically agreeing with this dependency, accepting the political legitimacy of the capitalist world order, and imitating the consumption model of developed countries, thereby removing their resistance and revolutionary awareness. Worldwide capitalist reproduction will become a reality through the popularization of western consumer goods. Ultimately, developed capitalist countries will fully control developing countries and prevent them from developing an independent national economy.

However, according to proponents of the associated-dependent development theory represented by Fernando Henrique Cardoso in the early 1970s, the backwardness of underdeveloped countries is no longer solely a matter of world economic structure, but an issue jointly created by the world economic structure and the domestic social structure and development strategies of the developing countries themselves.[5]

Admittedly, there are certain differences between the post-war underdevelopment theory and Marxist thought on the analysis of the causes of underdevelopment. According to Marx, the pre-capitalist economic and social structure was at the root of underdevelopment, while the post-war underdevelopment theorists, despite certain divergences, all agree that the economic structure of the capitalist world is the root cause of underdevelopment because this structure largely hinders or prohibits underdeveloped countries from fully developing capitalism. The dependency theory assumes that underdevelopment is caused jointly by the backwardness of domestic social structures, as Marx believes, and the economic structure of the capitalist world.

In terms of the road to development, there are also differences between Marxist thought and the post-war underdevelopment theory. In *The Future Results of British Rule in India*, Marx mentions that 'only when the great social revolution possesses the achievements in the bourgeois era and dominates the world market and modern productive forces, and subjects them all to the supervision of the most advanced nations, will the progress of mankind no longer be like the macabre pagan gods who drink sweet wine from human skulls'.[6] In the preface to *Das Kapital*, Marx expresses this more explicitly: 'What the more industrially developed countries have shown to the less developed ones is the future vision of the latter'.[7] 'Even if a society has discovered the natural laws of its own movement … it can neither skip nor use laws and regulations to eliminate the natural stages of development, but it can shorten and alleviate the pain of its birth'.[8] Here, Marx believes that the road to development of underdeveloped countries is a kind of 'stage theory'. The introduction of capitalism into the pre-capitalist society and the development of capitalism in this society are essential for

[5] Fernando Henrique Cardoso, "Associated-Dependent Development: Theoretical and Practical Implications," in Alfred Stepan, ed., *Authoritarian Brazil, Origins, Policies, and Future*, Yale University Press, 1973, pp. 144–152.

[6] *Marx/Engels Collected Works*, Vol. 1, Beijing: People's Publishing House, 1995, p. 773.

[7] *Marx/Engels Collected Works*, Vol. 2, Beijing: People's Publishing House, 1995, p. 100.

[8] *Marx/Engels Collected Works*, Vol. 2, Beijing: People's Publishing House, 1995, p. 101.

the realization of development, which also creates material conditions for future social change.

Structuralists believe that in order to transform the backward economy of developing countries, it is imperative to change the unreasonable international exchange pattern and improve the trade conditions for underdeveloped countries. For this purpose, the developing countries have to set up international organizations for primary products, establish robust programs to protect their export products, develop independent industrial manufacturing to replace imports from developed countries, encourage foreign capital to invest in the manufacturing industries, create a common marketplace for underdeveloped countries, and reduce their dependence on developed countries. One of the biggest achievements of structuralism is that it has triggered a movement among developing countries to reform the unjust international economic order, a movement that aims to foster a favorable environment for the development of developing countries by reshaping the international economic environment. In fact, this road to development is also a kind of stage theory.

Some post-war dependency theorists believe that because Western powers need to preserve the mixed economic structure of developing countries so as to provide surpluses for the world economy, it is impossible for developing countries to fully develop capitalism and join the ranks of developed countries. Therefore, only through national democratic revolution and a breakaway from the economic system of the capitalist world can developing countries truly achieve development, as other development models all have their limitations.[9] To put it simply, this is a 'leapfrog theory', which means undeveloped nations, after gaining their national independence, should firstly free themselves from the capitalist world market, and then develop themselves by constructing socialism (establishing a new mode of production), instead of going through the all-round development phase of capitalism. This idea is consistent with China's development thinking before its reform and opening-up. China's ideological maxims, such as 'the capitalist road to development does not work for China' and 'only socialism can save China', are the embodiment of this development thinking.

In the face of the investment of Western multinational companies in some emerging industrialized countries, especially the 'East Asian Miracle' of the 1960s and 1970s, some left-wing scholars put forward the so-called

[9] Theotonio Dos Santos, *Imperialism and Dependence*, Yang Yanyong et al., trans., Beijing: Social Sciences Academic Press, 1999, pp. 460–488.

associated-dependent development theory. Fernando Henrique Cardoso, who proposed this theory, believed that dependency and development may co-exist in some developing countries under a particular historical structure; a coordinated political and economic structure between the authoritarian government and transnational capital and the emerging middle class (i.e., the national industrial capital that is associated with the transnational capital) in developing countries. Under this political and economic structure, the authoritarian government guarantees the country's social stability and provides political security. The implementation of the modernization development strategy under state capitalism is the basic condition for domestic political and economic development. Multinational companies' investment in these developing countries is used to boost their economies and help nurture their middle classes, so as to ensure the continuation and expansion of sales and production, which is the external driving force of development. In association with transnational capital, local modern national capital can participate in and undertake the low-end production for multinational companies, which also provides certain room for development and forms a symbiosis between local capital and foreign capital. Under this political structure, dependent development occurs in some developing countries. Such 'associated-dependent development' or dependent development is not autonomous. In fact, these developing countries do not have full control over their technology nor the financial mechanisms for economic development; consequently, they are affected by transnational capital and the international market, as well as severely polarized distribution.[10] Another dependent development scholar, Peter Evans, supports this proposition that dependency and development can co-exist and believes the alliance of local capital, international capital, and national capital in the peripheral countries can provide an important condition for dependent development.[11] To some extent, this dependent development theory recognizes the opportunities brought about by transnational production and its role in promoting the development of developing countries. The theory has evolved from the stage of rejecting the influences of the world market and transnational capital, to the stage of

[10] Fernando Henrique Cardoso, "Associated-Dependent Development: Theoretical and Practical Implications," in Alfred Stepan, ed., *Authoritarian Brazil, Origins, Policies, and Future*, Yale University Press, 1973, pp. 144–152.

[11] Peter Evans, Dependent Development, *The Alliance of Multinational, State, and Local Capital in Brazil*, Princeton University Press, 1979.

accepting their significance. It shares considerable similarities with the theory of China's reform and opening-up. In a sense, the development of China's reform and opening-up is aligned with the dependent development theory.

2 China's Road to Development and Its Impact on the Underdevelopment Theory

Since the late 1970s, due to the economic woes caused by the Cultural Revolution, the implementation of China's old import substitution strategy and central planning has faced enormous challenges. As a practical response, China has embarked on the journey of reform and opening-up, with particular emphasis on learning lessons from some developing countries. Generally, it follows the path of those countries that have created 'the Asian Miracle', a path that conforms to the characteristics of associated-dependent development, that is, a nationalistic development strategy under the authoritarian political system, and market-driven, export-oriented, and international capital-attracting development strategies under government regulation. Although this road to development is not unique to China, China's development is unique in the world, and it has blazed a trail of dependent development. In fact, it has made even greater achievements than many other developing countries. What is even more commendable is that it is lesser dependent than many of its peers. China's economy keeps growing rapidly and sustainably, and the Chinese people's living standards have been improved correspondingly. In contrast, the economic growth of countries that adhere to the traditional central planning is sluggish, and for those which adopt the 'Washington Consensus' and the radical free market system, their growth is unstable. It proves that China is the most successful country in the past four decades in terms of dependent development, and its success also confirms the feasibility of the dependent road to development. China's dependent development also has its salient problems, such as a shortage of proprietary technologies, the constraints of external markets and capital in its economic development, a seriously polarized distribution, resource and energy bottlenecks, serious environmental and ecological problems, and severe corruption, and so on. However, compared with those developing countries which have a smaller market size and are radically integrating themselves into the international economic system, China is relatively less dependent and has greater autonomy in its development, such as a relatively larger number of proprietary technologies, a self-controlled financial system and less susceptibility to the international financial crisis, substantial foreign exchange reserves, and greater autonomy in economic and social development. Based on these considerations, we can see that China's development over the past 40 years has two basic characteristics: firstly, it follows the path of dependent development; secondly, it has relatively greater autonomy in its development than other non-Western nations. These two basic characteristics, especially the latter one, have provided significant insights for the enhancement and development of the underdevelopment theory, summarized as:

1. *It overcomes the weakness of the traditional underdevelopment theory which overemphasizes the negative impacts of the external economic environment without seeing the possible opportunities provided by the capitalist world economy to underdeveloped countries.* Since the Second World War, the United States has implemented gradual changes to the modes of production and organization all over the world. As this new global mode of production, characterized by the transnational mode of production and organization, began to develop,[12] especially after the end of the Cold War, such changes were accelerated.[13] With these changes in the capitalist mode of production and organization, the world economy provides developing countries with unprecedented opportunities for development. Under the transnational mode of production, capital aggregates according to factors of global production based on the comparative advantages of each country, resulting in a transnational production chain dominated by transnational capital wherein products are being manufactured in different countries. The organization mode of transnational production, as one of the main features of the current economy, is different from previous international production which was mainly characterized by domestic production and organization. The international mode of production used to be dominated by the

[12] Stephen Hymer, A pioneer in transnational production research with a Marxist tendency, has made a good analysis of the United States' promotion of overseas expansion of transnational corporations and their causes, see Stephen Hymer, "The Multinational Corporation and the Law of Uneven Development," in Jagdish Bhagwati, ed., *Economics and World Order*, New York: Macmillan, 1974, pp. 113–135.

[13] For related description, see Jeffry A. Frieden, *Global Capitalism: Its Fall and Rise in the Twentieth Century*, Yang Yuguang et al., trans., Shanghai: Shanghai People's Publishing House, 2009, pp. 383–386.

domestic production of developed countries, making products that were exported to global markets, including to developing countries, in exchange for raw materials. This mode severely hampered the industrialization of developing countries. However, under the new mode of transnational production, the transnational capital of developed countries is dependent on developing countries, with their comparative advantages in labor and environmental protection, for expanding the international production chain. This provides certain external conditions for the industrialization of developing countries, which is precisely evidenced by the practice of China's road to development.

2. *It stresses that in the capitalist world economy, underdeveloped countries should actively seek useful strategies rather than passively following a planned economy and isolating themselves from the external markets.* Developing countries should be adept at observing new changes in the world economy, proactively reforming their domestic economic and political systems, and making full use of their comparative advantages, so that they can also capture development opportunities offered by the capitalist world economic system. This approach can overcome the weakness of the early dependency theory which neglected the internal factors, a deficiency which has long been criticized by development theorists. Although the dependent development theory has addressed this deficiency theoretically, it is the relative success of China's road that has proved, in practice, the significance of the internal factors of developing countries in the capitalist world economy. In the process of developing countries' integration into the world economy, the more active role their internal factors play, the healthier their road to development will be.
3. *The problems in China's road to development, such as its dependency, have also proved the assumption of the underdevelopment theory that the external world economic order is structurally restraining the development of developing countries.* This confirms the necessity of reforming the international economic order. In addition, it not only provides a realistic basis for developing countries to participate in the global governance of the international economy and promote the development of the international economic order toward a fairer direction in the future, it also raises topics for the theorists to promote the further evolution of the underdevelopment theory. The problems posed to most developing countries in their opening-up

process are the same as those of China, and can only be fully addressed by adjusting the world economic structure for win-win cooperation at the global economic governance level. As such, theorists are required to put forward their own theory of global economic governance. Judging from the history of the underdevelopment theory, the proposition of the structuralism theory in the 1970s—that the unbalanced exchange caused by the international economic structure is the root cause of the underdevelopment of developing countries—laid the foundation for the establishment of a just international economic order. The early dependency theory believes that the external capitalist world economic order hinders the development of developing countries, which provides a theoretical basis for many developing countries to take a radical road to development and sever their connections with the capitalist world market. Today, the common problems many developing countries have encountered during their opening-up will certainly motivate the development theorists to provide a new theory of global economic governance.

Theoretical development comes from practice, and practice raises issues for theoretical development. China's road actually represents the common practice of most developing countries since the 1970s. As a role model for past theoretical practice, China's success has verified these early theories and provided excellent material for theoretical development. In summary, China's development experience is indisputably significant for the enhancement and development of the underdevelopment theory and it has also heralded new requirements for theoretical development.

3 Implications of China's Road for Developing Countries

Since the 1970s, China has been successful in shifting from inward development to outward development; this is manifested not only in its economic development but also in the fact it features the least dependency of the numerous countries that have taken the path of outward development. China's success has the following implications for developing countries:

Firstly, it proves that developing countries grow faster when they become a part of the capitalist world economic system rather than seeking independent development outside of the system. Prior to the introduction of capitalist industrialization, underdeveloped countries were feudal or semi-feudal, or even more socially backward than a feudal society. This meant that their historical social systems could not provide the conditions, resources, and skills for industrialization, so their societies were not capable of industrialization. Due to the lack of powerful determinants for modern development, and the strong internal social forces that impeded modernization, the modernization of these societies was beset by feudal influences and other backward factors. In this case, they needed to adopt capitalism to help them overcome their inherent resistance to development, and they needed external capital to provide them with the resources and skills for development. The internal impetus of the world capitalist system also needed to break through a closed feudal economy to achieve the free flow of capital worldwide. Marx said that the importation of capitalism has a dual effect on backward nations. Firstly, it undermines local social structure, and secondly, it contributes to the capitalist development,[14] both of which are exactly what developing countries need for their development. Although there is a belief, from Lenin to the early dependency theorists, that when capitalism becomes a monopoly, developed countries do not expect a complete industrialization of those backward nations, because they need to use a large amount of the profits from these nations to ease their domestic social conflicts. What they need is nothing but the monopoly profits provided by the backward countries.[15] However, the new reality of post-war transnational production has changed the situation where developed countries only seek profits from developing countries and do not promote their development. In order to avoid a downward trend in profits brought by the welfare state, transnational corporations, driven by profits and competition, have carried out the cross-border distribution of production, having provided certain conditions for the development of developing countries, as 'only transnational corporations can ensure the connections between technologies, finance, organizations and markets'.[16] This effectively enables transnational corporations to have a positive influence on the development of developing countries. They hope to invest in the development of the host country, which will in turn provide themselves with the bases and markets for reproduction. In fact, 'any attempt by the already backward developing countries to isolate or separate themselves from [the world market] will only lead to a more brutal dominance

[14] *Marx/Engels Collected Works*, Vol. 1, Beijing: People's Publishing House, 1995, p. 255.
[15] Dudley Seers, ed., *Dependency Theory*, London: Frances Printer, Ltd., 1981, pp. 29–50.
[16] Ibid., *Authoritarian Brazil, Origins, Policies, and Future*, p. 149.

of the global system, and a retrogression toward weakness and poverty',[17] because such an attempt will deprive developing countries of any opportunities to gain external resources when they already lack the resources for modern development. Unlike some developing countries that have not participated in economic globalization, China has gained rich experience in reform and opening-up over the past 40 years; experience that proves that integration into the world economic system is a more practical and wise choice for developing countries. Therefore, an outward-oriented road to development is an inevitable choice for backward, developing countries to achieve preliminary modernization.

Secondly, it proves that for those developing countries which have already been a part of the capitalist world economic system, even if they are unable to free themselves from dependent development immediately, they can still reduce their degree of dependency and enhance autonomous development based on their own conditions and through their own efforts. In the process of transnational production, it is inevitable that developing countries become dependent with respect to their own capabilities and subordinate status, because they are incapable of withstanding the international market fluctuations and navigating the international market, easily falling victim to the fluctuating international market environment.[18] However, joining the capitalist world economic system is only comparatively the better of the two disadvantageous choices. In spite of the possible development opportunities for developing countries, such a choice will unavoidably result in dependency. China is no exception in this respect, as can be seen in the problems occurring during its development process over the past 40 years, such as the predominance of foreign-invested enterprises in providing its export revenue, the lack of proprietary technologies, the meager profits it receives from the industrial transfer and division of labor required by developed countries, severe environmental pollution, serious problems in domestic income distribution, and inefficient financial mechanisms that fail to address the possible external financial risks after full liberalization, and so on.

[17] Michael Hardt and Antonio Negri, *Empire*, Harvard University Press, 2000, p. 284.

[18] Although some development economists believe that such theories as the 'dependency theory' are outdated, in recent years some left-wing scholars in Western academic circles still use the 'dependency theory' to analyze developing countries' falling victims to the world market and explain there are so many difficulties in development, even if a country joins the world market, from multiple perspectives. For related thesis, see Kema Irgbe, "Globalization and the Development of Underdevelopment of the Third World," *Journal of Third World Studies*, Spring 2005, pp. 41–67.

On the other hand, China's road to development has also shown that as long as developing countries learn from the successful experiences of their counterparts and create certain domestic conditions, they can reduce the degree of dependency and enhance the autonomous development through their own efforts. China's development provides notable experiences in this regard.

According to the associated-dependent development theory, the success of China's development is largely due to its unique political structure and the wise governance of its leadership. This motivates China to follow a more stable nationalist development strategy and attach more importance to autonomy in the process of its reform and opening-up. The following points illustrate China's experiences:

Firstly, China's one-party leadership system is an important political guarantee of economic development, ensuring the stability of its society and the sustainability of its nationalist development strategy. In the course of reform and opening-up, the Chinese Communist Party upheld the principles of 'one center, two basic points' and 'stability is of overriding importance', with a central focus on the balance between reform and opening-up and stability, as well as the pace and dynamics of reform and opening-up. Therefore, although China has experienced widespread political turmoil and abnormal leadership succession since 1989, it has always made development its top priority. Moreover, the success of its economic development has, in turn, strengthened the stability and legitimacy of its political system, and also enhanced the ruling party's confidence in its road to development, institutions, and theories, thus further consolidating the political foundation for this development.

Secondly, China attracts constant foreign investment in transnational production, such external resources becoming a driving force for its development. China has a stable social environment, preferential measures to attract capital (including sound infrastructure, government services and tax incentives, etc.), an available and cheap labor force, as well as a potentially huge, and growing, market (e.g., the middle classes who have achieved new wealth have become an increasingly large consumer group), and so on. Such a unique production environment, with its broad opportunities for profits, has attracted many multinational companies to invest in China and regard it as an important part of their transnational production chain. This in turn allows China to make full use of international resources for rapid development.

Thirdly, China's state capital and local national capital maintain an appropriate symbiotic relationship with transnational capital, making it possible for transnational production to drive the associated development of local national capital and state capital. In the form of joint ventures or non-equity partnerships, local companies in China can participate in transnational production to grow and thrive. Transnational corporations have not formed an enclave economy in China to distort or hinder the development of China's national economy. This laudable result would not be possible without the Chinese government's endeavor to push domestic enterprises to join the world economy by encouraging the development of private enterprise and promoting the reform of state-owned enterprises, as well as its policies of maintaining a well-paced opening-up, and protecting and supporting domestic enterprises.

The above-mentioned three achievements are the result of the domestic political structure of China and the wise development strategy of its leadership. It is under such circumstances that China has gained impressive capital accumulation from its participation in the international economic cycle, gradually developed its proprietary technologies, and substantially controlled the financial sector that is the economic lifeline of the country. All this has laid a foundation for the possibility of independent development in the future.

Dependent development is characterized by three interplaying factors: a relatively low degree of capital accumulation, a lack of proprietary technologies, and the absence of full control over financial mechanisms.

The reason developing countries accumulate less capital under dependent development is that the mode of production at different levels in underdeveloped countries is combined with that dominated by the capitalist world. In this way, 'the ranks formed between different types of production relations constitute a kind of accumulation structure. The extracted surplus flows from the subordinate, backward production level to the dominant, powerful level'.[19] Although China also receives unsatisfactory income under such a distribution system, it still outperforms many of its peers. China currently has over US$4 trillion in foreign exchange reserves, evidence that it has benefited substantially from its participation in the international economic cycle. Such profits provide a certain amount of capital accumulation for development, which serves as a material guarantee for China's future independent development. There

[19] Ibid., Robert Cox, *Production, Power, and World Order*, p. 5.

are two important factors that contribute to this accumulation: firstly, substantial deposits are generated locally from foreign capital, thanks to China's development environment, its attraction to transnational capital, and the symbiotic relationship between local capital and transnational capital (this can be verified by the data on stocks of direct investment in China); secondly, the accumulation from China's continuous rapid growth after its accession to the world market, as a result of the ability of Chinese companies to fill the gap in transnational production or to become an important part of the transnational production chain.

Dependency occurs when developing countries lack the proprietary technologies needed for the world's production process, so are unable to lead international production, resulting in meager profits and the weak momentum of sustainable development. The possession of proprietary technologies is one of the key conditions for a country to improve its economic position in the world, lead international production, and gain more benefits. In reality, China still has not made sufficient breakthroughs in this respect. However, compared with many other developing countries, China has mastered a number of modern and independent technologies in the course of reform and opening-up, such as high-speed railway locomotives, nuclear power plants, mobile communications technology, as well as some infrastructure construction technologies. Although there are many areas of technology in which China is still deficient, it is outperforming many of its peers. In particular, unlike many developing countries where military engineering relies entirely on foreign technology, China is definitely prominent in this field, thanks to its government's policy of placing a long-term emphasis on the development of science and technology education (an important part of the nationalist development strategy), and its ability to exchange market for technology, as well as its strategies and capabilities of acquiring technologies and talents.

Last but not least, China has a relatively autonomous and moderately open financial system. It has emphasized a gradual approach to opening-up, instead of indiscriminately following the trend of global financial integration over the past 40 years and more. China's financial sector has been in the tight grip of the government, with its capital accounts yet to be liberalized even if private finance is at the initial stage of development. Therefore, it is very difficult for international financial capital to control China's economic lifeline. This is why China has been insulated from most of the international financial crises, having avoided the great economic turmoil they caused during the past four decades. Moreover, this tight control over the process of reform and opening-up also protects the Chinese government from lapsing into a political crisis, thus consolidating the key sectors in the political structure that are vital to dependent development—the basis of a strong authoritative government. Marx proposes that the financial credit system under capitalism has a dual function: the 'prophet's' function and the 'devil's' function. The prophet's function is that it can pool social funds to ramp up production; and the devil's function is that it brings fraud, gambling, and crises.[20] To some extent, China's control over the opening-up of its financial sector has protected it from the devil's function of the international financial market and has prevented transnational financial capital from triggering potential crises to China via financial channels to committing fraud and plunder. This is in sharp contrast to some developing countries whose excessively open financial markets have involved them in the financial crises, plundering their historically accumulated capital. China's achievements would be impossible without a strong government that implements a nationalist development strategy.

China is unquestionably a 'straight-A student' among all the countries that follow a dependent road to development, featuring the least dependency and the greatest autonomy. It has achieved the best possible results in its dependent development as manifested in its rapid development, considerable profits under the unfair distribution system, a number of proprietary technologies, and a relatively autonomous financial system. This provides a paradigm for underdeveloped countries. China provides an alternative model as opposed to the Western model which advocates the democratic system, a completely free market, unrestrained openness, and comprehensive privatization (largely from the 'Washington Consensus'). Of course, many factors in China's experience cannot be practically replicated by some other developing countries. For example, in addition to its huge potential market size, China had a deeply rooted heritage before its reform and opening-up. It has also established a relatively complete industrial system and foundation, good infrastructure, and an excellent educational system and scientific-research force. Some of these factors are derived from China's unique history and culture, such as the emphasis on education and savings.[21] However, there is still much that developing countries can

[20] *Marx/Engels Collected Works*, Vol. 2, Beijing: People's Publishing House, 1995, p. 521.

[21] Giovanni Arrighi has analyzed the unique factors about China's development in the past 40 years. See Giovanni Arrighi, *Adam Smith in Beijing*, Lu Aiguo et al., trans., Beijing: Social Sciences Press, 2009, chapter 12.

learn from China, such as a stable political structure, the government's continuing pursuit of its nationalist development strategy, the wise governance strategy of its leadership, and its emphasis on the relationship between development, stability, and reform. However, it must be noted that there are also some deficiencies and lessons to be learned from such political factors, such as the problems of corruption and vested interest groups, which are exactly what China is now endeavoring to resolve. These negative experiences are also useful for other developing countries.

4 Conclusion

China's road to development over the past three decades or so shows that the integration of developing countries into the world economy is a pragmatic approach for their development. Although this inevitably leads to the problem of dependency as mentioned in the dependency theory, it is still a relatively autonomous and sustainable development model, because it enables developing countries to make full use of the resources brought by international capital to make up for their lack of resources and momentum for modernization. China's road to development can enhance the underdevelopment theory and provide informed suggestions for developing countries to reduce their degree of dependency and gradually increase their autonomous development. China's authoritative political structure, its government's persistent pursuit of a nationalist development strategy, and the wise governance strategy of its leadership are replicable. These characteristics enable developing countries to attract foreign capital, establish a symbiotic relationship between foreign capital and local capital, and spur the interactive development of the local economy, thereby improving their ability to negotiate foreign capital, gain more profits, and to acquire and develop autonomous technologies. Moreover, they should open up in a moderate manner, especially when opening up their financial markets, so as to prevent the risks and negative effects of the international financial market.

PART V

China's Road and the World's Future

CHAPTER 10

Aligning National Development Strategies and Building a New Type of International Relationship: A Case Study of China's Belt and Road Initiative

Wang Cungang

1 Introduction

As a major part of its diplomatic pursuits in the new era and its ideal vision of "peaceful development", China needs to build a new type of international relations that is oriented to win-win cooperation and conducive to the transformation of international systems and the world order. It will take great effort to accomplish this unprecedented undertaking for the benefit of later generations. As an extremely significant and effective approach to fulfilling this undertaking, the promotion of the alignment of national development strategies can foster and strengthen the strategic mutual trust between countries with different historical and cultural traditions, social systems and development levels and concepts, and can enhance the level and quality of international cooperation, with the ultimate goal being the achievement of a win-win outcome.

W. Cungang (✉)
Institute for China & World Studies, Tongji University, Shanghai, China

H. Men (ed.), *On China's Road*,
https://doi.org/10.1007/978-981-13-7880-5_10

There have been a great number of academic publications on the establishment of a new type of international relations to date, but as yet there have been no theoretical discussions on the alignment of national development strategies nor any specific literature combining the two. Therefore, this study has important theoretical value and practical significance. This chapter will first elaborate on the connotations and possibilities of the alignment of national development strategies, then discuss their value to the development of a new type of international relations; in addition, it will use the alignment of China's Belt and Road Initiative (or the Belt and Road initiative) with the national development strategies of relevant countries as an example to support this contention and identify problems in the process of alignment; finally, it will propose strategies to implement this form of alignment and facilitate the building of a new type of international relations. Interpretation and case studies are the main research methods.

2 Connotations and Possibilities of the Alignment of National Development Strategies

2.1 *Connotations of the Alignment of National Development Strategies*

To explore the alignment of national development strategies, first and foremost, it is necessary to clarify the connotations of such strategies. As an integral part of a national strategy,[1] the national development strategy embodies the overarching design formed by the top leadership of a country for its development in a given period, based on such important factors as the fundamental goals, realization approaches and supporting measures. It covers both domestic and foreign affairs and involves a wide range of fields, such as economics, politics, security, society, science and technology, and culture. The national development strategy of a country epitomizes how its leadership views the era, the world, other nations, and its own development and interests. The fundamental national development goal, established on the basis of such a strategy, provides the overall direction and basic path for the country to develop in a given period, and it

[1] See Bo Guili, "On the Scientific Connotation of National Strategies," *China Administration*, Vol. 7, 2015, pp. 70–75; Zhou Jianming and Wang Hailiang, "National Grand Strategies, National Security Strategies and National Interests," *World Economy and Politics*, Vol. 4, 2002, pp. 21–26.

influences the choice of its domestic and foreign policies. Historical experience and theoretical studies have shown that an appropriate national development strategy must comply with the basic characteristics of the era and align with the country's actual conditions and core needs.

This "docking"[2] of national development strategies refers to a new form of opening-up and international cooperation in a new historical context. It focuses on the convergence of development ideas, development goals and development plans among different countries, and the integration of multiple areas such as the operation of institutional mechanisms, infrastructure construction and industrial operations. The prerequisites for alignment are a mutual respect and mutual understanding based on sovereign equality, whereby countries support and complement each other in the process of cooperation. Thus, the main goal of alignment is to consolidate and expand these overlapping interests, and to identify opportunities for new common interests and a win-win result. This alignment strategy is not about a country imposing its own will and interests on other countries, but a vision that countries are allowed to freely express their will and pursue their interests without interference. Its nature and implementation approach are completely different from the long-standing colonial division-of-labor system and its variants, which reflect the will and interests of only a few suzerains. As pointed out by Chinese State Councilor, Yang Jiechi, "Alignment means neither you have to accept my rules, nor I have to accept yours. In fact, we look forward to finding common ground for cooperation, and then developing rules together on the basis of mutual respect".[3]

2.2 *Possibilities of the Alignment of National Development Strategies*

First, some related countries have shared similarities in terms of development ideas. American scholars, Judith Goldstein and Robert O. Keohane, state that "Ideas are often an important determinant of government policies

[2] "Docking" was originally a concept of space science. "It means that two or more flying space craft (space shuttles, spaceships, etc.) converge and combine into one." Dictionary Editing Office, Institute of Linguistics, Chinese Academy of Social Sciences, *Modern Chinese Dictionary (Chinese–English Bilingual)*, Beijing: Foreign Language Teaching and Research Press, 2002, p. 491.

[3] Yang Jiechi, "Deepening Mutual Trust and Strengthening Alignment to Co-Build the 21st Century Maritime Silk Road," http://www.fmprc.gov.cn/mfa_chn/ziliao_611306/zyjh_611308/t1249710.shtml, May 9, 2015.

... The principled or causal beliefs embodied in ideas provide a roadmap for players, allowing them have a clearer picture of the relationship between goals/objectives and means; under the circumstances where there is no unique equilibrium, ideas will influence the outcome of the strategic situation; they can be embedded in the institution".[4] In recent years, in the face of the numerous challenges posed by economic globalization and the rapid development of social informatization, especially with the collapse of the "“Washington Consensus" after the international financial crisis of 2008, many countries have made significant adjustments to their national development ideas and have formulated new concepts for national development. For example, since its reform and opening-up, China has gradually established a national development strategy that highlights economic development and aims to meet the people's basic living needs. Based on these considerations, China adjusted its development concept and proposed the "Scientific Outlook on Development", which emphasizes comprehensiveness, coordination and sustainability, at the 18th National Congress of the Communist Party of China in 2012.[5] Similarly, since Vladimir Putin came into power, Russia's national development concept has been continuously adjusted and become increasingly explicit. In 1999, when Putin was appointed as Russian President, he published a paper entitled "Russia at the Turn of the Millennium", in which he systematically summed up and reflected on Russia's development road. He believed that, having grown into an industrial powerhouse, Russia's development road was distinctly different from that of East Asian countries which were struggling to catch up with the advanced ones, and its future depended on the progress of those sectors that were based on high-tech-intensive products. In February 2008, Putin delivered a speech entitled "Russia's National Development Strategy for 2020", which prioritized innovative development as the core of its strategy. Although the subsequent international financial crisis had a huge impact on the Russian economy, Dmitry Medvedev, by then the third President of Russia, did not make any drastic changes to Putin's national development

[4] Judith Goldstein and Robert O. Keohane, eds., Liu Dongguo and Yu Jun, trans., *Ideas and Foreign Policy*, Beijing: Peking University Press, 2005, p. 3.

[5] *Mao Zedong, Deng Xiaoping and Jiang Zemin's Outlook on Scientific Development*, Beijing: Central Literature Press, Party Building Books Publishing House, 2008; Party Literature Research Center, *Excerpts of Important Statements on Scientific Outlook on Development*, Beijing: Central Literature Press, Party Building Books Publishing House, 2008; Li Lasheng, *Research on National Development Strategies of the Communist Party of China*, Beijing: People's Publishing House, 2013.

philosophy and ideals, which were clearly reflected in his article "Go Russia!"', published in September 2009. Since Putin was re-elected as President in 2012, under his long-term leadership, the Russian national development concept has been extended and strengthened. In comparison, Kazakhstan emphasizes economic diversification, investment in the future, service to the people and innovation in social governance models in its process of national development.[6] Mongolia's national development idea is "to promote the building of a humane, civilized and democratic society and to vigorously develop its economy, society, science, technology, culture and civilization" in an all-round manner.[7] If we compare the new development ideas of these different countries, it is not difficult to find many similarities, laying a solid foundation for the alignment of national development strategies.[8]

Secondly, these associated countries have successively developed new national development strategies. The change in their development ideas has instigated a new formulation or transformation of their own development strategies, with developed countries taking the lead in this regard. For example, Germany formulated its "National Sustainable Development Strategy" in 2001, focusing on the organic integration of environmental, economic and social policy goals, as well as the promotion of sustainable development driven by specific projects in priority areas. In 2010, Germany proposed the Industry 4.0 strategy in its "High-Tech Strategy 2020". Specifically, this strategy aims to capitalize on the Cyber-Physical System (CPS) to comprehensively enhance intelligent manufacturing, to establish smart factories featuring flexibility, resource efficiency and human-factors engineering, and to integrate customers and business partners in both the business and value processes. The developing countries are certainly not willing to be outdone. For instance, Kazakhstan has developed "The 2050 National Development Strategy", in an attempt to become one of the top 30 most advanced coun-

[6] Zhao Changqing, "Kazakhstan's Strategy 2030/2050 and Discussing Its Leapfrog Development," *Journal of Xinjiang Normal University (Philosophy and Social Science Edition)*, Vol. 3, 2013, pp. 37–42.

[7] Feng Weijiang and Cai Dan, "Mongolia's National Comprehensive Development Strategy and China's Economic and Trade Strategy to Mongolia," *China Market*, Vol. 16, 2011, pp. 87–95.

[8] Dmitri Trenin, *Post-Imperium: A Eurasian Story*, Han Ning, trans., Beijing: Xinhua Publishing House, 2015; Xu Poling, "A New Strategy for Russian National Development," *International Economic Review*, Vol. 3, 2012, pp. 45–58; Pang Dapeng, "Russia's Development Road," *Russian Studies*, Vol. 2, 2012, pp. 53–81.

tries in the world by 2050 through the implementation of the principles and standards promoted by OECD member countries, and by means of the development of different themes in two major phases. Mongolia has proposed "The Millennium Development Goals-Based Comprehensive National Development Strategy of Mongolia", which involves four key policy aspects: Mongolia's human and social development, its economic growth and development, its environment, and the development of its legislative and government organization. In the process of formulating national development strategies, the top leadership of all countries must fully consider both their domestic environment and the international one. In other words, it is important to consider the domestic and international situations in combination, by making full use of both kinds of resources and markets, and adhering to the principle of the harmonious integration of domestic and international factors. If national development strategies are implemented which fail to reflect the basic characteristics of a country's internal and external environment and disregard the national interests of other countries, especially their core interests, they will incur resentment, resistance and confrontation from other countries. This will lead to the deterioration of the external environment for national development and to various domestic destabilizing factors, ultimately leaving the desired goals of national development unfulfilled.

Thirdly, these associated countries have expressed a strong desire for cooperation. Nowadays, with growing interdependence among countries, international cooperation is an appropriate strategy for a country to expand its presence on the world stage. The alignment of national development strategies, as a new approach to international cooperation, is not possible without other countries' desire for international cooperation. As a responsible power and the world's largest developing country at present, China continues to send a clear and strong signal to the international community that "China remains committed to the peaceful development road and the concept of win-win cooperation",[9] and that "China's development is connected with global development and the interests of the Chinese people is combined with those of people all over the world".[10]

[9] The Publicity Department of the CPC Central Committee, ed., *Collection of Important Speeches by General Secretary Xi Jinping*, Beijing: Xue Xi Publishing Housing, People's Publishing House, 2014, p. 154.

[10] "Considering the Overall Domestic and International Situations, Laying a Solid Foundation for the Road of Peaceful Development," *Guangming Daily*, January 30, 2013, 1st edition.

China is willing and able to help accelerate the development of other countries, providing them with real development opportunities and practical interests. It seeks to drive the world economy to grow in a more open, balanced, reasonable and inclusive way, to build a fully integrated community of shared interests and outcomes. China's goodwill has seen a positive response from other countries. These associated countries have responded positively to the cooperation signals emitted by China. For example, Russian President Putin has pointed out that China is one of Russia's key partners in the world and the Asia-Pacific region. Kazakhstan's President Nursultan Nazarbayev also said that "Kazakhstan is committed to developing a comprehensive strategic partnership with China and places high hopes on deepening the pragmatic cooperation between the two countries".[11]

3 The Alignment of National Development Strategies to Help Build a New Type of International Relations

The impacts of the alignment of national development strategies are multifaceted. In terms of their impact on international relations, the alignment of national development strategies can help in the following ways:

3.1 To Expand Overlapping Interests Among Countries

The ongoing globalization and increasing prominence of global issues have intensified the interdependence of different human communities, and significantly changed contemporary international relations. In particular, there has been an increasing overlap of national interests and core interests among countries.[12] A national development strategy is, by

[11] "Xi Jinping meets with Kazakhstan President Nursultan Nazarbayev, pointing out that a deeper China-Kazakhstan strategic partnership is promising," http://www.fmprc.gov.cn/mfa_chn/zyxw_602251/t1157486.shtml, July 19, 2015.

[12] Although the basic dimension of national interests has remained unchanged for a long time, its specific content has changed with the changing of the times and the country's strength, status and willingness. For example, as countries are racing in the fields of outer space, deep sea exploration and internet, the scope and content of the national interests of related countries have undergone significant changes. As another example, with the vigorous promotion of the business "going out" strategy, China continues to expand the scope and enrich the content of its overseas interests.

definition, an overarching design that guides a country to improve its own strength over a period of time. In a sense, it is also a basic roadmap for maintaining and expanding national interests. Different countries can align their national development strategies, provided their interests are overlapping or complementary to some extent, or at least without a serious conflict of interests. Otherwise, the associated countries will be unwilling to do so. The more overlapping interests there are, the more willing they will be to expand cooperation, and the more likely a win-win result will be realized.

3.2 To Increase In-depth Communications among National Agencies

In order to truly align national development strategies, the policy implementation departments of the associated countries (including those of both central and local government) should carry out full and detailed communications and coordination in a wide range of areas, to ensure the alignment is uninterrupted and the desired goals can be achieved. These ongoing in-depth communications, conducted in a variety of forms and involving numerous participants and extensive topics, will enable countries to enhance their mutual understanding and trust, thereby promoting the predictability of actions, the credibility of commitments and the expectations of the good intentions of the other parties. As a result, the trust on which this understanding is based will not only promote further cooperation, but also foster and develop the trust.[13]

3.3 To Promote Positive Social Interaction and Cement the Foundation of Public Opinion

International communication is about people-to-people exchange. Support from the people in the relevant countries is required for the alignment of national development strategies. In particular, these countries are expected to participate in in-depth discussions on the integration and

[13] Cao Dejun, "Generation of Trust between Countries: A Process-oriented Social Network Analysis," *Contemporary Asia-Pacific Studies*, Vol. 5, 2010, p. 125. Research shows that "there is a positive correlation between the degree of trust and the institutional level of cooperation." Yin Jiwu, *Shaping Social Cognition and Alliance Trust*, Shanghai: Shanghai People's Publishing House, 2009, p. 115.

complementarity of infrastructure, institutional mechanisms and advantageous industries, and take concrete actions in relevant areas accordingly. This will enhance the communication between different countries and increase their connection in the global supply chain, industrial chain and value chain. What is particularly important is that this increasingly frequent and intimate people-to-people exchange will empower these countries to realize the important common goal of promoting mutual understanding among different nationalities in the process of sharing their cooperation and developmental achievements.

3.4 To Achieve the Long-term Stability of Strategic Relations among Countries

The stability of strategic relations is the basic premise and important guarantee for long-term cooperation among countries. It enables the relevant countries to maintain stable expectations for their interactive relations over a period of time and to continue to invest diplomatic resources accordingly. As a result, the overall practice of cooperation will not be hampered by trivial conflicts, temporary setbacks, accidental events nor by interference and destruction by third parties. A country is willing to engage with other countries' national development strategies because it has recognized the national development strategies of its counterparts. In the process of such engagement, this complex and diverse "non-zero-sum" game that countries play can substantially improve their interdependence in a wide range of areas, increase the resilience of their bilateral relations, and strengthen their sense of community. This is especially true for emerging economies and developing countries that have to address the ongoing situation of an unstable, weak and imbalanced global economic recovery, as well as such challenges as a lack of endogenous power, difficulty in expanding international demands, and the spillover effects of developed countries' economic policies. This alignment of national development strategies can not only prevent the possible negative spillover effects of policy changes in different economies but also enhance the overall strength of emerging economies, thus promoting the multipolarization of the world economic pattern.

In summary, it can be observed that the alignment of national development strategies, which cover a wide range of areas and engage a large number of players, is highly valuable for the healthy development of international relations, serving as both a stabilizer and an impetus to bilateral relations. In particular, the alignment of development strategies between major powers has a direct and positive impact on regional and global stability, with an influence that goes beyond the bilateral level. Such alignment is carried out cooperatively in both means and form, to achieve a win-win result.

4 Successful Practice of the Alignment of National Development Strategies: Case Studies of China's Belt and Road Initiative

The "One Belt, One Road" initiative is an integral component of China's national development strategy. In particular, it forms part of China's new-era opening-up strategy, supporting the principle of achieving shared growth through discussion and collaboration.[14] Under the leadership of President Xi Jinping and Premier Li Keqiang, China has aligned this strategy with the national development strategies of several countries along the way, and has pushed corresponding bilateral relations to a new level. The following is a selection of four typical cases, involving one world power, two regional powers and one small country, to test these contentions and discuss the problems that exist in the process of alignment.

4.1 Case #1: The Alignment with the Russian-led Construction of the Eurasian Economic Union (EEU) and Its Performance

Russia is a world power that spans the two continents of Europe and Asia. As part of the Eurasia Strategy put forward by Putin after he was re-elected as President of Russia in 2012, the construction of the Eurasian Economic Union (EEU) project mainly focuses on developing regional cooperation, unleashing the potential of former Soviet states that share the common economic foundation, improving mutual trade and investment, and striving to achieve the long-term goal of economic diversification and development.[15] This strategy has attracted widespread opposition from Western countries because of the possible far-reaching impacts of its geo-economic

[14] "Vision and Actions on Jointly Building Silk Road Economic Belt and 21st Century Maritime Silk Road," people.com.cn, http://politics.people.com.cn/n/2015/0328/c70731-26764643.html, August 23, 2015.

[15] Li Jianmin, *The Silk Road Economic Belt, Eurasian Economic Union and Sino-Russian Cooperation*, pp. 11–12.

and geopolitical goals. In contrast, China has responded positively and offered its strong support. During President Xi Jinping's visit to Moscow on May 8, 2015, China and Russia issued a joint statement to confirm their interactive cooperation in the construction of the Silk Road Economic Belt and the EEU to "ensure the sustained and stable growth of the regional economy, strengthen regional economic integration, and maintain regional peace and development".[16] This also marks the first joint statement issued by China and another country on the theme of aligning their national development strategies. On July 10 of the same year, China and Russia jointly issued the "Mid-term Roadmap for Development of Trilateral Cooperation" with Mongolia, announcing that the trio would "prepare the 'Cooperation Framework for the China-Mongolia-Russia Economic Corridor' on the basis of the cooperation between the Silk Road Economic Belt and the EEU as well as the Prairie Road initiative"[17] On the same day, President Xi Jinping met President Putin and stressed again that, "China and Russia will use the Shanghai Cooperation Organization (SCO) as an important platform for the integration of the Silk Road Economic Belt and the EEU in order to expand the space for practical cooperation between the two countries, and drive the development, cooperation and prosperity across Eurasia".[18]

China and Russia have achieved fruitful results from the alignment of national development strategies. Firstly, China's investment in Russia continues to grow. By the end of 2014, China had invested nearly US$33 billion in Russia.[19] With this steady increase in the amount of investment, China has been gradually expanding its investment fields in Russia, from energy, raw materials and forestry, to infrastructure construction, manufacturing, technological innovation and other fields. Furthermore, Russia

[16] "Joint Statement of the People's Republic of China and the Russian Federation on the Joint Cooperation of the Construction of the Silk Road Economic Belt and the Eurasian Economic Union," http://www.fmprc.gov.cn/mfa_chn/zyxw_602251/t1262143.shtml, May 9, 2015.

[17] "Mid-term Roadmap for Development of Trilateral Cooperation of the People's Republic of China, the Russian Federation and Mongolia," http://www.fmprc.gov.cn/mfa_chn/zyxw_602251/t1280229.shtml, July 19, 2015.

[18] "Xi Jinping meets Putin: China and Russia should continue to maintain high-level strategic cooperation in SCO," http://politics.people.com.cn/n/2015/0709/c70731-27278218.html, July 20, 2015.

[19] "Investment and finance have become the new growth points for Sino-Russian economic trade cooperation," http://news.xinhuanet.com/finance/2015-06/18/c_1115660424.htm, August 17, 2015.

has extended an olive branch to China, inviting it to invest in some strategic industries. In March 2015, senior officials of Russia said for the first time that they were considering the possibility of allowing Chinese companies to acquire a majority stake in a series of strategic oilfields in Russia.[20] Secondly, Sino-Russian financial cooperation is growing rapidly. In October 2014, the central banks of the two countries signed a bilateral local currency swap agreement with a scale of RMB 150 billion. In May 2015, China and Russia issued a joint statement to announce the further promotion of settlements in local currency to cover the sectors of bilateral trade, mutual investment and credit. Now RMB is beginning to be widely used in settlements between Chinese and Russian businesses.[21]

Since the beginning of 2015, the China Development Bank (CDB) and The Export-Import Bank of China have signed facility agreements with several Russian financial institutions, including Sberbank, VEB and VTB, to jointly support the construction of large-scale projects. This is the first time that RMB has been used to finance Russian construction projects, marking a new milestone in the financial strategic cooperation between the two countries.

The achievements made by China and Russia in economics and trade have ensured a long-term and high-level strategic partnership, acting as a role model for contemporary new relationships between major powers. On May 9, 2015, China and Russia announced in the Joint Statement on Deepening Comprehensive Strategic Partnership of Coordination and Advocating Win-win Cooperation that "the two sides regard further

[20] "Russia is expected to open strategic industries to China, a new chapter for Sino-Russian investment cooperation," http://news.xinhuanet.com/2015-03/02/c_1114492774.htm, August 17, 2015. Russia's 2008 law stipulates that foreign investment in the country's strategic industrial companies shall not exceed 50%. If foreign investors wish to obtain a controlling stake of more than 10%, they must file with the Federal Anti-monopoly Service (FAS) of Russia and be subject to review by an interdepartmental committee led by the Federal Security Council of Russia. As such, the Russian side clearly makes a friendly gesture to China this time. In addition, Chinese investors will be given more favors in Russia than Western investors.

[21] In the first quarter of this year, the RUB/RMB exchange amount has increased more than five-fold year-on-year, and the number of Russian companies that opened renminbi accounts rose significantly. According to data provided by the Ministry of Commerce of the People's Republic of China, in the first five months of this year, the amount of settlement in local currency between Chinese and Russian enterprises has quadrupled year-on-year. See "Investment and finance have become the new growth points for Sino-Russian economic trade cooperation."

deepening bilateral relations as a priority in their respective diplomacy", and "will consolidate mutual support and assistance in the fields that interest both parties such as maintaining respective sovereignty, territorial integrity and security, preventing foreign interference and choosing the development road independently, as well as preserving their respective history, culture and moral values".

4.2 *Case #2: The Alignment with Indonesia's Global Maritime Axis Strategy and Its Performance*

Indonesia is a large ASEAN country and an important global emerging economy. The Global Maritime Axis (*poros maritim dunia*) development strategy announced by the Indonesian President Joko Widodo in 2014, proposes to raise people's maritime awareness, build a marine highway, promote maritime connectivity, develop the marine economy, maintain maritime security, develop maritime diplomacy and build Indonesia into a maritime power.[22] This strategy is closely aligned with China's Maritime Silk Road initiative in terms of its content and spirit, and has therefore received a positive response from China. In a meeting on March 26, 2015, when President Joko Widodo visited China, President Xi Jinping said that "China is willing to leverage the Asian Infrastructure Investment Bank (AIIB), the Silk Road Fund and other financial institutions, to support Indonesia's development of the maritime highway, and actively participate in the construction of ports, high-speed rail, airports, shipbuilding and coastal special economic zones in Indonesia"[23] On April 22, in a meeting with President Xi Jinping at the Boao Forum for Asia held in China, President Joko Widodo said that Indonesia hoped to expand cooperation with China in various fields and was willing to explore opportunities for cooperation provided by Indonesia's new development strategy and China's 21st Century Maritime Silk Road initiative. In the Joint Press Communiqué issued on the same day, China and Indonesia announced that "The two heads of state have reaffirmed that the two parties will

[22] For details, see Liu Chang, "Re-focusing on the Ocean: Comment on Indonesia's Global Maritime Axis Vision," http://www.ciis.org.cn/chinese/2015-06/10/content_7979599.htm, July 19, 2015.

[23] "Xi Jinping meets Indonesian President, emphasizing the promotion of sustainable and sound development of China-Indonesia comprehensive strategic partnership," http://www.chinanews.com/gn/2015/03-26/7162209.shtml, July 19, 2015.

promote the comprehensive integration of China's strategic vision of building a 21st Century Maritime Silk Road and Indonesia's Global Maritime Axis development plan, as two maritime partners that share prosperity through joint efforts, strengthened policy coordination, pragmatic cooperation and cultural exchange". The two parties undertook to work together to increase the bilateral trade volume to more than US$150 billion by 2020, reduce tariff and non-tariff trade barriers and strengthen exchanges between the trade departments of the two countries, jointly implement the agreement between the two governments on the China-Indonesia Integrated Industrial Park, vigorously carry out the Five-Year Development Plan for China-Indonesia Economic and Trade Cooperation, sign off the list of priority projects as soon as possible, and encourage more effective execution of the bilateral local currency swap agreement.[24]

China and Indonesia have also achieved many successes in the alignment of their national development strategies. First, the two sides have steadily promoted their mutually beneficial cooperation in the fields of economics, trade and investment. According to Indonesian officials, in the first seven months of 2015, China has become Indonesia's second largest export market and its largest source of imports; China will also invest a total of US$100 billion in Indonesia's electricity, railway, smelting and other sectors.[25] Secondly, the people-to-people exchanges between the two countries are going smoothly. At the end of May 2015, China and Indonesia held the first high-level People-to-People Exchange Mechanism (PPEM) at the vice premier's level, representing the first-ever high-level PPEM to be established between China and the developing countries, and seven cooperation documents were signed. Economic cooperation and people-to-people exchanges have effectively promoted the development of China-Indonesia relations. China and Indonesia also acknowledged in the aforementioned Joint Press Communiqué that the two sides will become maritime partners, sharing prosperity based on joint efforts, strengthening coordination

[24] "Joint Press Communique between the People's Republic of China and the Republic of Indonesia (full text)," http://www.fmprc.gov.cn/mfa_chn/zyxw_602251/t1257081.shtml, July 21, 2015.

[25] "China and the US are the largest export market and import source to Indonesia respectively," http://www.cic.mofcom.gov.cn/ciweb/cic/info/Article.jsp?a_no=380740&col_no=459; "China will invest a total of US$ 100 billion in Indonesia," http://www.cic.mofcom.gov.cn/ciweb/cic/info/Article.jsp?a_no=380145&col_no=459, August 25, 2015.

and cooperation in regional and international affairs, and shaping a new type of international relations that delivers mutual benefits and a win-win result.[26]

4.3 *Case #3: The Alignment with the Bright Path, Kazakhstan's New Economic Policy and Its Performance*

Kazakhstan is a major Central Asian country and an important EEU state. In a state-of-the-union address delivered in November 2014, the President of Kazakhstan Nursultan Nazarbayev announced a new economic policy called "Nurly Zhol"—the Bright Path—(also known as the "Bright Path plan" or the "Bright Path initiative"), as an important part of its 2050 National Development Strategy. According to this initiative, Kazakhstan is committed to improving its infrastructure construction in the fields of transportation, industry, energy, society and culture to ensure sustainable economic development and social stability. Given Kazakhstan's special geopolitical position, its great potential for economic development and its role as the starting point of the Silk Road Economic Belt, China has taken a positive stance on the new economic policy of Bright Path. In December 2014, Premier Li Keqiang stated clearly during his visit to Kazakhstan that "China is willing to actively engage in the Bright Path plan to help Kazakhstan revive its economy" and proposed the important idea of "capacity cooperation".[27] In May 2015 in Astana, President Xi Jinping emphasized again that "we are willing to promote the alignment of China's Silk Road Economic Belt construction plan with Kazakhstan's Bright Path new economic policy on the basis of equality and mutual benefit, so as to achieve common development and prosperity". President Nursultan Nazarbayev said that "Kazakhstan supports China's Belt and Road initiative and is willing to become an important partner in the construction of the Silk Road Economic Belt. We will spare no efforts to promote the alignment of China's Silk Road Economic Belt construction plan with our Bright Path strategy for economic development and strengthen cooperation

[26] "Joint Press Communique between the People's Republic of China and the Republic of Indonesia (full text)," http://www.fmprc.gov.cn/mfa_chn/zyxw_602251/t1257081.shtml, July 6, 2015.

[27] "Li Keqiang meets President of Kazakhstan, willingness to participate in the Bright Path initiative of Kazakhstan," http://news.china.com.cn/world/2014-12/15/content_34315248.htm, July 19, 2015.

with China in various fields including economy and trade, production capacity, energy, science and technology".[28]

The alignment of national development strategies between China and Kazakhstan has also delivered remarkable results. During his visit to China at the end of March 2015, Kazakhstan Prime Minister Karim Massimov signed 33 cooperation documents with China, covering a wide range of subjects and totaling US$23.6 billion, on behalf of the government of Kazakhstan.[29] The two parties agreed that this Sino-Kazakhstan capacity cooperation will effectively propel the industrialization of the two countries and help them make new economic breakthroughs in the general context of the weak global economic recovery, and will also provide a model for other countries which engage in similar cooperation. Government departments from both countries should cooperate strongly in this process.[30] The two sides also agreed to jointly hold a series of activities to commemorate major historic events, such as the 70th anniversary of the victory of the World Anti-Fascist War and the 70th anniversary of the victory of the Chinese People's War of Resistance against Japanese Aggression, in an effort to further consolidate the friendship that has grown from generation to generation. The alignment of national development strategies between China and Kazakhstan has helped deepen their comprehensive strategic partnership and make new and positive progress within the framework of the Conference on Interaction and Confidence-Building Measures in Asia (CICA) and AIIB.

4.4 *Case #4: The Alignment with Mongolia's Prairie Road Initiative and Its Performance*

Mongolia is a small country in Northeast Asia. In September 2014, the Mongolian government officially announced that, as a country between Europe and Asia, it planned to implement the Prairie Road initiative

[28] "Xi Jinping holds talks with President of Kazakhstan Nursultan Nazarbayev," http://politics.people.com.cn/n/2015/0507/c1024-26965829.html, July 19, 2015.

[29] "China and Kazakhstan sign capacity cooperation projects worth of US$ 23.6 billion," http://politics.people.com.cn/n/2015/0329/c70731-26765355.html, July 19, 2015.

[30] "China-Kazakhstan capacity cooperation: a new specimen of Li Keqiang's pragmatic diplomacy," http://news.xinhuanet.com/2015-03/29/c_1114799174.htm, August 24, 2015.

consisting of five projects and totaling US$50 billion, to revitalize the Mongolian economy by developing the transportation trade. Previously, in an exclusive interview with the Chinese media, President Tsakhiagiin Elbegdorj of Mongolia said that Mongolia was discussing and actively participating in the Silk Road Economic Belt initiative. It was hoped that as two neighboring countries, sharing a 4710-kilometer-long border, Mongolia and China would strengthen cooperation to help Mongolia build railways, gas pipelines, highways and other infrastructure.[31] China also gave a positive response to this Prairie Road initiative. In August of the same year, President Xi Jinping said, during his visit to Mongolia, that "China is willing to strengthen cooperation with Mongolia under the Silk Road Economic Belt initiative and is open to the Prairie Road initiative of Mongolia. The two sides can strengthen cooperation and achieve development and benefits together based on new platforms such as the Asian Infrastructure Investment Banks".[32] In May 2015, the Prime Minister of Mongolia, Mendsaikhany Enkhsaikhan, also stated that Mongolia's Prairie Road initiative was a positive echo of China's Belt and Road initiative. The two closely-linked national development strategies are crucial to the economic development of Mongolia,[33] which is reaffirmed by the aforementioned "Mid-term Roadmap for Development of Trilateral Cooperation" between China, Russia and Mongolia.

To date, China and Mongolia have reached a series of agreements on the export of Mongolian goods via China to a third country and have signed a number of bilateral agreements. China has agreed to use six of its ports, including Tianjin port, to export Mongolian goods, helping Mongolia solve its long-standing difficulties with transit transportation and access to seaports. This opens a golden era for China-Mongolia relations. During President Xi Jinping's visit to Mongolia in 2014, the leaders of the two countries jointly announced the escalation of their "strategic partnership" to a "comprehensive strategic partnership"

[31] "Exclusive interview with President Tsakhiagiin Elbegdorj of Mongolia: Mongolia wishes to further enhance strategic partnership level with China," http://news.xinhuanet.com/world/2014-08/19/c_1112127543.htm, July 21, 2015.

[32] "President Xi Jinping delivers a speech at the State Great Khural of Mongolia," http://news.xinhuanet.com/world/2014-08/22/c_1112195359.htm, May 10, 2015.

[33] "China's Belt and Road initiative helps Mongolia pave the Prairie Road," http://news.xinhuanet.com/world/2015-04/23/c_1115066487.htm, May 9, 2015.

4.5 Conclusion

4.5.1 Performance Evaluation of Strategy Alignment

First, the alignment of development strategies can be achieved in countries with marked differences. Although the four countries discussed above are significantly different from China in historical and cultural traditions, social and political systems, and economic and social development, and also have their own distinct national development ideas, all of them have realized the preliminary alignment of their national development strategies with China's. This alignment has enabled these four countries and China to further expand their common interests and has facilitated more in-depth exchanges between their state institutions.

Secondly, the alignment of national development strategies can serve as an important lever to achieving a new, more meaningful, type of international relations. Instead of being an empty diplomatic parlance, this new type of international relations will give more impetus and significance to the strategy of alignment. This interaction between the different countries will facilitate smoother and more substantial progress for each of them.

4.5.2 Problems in the Process of Strategy Alignment

First, the level of strategic mutual trust needs to be improved. Strategic mutual trust is the basis for sustained and effective cooperation between countries, while strategic suspicion will inevitably erode this basis. If strategic confrontation occurs, international cooperation will be seriously damaged and disrupted. Currently, basic strategic mutual trust has already been established among the countries that have announced, and actually engaged in, the alignment of national development strategies. However, the level of such trust varies between different countries, and its basis is not sufficiently solid. For example, Russia is suspicious of China's actions in Central Asia. In a survey of the Kazakhs, 70% of the respondents believed that China is the biggest threat to the economy of Kazakhstan.[34] The main reason for such suspicion is that these associated countries have doubts about China's development strategy, especially regarding how China will capitalize on its growing strength.

[34] "Ambassador Yao Peisheng: The Belt and Road Initiative is exposed to political instability in Central Asia," http://ydyl.takungpao.com/spft/2015-07/3037868.html, August 23, 2015.

Secondly, different countries have a different focus on the alignment of development strategies. Among the participating countries, there are both post-industrialized countries such as Russia, and industrialized countries such as China and Kazakhstan. China has developed an advanced manufacturing industry, equipped with a sound infrastructure. Russia, Mongolia and other countries boast rich energy and natural resources. With differences in development levels, development priorities and resource endowments, each country has different aims and focuses regarding the process of strategy alignment. Such differences are the chief concerns of this "cooperative game", which, if not addressed properly, will cause ongoing disagreements and friction in the process of alignment and will ultimately damage their mutual trust.

Thirdly, the difference in institutional mechanisms makes it more difficult for alignment to proceed. As mentioned above, the countries that currently participate in an alignment strategy are considerably different from each other in political systems, economic operation mechanisms and social management systems. While alignment has been strongly promoted and endorsed by the major leaders of these countries, it is hoped that government departments will take the lead, and the business community and civil institutions will participate extensively in the actual implementation process. The effect of the alignment on different countries varies because of differences in their governance approaches and the administrative efficiencies of their government departments, the transparency of economic trends and policy stability, the degree of internationalization of their companies, and the companies' awareness and ability to fulfill corporate social responsibilities.

Fourthly, some countries are severely challenged by potential political instability. There have been many academic discussions on the positive relationship between political stability and national development, so this chapter will not elaborate. However, the political stability of the associated countries is a basic prerequisite for the alignment of national development strategies. It is therefore of concern that some of the participating countries are not sufficiently politically stable. For example, in Kazakhstan, a country in the shadow of a "Color Revolution", the three forces of extremism, separatism and terrorism are still rampant, and there is also the possibility of a change in its regime because its major political leaders are getting older. Therefore, although its domestic political situation remains generally stable, the occurrence of future large-scale political and social turmoil cannot be ruled out. In Indonesia, deep-rooted corruption, intense nationalist sentiment, and well-organized and highly destructive religious extremism and terrorism pose a serious threat to its political and social stability. Consequently, these problems will have negative impacts on the alignment of national development strategies.

5 The Expansion of the Form and Content of Alignment to Push the Building of a New Type of International Relations to the Next Level

As a highly complex systematic project involving all aspects of society, both the alignment of national development strategies and the building of a new type of international relations are based on the ongoing investment and efforts of the participating countries. It is therefore essential to include the following measures to assure its future:

5.1 Promotion of the Alignment by the Top Leadership and their Emphasis on Its Importance

The above cases have clearly indicated that the top leadership of a country provides the most powerful, direct and effective impetus for the formulation and implementation of the national development strategy and its alignment with the development strategies of other countries. Without doubt, a successful alignment of the national development strategies of different countries hinges on their leaders' strategic vision and intentions, their ability to make strategic decisions, to integrate domestic resources, and to communicate with external forces, especially with their counterparts. In future, the content and form of summit diplomacy needs to be further enriched and innovated in order to reinforce the consensus between the top leaders, consolidate the underlying ideals, and maintain the driving force for alignment.

5.2 Improvement of the Combination of Bilateral Alignments with the Creation of Regional Cooperation Mechanisms

International mechanisms play an important role in reducing the cost of international cooperation, reinforcing the stable expectations of participating countries, and forming and maintaining an international order.[35] Such mechanisms can be either multilateral (global or regional) or bilateral. The alignment of national development strategies is a cross-border engagement based on bilateral mechanisms. In future, such mechanisms will be further leveraged, particularly to coordinate the macro-policies of the countries involved, and to urge a degree of reform to their domestic administrative systems. In addition, it is necessary to further explore the potential of existing regional cooperation mechanisms and initiatives, actively promote the creation of new regional, sub-regional and trans-regional multilateral cooperation platforms for win-win cooperation, and to form a multilevel mechanism for policy synergy and a multisource dynamic mechanism for development.

5.3 Strengthening of Cooperation on National Early Warning Mechanisms

Risks permeate every corner of our unprecedentedly complicated modern society, and they are intensified on the international level where complicated and diverse international relations are essentially in a state of disorder. Risks are unavoidable in the implementation of national development strategies and the alignment of such strategies with other countries. Immediate and accurate early warning mechanisms, as well as corresponding actions, are required to reduce such risks. In future, all associated countries should enhance their early warning systems and strengthen their cooperation with other countries in this regard. As part of this process, particular efforts should be made to capitalize on big data and break open the "data silos" without compromising national sovereignty and security, making global information-sharing a reality. Through these approaches, it will be possible to minimize the uncertainties and risks that may arise during the alignment of national development strategies, encourage countries to participate in a more proactive manner, and improve the performance of alignment.

5.4 Giving Full Play to the Enterprises' Initiative and Creativity

Enterprises, as active players in the promotion of national development, should also serve as an important source of power for facilitating the

[35] Peter J. Katzenstein, Robert O. Keohane, and Stephan D. Krasner, eds., *Explanation and Contestation in the Study of World Politics*, Qin Yaqing et al., trans., Shanghai: Shanghai Century Publishing Group, 2006, pp. 120–135.

alignment of national development strategies. On the national level, alignment will be impossible without the active and effective participation of enterprises; on the corporate level, alignment also provides rare opportunities and space for enterprises to grow bigger and stronger. In future, government departments need to create more opportunities and build more platforms for these market players, and protect their overseas interests more actively and effectively. Enterprises also need to take more active measures to align their own development strategies with the national ones, by reforming their internal governance mechanisms and improving their efficiency in using both local and international resources and markets. While pursuing their own development and benefiting the people in their home country, enterprises are also expected to deliver more benefits to the people of the countries in which they invest and operate, and to lay a solid social foundation for the sound development of international relations.

5.5 Furthering the Consolidation of the Foundation of Mutual Understanding between Peoples by Promoting Public Diplomacy

As discussed above, a mutual understanding between nationalities is an important social basis for the realization of alignment, and public diplomacy influences the way people from different countries understand each other, because "public diplomacy is an important strategy for a country to secure its legitimacy and the recognition of the international community".[36] People will be reluctant to take an active part in international cooperation if the legitimacy and development strategies of their own country, and other involved countries, are not recognized. In order to gain such recognition, two things have to be accomplished. First, the country pursuing public diplomacy should conduct an in-depth study of its counterparts, so as to gain an insight into their historical and cultural traditions, the status quo of their development, and the intrinsic characteristics of their people. To achieve this, it will be helpful to study their respective history, geography, comparative politics and comparative culture. Secondly, the country pursuing public diplomacy must achieve good internal governance. To this end, both its ruling party and its government need to

[36] Han Fangming ed., *An Introduction to Public Diplomacy*, Beijing: Peking University Press, 2011, p. 7.

constantly improve their own governance capabilities, steadily promote the reform of administrative systems and social management systems, and actively implement a universal value system.

6 Conclusion

As an important part of national strategy, a national development strategy reflects the primary value orientation and direction of a country, serves as a roadmap that guides its development in a certain period of time, and regulates the choice of domestic and foreign policies, as well as its underlying actions. The alignment of national development strategies provides a new and important opportunity for countries to open up and accomplish international cooperation, as well helping to shape a new type of international relations. This alignment of national development strategies is made possible by ongoing globalization, increasingly salient global issues, and the widespread use of information technology strategies. The case studies show that the alignment of national development strategies will contribute significantly to the building of a new type of international relations focused on win-win cooperation.

As an emerging developing socialist country, China can make a remarkable contribution to the alignment of national development strategies and the construction of a new type of international relations. The recent implementation of its Belt and Road Initiative has enabled China to align its national development strategies with some countries along the route, with promising early results. In future, China needs to continue to promote its alignment with other countries by continuously enriching the connotations of such alignment, expanding the scope of participating countries, innovating the form of alignment, focusing on the performance of its alignment, organically combining bilateral alignment with the creation of international mechanisms, while giving full play to enterprises and the many other players in the alignment, and actively carrying out public diplomacy, so as to push international cooperation to a new level, to achieve the important goal of a win-win situation.

CHAPTER 11

China as Methods While the World as Objective

Wu Xinbo

China's Road is neither a political slogan nor a fashion tag; it has a rich meaning that deserves our in-depth thinking. The chapter is going to discuss the issue of China's Road from four dimensions: Road, expression, method, and purpose. It is not meant to be comprehensive but to inspire further discussions and debates.

1 The Choice of China's Road

The biggest challenge of China's Road is how to resolve the relationship between "methodology" and "purpose" from a philosophical perspective. In other words, should China's Road take China being the purpose and the world (Western) being the method, or should we use China as the method and the world (Western) as the purpose?

So far, we have been taking the Road with the world (western) being a method and China being the purpose. China is just a case within the Western discourse and methodology. We use Western concepts and follow Western logics to design, build, and develop ourselves.

W. Xinbo (✉)
Institute for Sinology Studies, Shanghai International Studies University, Shanghai, China
e-mail: 1608@shisu.edu.cn

H. Men (ed.), *On China's Road*,
https://doi.org/10.1007/978-981-13-7880-5_11

In this unfamiliar framework, we completed the construction of a sovereign state in the modern sense with the help of Western theory. We also found the correct development direction to modernization with the help of Western knowledge after a long period of trial and error. With the help of Western experience, we have completed two transformations (the transition from an agricultural society to an industrial society and from a planned economy to a market economy). It can be said that we have learned from other people's theories and reached great accomplishments based on China's case.

However, this development framework, platform, and logic have gradually lost its original motivation and significance to current China. The development of China as a case has far exceeded the scope that Western theory can cover and explain. China is revealing its true colors and quietly forming its own development logics. It has been unconsciously creating its own Road, although this Road has not yet been able to be summarized in an abstract way and be advanced to the height of theory and methodology so as to form a powerful discourse system with an explanation capability.

The opportunity has gradually arrived. Now it is high time we begin to consciously transform from the past experience to cultural and theoretical consciousness, we must return to the self, form active consciousness, build our own discourse system, and use our own academic language to seriously summarize our own way and express our own Road. Therefore, the selection and development of China's Road should be based on a high degree of cultural consciousness.[1] Without cultural consciousness of a high level, there is no high degree of theoretical and practical self-consciousness, thus lacking a conscious awareness of its Road. As Mr. Fei Xiaotong said, "Cultural awareness is an arduous process. Only by understanding one's own culture and understanding and interacting with a variety of cultures can we have the conditions to establish ourselves and find our position in this emerging multicultural world. And then through self-adaptation, together with other cultures, we are able to complement each other and establish a basic order with mutual recognition and a set of coexistence principles in which multiple cultures can coexist peacefully, develop their abilities, and develop together."[2]

[1] "Cultural Consciousness" was first proposed by Mr. Fei Xiaotong in the second seminar on socio-cultural anthropology organized by the Institute of Sociology and Anthropology of Peking University in 1997. The purpose was to respond to the inevitable development of globalization and to propose a solution for people relationships.

[2] See Fei Xiaotong, *Globalization and Cultural Consciousness.*

Cultural consciousness is an arduous process. For contemporary China, the author believes that this process includes at least four stages. The first stage is the return of the actor, which refers to Fei Xiaotong's "self-awakening" or the establishment of Chinese consciousness (Chinese perspective). The second stage is to rediscover and understand China, or Fei Xiaotong's "self-reflection." The third is theoretical self-consciousness, that is, Fei Xiaotong's self-creation. The fourth stage is conscientious practice, to be yourself, and to explain China to the world.

The first stage is the return of the actor. China's loss in modern times was in all aspects. The most heart-wrenching among them was the loss of traditional Chinese culture, which was unprecedentedly catastrophic and devastating. The situation of Chinese culture can be described as tragic. Now China has risen, but the rise of the economy and the military alone are far from enough. With the material strength, there will inevitably be a massive renaissance. Like the rise of modern Western countries, we must regain the once lost China, find China, understand China, read China, and rebuild China.

The second stage is to rediscover China. The meaning of "cultural self-consciousness" should include reflections on its own civilization and other civilizations. Reflections on itself often help to understand the relationship between different civilizations. We need to contemplate and prepare a painstaking process of exploration, discovery, and thinking. We must discover China and discover a true and objective China. China is a mystery. Chinese people do not necessarily understand China.

The third stage is the theoretical self-consciousness. "Self-consciousness" means "self-consciousness of necessity and negation of spontaneity." Spontaneity refers to the fact that people are blindly dictated by historical inevitability in social activities and cannot foresee the consequences of their activities. Self-consciousness means that people understand the meaning of their activities to a certain extent in social activities and have clearer objectives and calculation.

The fourth stage is the practice of self-awareness, explaining China to the world. Once we understand China and move from a highly conscious culture to a highly conscious theory, from historical inevitability to the realm of freedom, once we have our own discourse power, build a complete system of perception as well as knowledge to interact and communicate with the West, we will be not only more willing but also more confident to explain China and China's Road to the world in a complete, systematic, comprehensive, and profound manner.

Therefore, the selection and development of China's Road is essentially a process moving from unconsciousness toward self-consciousness, from experience orientation to cultural self-awareness as well as self-awareness of theory and practice. It is a long process of cultural self-consciousness of returning to ourselves.

2 China's Academic Expression

The appearance of new terms such as the Beijing Consensus, China Model, and China's Road have actually told the people that China is quietly saying goodbye to the old-fashioned development Road with the world (western) being the method and China being the purpose. China is now, consciously and unconsciously, taking a Road of China as being the method and the world as being the purpose. During this major change, Chinese social science scholars must speak up, make explanations, give explanations, and conduct academic research. However, with Western learning in modern times, we have gradually lost our right to speak and have been seriously Westernized. We have long been accustomed to relying on the Western discourse system (let alone having our own discourse system), which made us dumb without the Western discourse system. We are in a state of serious aphasia.

Our academic research and expression have been frustrating and disappointing in regard to China's rise and China's Road. We seriously lag behind our great practices and rich experience and are unable to give academic explanation. "Over the past 30 years of reform and opening up, although our academic research has achieved great results, this achievement has mainly developed under the new trend of 'Western learning,' and people are increasingly feeling that in order to develop innovation, some bottlenecks need to be overcome. The most prominent issue is the dependence on Western academics. Our academic originality is far from adequate. There is no academic discourse system with Chinese characteristics."[3]

Even in the field of "China Studies," there is a bad habit that is too much translation from and imitation of the "overseas Chinese studies." "A lot of people equate China studies in foreign academic circles with our own research on China, thinking that we are studying the same China, and

[3] Li Shumin and Liuhuachu, "Reflection on the Rebuilding Evaluation System of Chinese Academia," *Chinese Social Science Today*, March 4, 2015.

that problem awareness, research methods, and research materials are all shared."[4] This is related to the Western discourse system and research methods that we have long been immersed in, accustomed to, relying on, and worshipping. Even if we study China and ourselves, we have to rely on translation and imitation of the West, and even blindly follow the West. This has resulted in an overwhelming imitation of "overseas China studies." "People feel refreshing towards Western culture. It is a bit like fashion trends, as if the newer the better. One is often shocked by the Western new methods and theories, so they cannot communicate with and criticize the West on an equal platform."[5] We did not see that "although the foreign China studies are called so, they are essentially 'foreign studies.'" No wonder Qian Chengdan sighed, "Chinese academic history can be divided into two periods, 'ancient' and 'modern.' 'Ancient' academics lasted for thousands of years, forming a set of Chinese discourse systems and research methods. 'Modern' academics began with the Western learning movement. Now that we have basically incorporated Western templates, even 'China Studies' has been almost placed into the Western frameworks and methods."[6]

Some scholars regard the above phenomenon as a crisis in China's social sciences. This "crisis of China's social sciences" is mainly manifested in the inability to effectively explain China's experience, which lags far behind China's practice. The historical roots of the current academic crisis are relying heavily on external theories which have led to the lack of "discourse power" constituted by our own concepts, theories, and methods in current social sciences. It shows "ideological poverty." The current model of "scientific management of social sciences" not only fails to rejuvenate "China Studies" but also endangers China's national security. The subject of China's "new concepts, new categories, and new expressions" can only be Chinese and Chinese scholars.[7] Some senior predecessors and scholars even shouted that Chinese academics can no longer follow the "external" model.[8]

[4] Ge Zhaoguang, "Overseas China Studies Is Essentially 'Foreign Studies,'" *Wen Hui Bao*, October 5, 2008.

[5] Ibid.

[6] Qian Chengdan, "Chinese Academia Must Not Follow 'Outsiders,'" *Beijing Daily*, March 11, 2013.

[7] Yang Guangbin, "Thought Poverty in Prosperity: Also on Issues and Solutions of Chinese Education-Scientific Management System."

[8] Qian Chengdan, "Chinese Academia Must Not Follow 'Outsiders.'"

Our academic research is about to throw away the Western crutches and rely on our legs and feet to walk our own Road. Faced with new situations and issues—the brand new China Road, how to provide our academic perspectives may not depend on how we express it but on how we rediscover and profoundly understand China.

What is lacking in academic expression in China is not rhetoric and translatology training, but self-confidence and self-understanding. The long-lost "self" in Chinese modern times has resulted in the lack of confidence, the ability to express ourselves, and articulation about our own discourse system. To this end, we must establish confidence. We must find ourselves again, to discover China and understand China deeply. Only in this way can we establish our own method and discourse system so that we can use our own words and concepts to think and speak.

So how can we find, discover, and understand China?

3 China as "Method"

Discovering and truly understanding China is a seemingly simple but extremely difficult task. While the West is like Western paintings, which are easy to be recognized and grasped because of their objectivity and realism, China is more like Chinese traditional painting which is difficult to grasp and control because it advocates freehand brushwork and pursuits artistic conception (or more like the meridian and qi). For this reason, we cannot take it for granted that as long as we are Chinese, we will be able to read and understand China. On the contrary, our discovery and understanding of China has so far only stayed on the surface or the middle layer, and we have not discovered a China that exists as a system or method at a deeper level.

A Japanese scholar, Yūzō Mizoguchi, recognized China as a philosophical method. One of his most famous works is *China as Methodology* published in 1990. He expressed in his book that he was dissatisfied with the Japanese research approach on China Studies and put forward the idea of "China studies with China as the method." His "China-centered" approach and his focus on exploring the "Chinese principles" are indeed unique, invigorating, and far-reaching. Mizoguchi objected to using the world (Europe) as a standard (method) to measure China's practice and argued that both Chinese history and European history should be regarded as special existence. We need to construct a "world" vision based on the premise of understanding their particularities.

We need to use the power of academic discipline to understand and discover China. This specialized discipline is called "Chinese Studies."[9] The earliest China studies were formed overseas. Now, a few Chinese universities and research institutions have also established China studies or overseas China studies institutions and teaching institutions. The return of "China Studies" to China is not only to establish an actor status and subject consciousness but also to advocate a clear awareness on issues and methods. The biggest problem facing the current "local China studies" is that we have been relying on the eyes of Westerners to study China's problems. We lack confidence. We have not yet formed our own concepts and categories; we have no discourse system or our own methods. These are essential elements for building "local China Studies."

For this reason, "China Studies" set up by universities and research institutes not only needs to offer courses but also has to study "China as a method" and to use "China as a method" to study problems. We must realize that the Eastern world represented by China, like the Western world, has its own complete system with its own concepts, categories, principles, and methods. On the level of epistemology, ontology, and methodology, both the East and West also have their own definitions and have formed their own different Road dependences and cultural preferences. Although the East and West have formed distinct systems, they are not isolated from each other. With the past 10 million years of evolution and development, an amazing and wonderful interdependent relationship has been formed, in which exist various laws of interaction between the East and the West. As methods, the East and the West have formed a contradictory unity that promotes human development, such as yin and yang making up a perfect world.

How can we enter the world of methods and discover this wonderful and magical realm? The author believes that the East and the West are mirror images of each other. From comparison and analysis of the differences between the two, one can enter the world of methods and thus realize each other by discovering each other. In other words, to understand China

[9] "China Studies" is a comprehensive discipline. It is similar to "American Studies," "French Studies," "German Studies," and "Japanese Studies." They are comprehensive areas of discipline and knowledge in regional studies that focus on political, economic, military, cultural, social, historical, and diplomacy in countries like China, the United States, France, Germany, Japan, and so on. In other words, it is a comprehensive research area that treats various fields and problems of a country as a whole. Its research methods are often multidisciplinary and interdisciplinary.

as a method, we must first start with the differences caused by the cultural preferences of the East and the West to fully understand China (the East) and the world (the West). In this way, we can open this magical gate and discover a wonderful world. We will find that this difference is reflected not only on the system level with attribute meanings, but also on many basic elements that make up the system, such as hypothesis of human nature theory, cultural gene, minimum unit, ontology, methodology, epistemology, basic categories, as well as basic interaction laws that decide Eastern and Western cultures and thus profoundly affect the basic interaction of civilizations.

Although Eastern and Western civilizations have their commonalities and coexist with each other, they also have their own different cultural attributes, characteristics, and preferences. The result of these differences is not only in class, but also in its nature. Due to the limitation of space, the author only chooses three of them, such as cultural attributes (genes), social minimum units, and ontology, to talk about the author's superficial understanding of China as a method.

First, let us take a look at the difference in "cultural gene."

The so-called cultural gene refers to "the basic concept of fundamental spirit underlying various cultural phenomena," and it "has the ability to reproduce and develop in time and space, and possesses the basic characteristic of the cultural expression or manifestation of such ability."[10] When talking about Western cultural genes, Chinese Canadian scholar Liang Henian believes that "Western people's perceptions of heaven and earth, self and other determine Western civilization. Why do they have this idea? The answers to this question represent the cultural genes that govern Western civilization."[11]

The author believes that cultural genes cause fundamental differences between the Western and Eastern cultures and also are the different logical starting points for the formation of Eastern and Western discourse systems. The formation of this bifurcation is the result of the evolution of thousands of years. It eventually became a historical and cultural accumulation, a cultural inheritance in a biological sense.

[10] Armand Clesse and Mingqi Xu, *The Vitality of China and the Chinese*, Rozenberg Publishers, 2004, p. 97.

[11] Liang Henian, *Cultural Gene in Western Civilization*, SDX Joint Publishing Company, November 2013.

From the ontological perspective of social culture, the ontological status and role of human beings in social culture constitute cultural genes. The Eastern and Western societies and cultures are the opposing two poles, and the root cause of this opposite polarity lies in the diametrically opposed Eastern "group-based" cultural gene and Western "individual-based" cultural gene. "Group-based" and "individual-based" as the "cultural genes" of the East and the West may be stipulated subtly and profoundly at the creation of human being, thus forming two highly opposing yet complementary world systems and logic systems.

The "cultural gene" profoundly decides the different cultural attributes and preferences of the East and West, and it forms different discourse systems. In other words, all the systemic existence of the Eastern and Western cultures and the differences in all methods are all derived from this "cultural gene." The difference between the two cultures is due to the distinctions in this cultural gene.

Second, we need to look at the difference in "the smallest unit of society."

The smallest unit of society is determined by cultural genes. The smallest unit of society in the Eastern World is obviously different from the West. In the West, it is individuals not groups. Due to the different historical and national conditions of the Eastern countries, group behavior patterns are different. For example, the Middle East nation is based on clan tribes, while Chinese society is based on family. As the smallest group unit in Chinese society, "family" should be the smallest and most basic unit that can no longer be divided in China's social organization. Family is the eternal and unchanged existence of Chinese society. It is the foundation of Chinese society and the identity and lifeblood of the Chinese nation. It cannot be changed. Home can be assimilated to everything but not assimilated by other forces. Family is natural and the cultural result of the Chinese society that has evolved through thousands of years of historical changes and natural selection.

The most basic and smallest unit that constitutes a Western society is the individual, defined by the cultural gene of "personal orientation." The personal orientation theory highly values personal values and dignity. The so-called personal value and dignity, in Kant's words, is to regard the individual as an end, rather than merely treating the individual as a means and tool to satisfy the will of other individuals or groups.

The better and more complete the minimum unit that constitutes society, the better and healthier this society will be. The West is individual oriented, and everything in Western society can be restored to individuals. Therefore, in the social governance, the West attaches great importance to the development and cultivation of an individual's healthy personality and strives to protect individual rights and human rights. In sharp contrast to this, the East is group-based, and China's group unit is home and family. Building a sound and perfect family is the basic premise and condition for social governance.

From this we can see that in the theoretical construction and application, we cannot simply copy the western economic man hypothesis theory, the civil society theory, the social governance theory, the human rights theory and so on which are all based on individual orientation. Even if we learn from it, we must transform the concepts and logics; otherwise, it will inevitably lead to a messy narrative, and even make ways in the wrong direction.

Third, we should consider the difference in the Eastern and Western ontology.

The ontology issue of Eastern and Chinese culture is closer to a "conceptual ontology" or "relative orientation." This kind of ontology is directed at the socio-cultural genes of the "group-based" origin and is controlled by this social material organization, which is defined by this social and cultural gene.

Since ancient times, Chinese culture has been emphasizing the (group) relationship as the essence of all things and believing that the material world is homogenous with people. In the myth of world origin, Pangu and heaven coexist in chaos. Chaos has both objects and people. In Daodejing, Dao as a concept similar to ontology refers not only to the origin of human beings but also to the origin of things. "Dao" is the unity of the nature of the material world and the essence of human beings. In addition, we can also find the "conceptual ontological" of Chinese culture (i.e. its non-material ontological characteristics) from Taoism. "In ancient Chinese culture, there are saying like 'using Dao to view things' and achieve 'being one body with Dao' and 'Unity of Universe and Human,' as well as 'the wisdom of contemplation' in Buddhism to find the 'doctrine of non-duality,' 'harmony and mutual identification,' and 'the ordinary mind is the way.'" These ancient sayings are all different from the Western culture's thinking and "transcends binary opposition."[12]

[12] Zhou Quantian, "The Non-Indigenous Nature of Chinese Traditional Culture," *Journal of Zhoukou Normal University*, July 2011.

The ontology of Western culture is "object oriented"; it is a "binary opposition" based on systems. This concept resonates with the Western cultural gene of "individual orientation," and its ontology points to this social material organizational form which is regulated by its social and cultural gene. Western culture that is "ontologically material" starts from the "personal standard" and has a very clear boundary between "I" and "other." Being accustomed to understanding the world with an independent "I," over time, the Western world has developed a logical habit with clear boundaries in concept, reasoning, and arguments. Driven by the "binary opposition" mentality and the materialistic objectivity preference, a set of logical systems that are different from the East in terms of ontology, epistemology, and methodology are formed.

The God who created "human" and "world" as being of "one-dimensional origin" is also a third party. In the dialogue with the "individual" (Western people are constantly praying and confessing to God), they form a corresponding cause-effect relationship. The "system" is a secret agreement between God and independent individuals which is reached through secret negotiations. God as a creator is also an intermediary and continues to perform the sacred duty of coordinating the eternal relationship among humans as well as human and objects in binary opposition and conflicts through the "system." For this reason, once the principle of social operation of the "system standard" has been established in Western societies, it will always be distinguished from the Eastern society that emphasizes the "relationship standard."

In addition, from the differences in the hypothesis of human nature, the debate of human nature being good or evil can also find its own cultural origin from the Eastern and Western civilizations. In general, Western civilization is more accustomed to interpreting the world from the perspective of evil human nature, while Eastern civilization is relatively more willing to accept the hypothesis of good human nature. The hypothesis of human nature as a starting point of logic has now been fully demonstrated through the long development of the Eastern and Western civilizations.

In short, the world of methods is vast with rich content. There are still many unexplored areas that need to be explored and discovered by us. When we retreat complex phenomena to the highest levels of philosophy and methodology, we can discover the hidden differences between Eastern and Western cultures, thus forming an ultimate way of thinking to look at the world.

East-West comparison is the best way to discover China. Only by using the West as a mirror to profoundly understand the West can we better understand the East and China. As a systematic existence, China has a very rich logical vocabulary. How to dust off the history that has been covered by thick dirt and discover China's logics one by one? It will be a very difficult process of exploration, and of course it is a very long process with theoretical self-consciousness and theoretical innovation.

4 World as "Purpose"

From a phylogenetic perspective and the theory of evolution, China as a method will not only not disappear, but it will sooner or later have to face the world problems in a status equivalent to the West. In the balanced development of global cultural ecology, the discovery of China is conducive to restoring the global cultural system that has been tilted and unbalanced, and to ensuring the harmonious and stable global cultural system. (This is the biggest contribution and the most important public product that China can provide for the world.) The collapse of China in modern times was an important cause of the rapid deterioration of the ecological environment in which the world's cultural system was located. Discovering and recovering China and establishing a Chinese system and method are not only strategic for China's rise, but also a pressing need of balanced and harmonious development of the world. The need to build a new cultural and ecological system and the environment with balanced development are inevitably required for the sustainable development of mankind to reconstruct a cultural and ecological system to achieve symbiosis harmony.

The existence of Eastern and Western cultures as methods and systems determines that the Western methods are not universal, and therefore it does not have the universal and absolute capability to interpret the world. This has left a huge space for survival and development for finding and rebuilding China as a method. But when we have established our own methods, we must also see that not only Western methods are not universal, Chinese methods are also not universal. In fact, any one method does not have the capability to unilaterally interpret the entire world, because they all belong to the specialty of universality. "That is to say, the Western experience is a particularity, and the Eastern experience is also a particularity. Only through observation and comparison of specific experiences among the East and West countries (such as the Britain, France, German, United States, Russia, China, Japan, India, Egypt, Brazil, etc.) can we truly understand and deduct the universal logic and historical connotation of 'modernization.'"[13] For this reason, we cannot universalize our methods.

Although neither East or West can universalize their methods one-sidedly, this does not mean that they do not have the possibility of co-building universality. As the other side of the problem, we should also see that both the Eastern and Western cultures have their own particularity and universality, but this universal realization is not a unilateral appeal with the exclusion of the other as the premise, but the result of mutual coexistence and benefit. In other words, the East and West can coexist (integrate the East and West together) and interact, learn from each other, and achieve mutual assistance. Only in this way can we achieve universality in the true sense. Only in this way, we can face the world's problems together and jointly solve world problems.

Judging from the historical development of modern China, the Chinese method can gain universality through its interaction with the West. For example, China's growth in modern times was to regain rebirth under the impact of Western civilization. The success of Reform and Opening Up was the result of the interaction between the Eastern and Western civilizations. China's model and plan can offer constructive solutions to the problems of global governance led by the West. To this end, the experience of China's growth and development should have universal significance for the world.

Similarly, the West can only obtain its universality through its interaction with the East and China. For example, some scholars believe that China enlightened Western modernization.[14] This argument is not groundless. In the eighteenth-century Europe, known as the "rational" era, some great thinkers used rational authority to replace the worship of God. The missionaries brought the Chinese cultural spirit to Europe, such as the idea of advocating nature, the concept of heaven, the Cheng-Zhu School, the imperial examination system, and good human nature which were deeply welcomed by the famous French Enlightenment thinker, Voltaire (1694–1778), and others, which became their spiritual weapons against theology. What is worth mentioning in particular is Taoism's assertion of "governing by non-action" has greatly enlightened European intellectual elites, through the widespread dissemination of missionaries in

[13] Xu Jilin, "China as Method, World as Purpose," *Social Sciences Abroad*, Vol. 1, 1998.

[14] The author went to South Korea to participate in the Sino-Japanese-Korea academic symposium in 2013. He exchanged views with Professor Dae-Kyu Yoon, the Vice President of South Korea's Kyungnam University, and Director of the Institute for Far Eastern Studies. He firmly believes that China enlightened the Western modernization.

Europe, and it continues to receive their recognition. The concept "laissez-faire" was first used by French businessmen M. Le Gendre in the mid-seventeenth century.[15] Later the leading figure of the French Physiocratic school, François Quesnay, promoted the term that came from the ancient China,[16] greatly impacting the European academic community including a group of economists such as Adam Smith and David Ricardo. Especially it had the most profound influence on Adam Smith, the father of the Western market economy. The idea of "laissez-faire" that came from the East has almost become the core concept of his economic ideology (Adam Smith describes it as an "invisible hand"), thus forming an important school of Western economics—Libertarianism, which laid the foundation for classical economics in modern Western market economy. This principle of market economy, which incorporates Eastern and Western wisdom, has a profound and widespread impact not only on Europe but also on the entire world. It has universal significance.

It can be seen that the common growth of the East and the West should be the ultimate pursuit for a perfect world. The situation of one-sidedness should be replaced by the situation of coexistence and win-win. Interaction and mutual complementarity are the driving forces for balanced development.

We have been on the Road of "using the world (West) as a method for the purpose of China" for more than 160 years. It seems that it is time for us to take "China's Road that uses China as a method and world as a purpose." Currently, China and the world should discover China, find China, rebuild China, and establish a Chinese discourse system with oriental implication. Only by building a harmonious symbiotic relationship between China and the world at a global level can China truly rise and the world achieve sustained and stable development. China's rise can inspire the world by its Road and method.

[15] In the middle of the seventeenth century, French businessman M. Le Gendre responded to the question raised by Louis XIV's Minister of Finance Jean Baptiste Colbert, "What is the best way to protect French business?" by "Freedom. Allowance" (Laissez-faire, Laissez-passer), which is translated into English as "leave us alone."

[16] In 1747, François Quesnay also put forward the idea of "freedom and laissez-faire" from the viewpoint of natural law in the second edition of *Essai Physique sur l'Econolnie animale.*